ABRAHAM LINCOLN

AS A MAN OF IDEAS

ABRAHAM LINCOLN
AS A MAN OF IDEAS

ALLEN C. GUELZO
WITH A FOREWORD BY MICHAEL LIND

SOUTHERN ILLINOIS UNIVERSITY PRESS
CARBONDALE

12   11   10   09   4   3   2   1

Frontispiece: Lincoln at City Point by Albert Hunt. Charcoal sketch drawn from life during Lincoln's visit to General Ulysses S. Grant's headquarters in City Point, Virginia, on March 27, 1865.

Library of Congress Cataloging-in-Publication Data
Guelzo, Allen C.
  Abraham Lincoln as a man of ideas / Allen C. Guelzo ; with a foreword by Michael Lind.
    p. cm.
  Includes bibliographical references and index.
  ISBN-13: 978-0-8093-2861-1 (alk. paper)
  ISBN-10: 0-8093-2861-5 (alk. paper)
  1. Lincoln, Abraham, 1809–1865—Political and social views. 2. Lincoln, Abraham, 1809–1865—Philosophy. 3. United States—Politics and government—1861–1865. 4. United States—Politics and government—1845–1861. 5. United States—Politics and government—Philosophy. 6. Slaves—Emancipation—United States. 7. United States—Intellectual life—1783–1865. 8. Presidents—United States—Biography. I. Title.
  E457.2.G875 2009
  973.7092—dc22   2008025089

CONTENTS

Foreword

Michael Lind

"Whenever this question shall be settled," Abraham Lincoln said of the question of slavery in New Haven, Connecticut, on March 6, 1860, "it must be settled on some philosophical basis. No policy that does not rest upon some philosophical public opinion can be permanently maintained."

This conviction guided Lincoln throughout his career, from his early days as a promoter of public works and economic development to his leadership in the campaign against the extension of slavery and his struggles as president to save the Union during the Civil War. To a degree uncommon in American statesmen, Lincoln felt compelled to justify his statecraft, however expedient and adapted to circumstance, by reference to enduring principles—the same enduring principles upon which a nation "conceived in liberty" itself was founded and by which at great cost, including Lincoln's own death, it was saved.

The story of Lincoln and the titanic struggles in which he took part can hardly be told except in terms of a clash of ideals as well as interests. All too often, however, the ideas that guided and inspired the greatest of America's leaders are lost in mounds of biographical detail, or jettisoned for fear that any adequate discussion of his view of the world will hamper the flow of a dramatic narrative. The histories that result from such omissions can be moving and popular, full of character and incident—but they can also be "full of sound and fury, signifying nothing." To contemplate the life and times of Abraham Lincoln deprived of his ideas would be like watching a reenactment of the Gettysburg Address with the sound turned off.

In Allen C. Guelzo, the thought of Abraham Lincoln has found a historian worthy of its subject. Each year, it seems, more books are published on Lincoln, each more perishable than the last. One of the small handful of books that are permanent contributions to Lincoln scholarship is Guelzo's *Abraham Lincoln: Redeemer President*, a biography not only of a public figure but of a public philosophy. In *Abraham Lincoln as a Man of Ideas*, Guelzo secures his position not only as a Lincoln scholar of the first rank but also as an eminent historian of ideas.

In this collection of essays, as well-written as they are well-informed, readers can share the pleasure of Guelzo's discovery "that there was a great deal more going on in Lincoln's mind than incidental notions of politics and liberty" and that Lincoln "had the temperament of a thinker, and his reading was much more formidable in its breadth than I had ever been led to suspect." Lincoln was no philosopher-king, Guelzo insists in his essay "Lincoln and Natural Law": "It would, I think, be a mistake to attempt a description of Lincoln as a natural law *philosopher*, or a philosopher at all. He was, after all, a man of practical intellectual application; just as he once remarked about his fund of jokes and stories, that he was a wholesaler, not a retailer, so he was as a thinker."

As eloquent and amiable as he is erudite, Guelzo serves as the perfect guide in exploring the thought and practice of Abraham Lincoln while avoiding the pitfalls presented by alternate forms of "presentism." One kind of presentism condemns Lincoln according to the standards of a later age. Guelzo points out the dangers of judging Lincoln's racial views, which were extraordinarily enlightened for a white American of his era, by the assumptions of our own. Yet another form of presentism foregoes such denunciation at the price of erasing the distinctions between past and present and turning Lincoln into a contemporary in antique clothes. Guelzo shows us how to avoid such anachronism, without lapsing into the opposite error of ignoring the truth of Secretary of War Edwin M. Stanton's observation at Lincoln's deathbed: "Now he belongs to the ages."

While Guelzo's Lincoln in many ways belongs to the ages, seen from another aspect he is a figure whose deepest convictions are at odds with much of modern American culture. Even in his own time, Guelzo argues, Lincoln's attachment to the natural rights philosophy of the American Founding and the Enlightenment seemed old-fashioned from the perspective of votaries of nineteenth-century romanticism, a movement whose influence Guelzo sees in abolitionism and evangelical Protestant revivalism as well as the South's romanticism of the right to own slaves. Today the hegemony of romanticism is so complete in American culture that it is commonly identified with American culture itself, which, according to many scholars, truly originated only with Ralph Waldo Emerson and Walt Whitman.

In one of the most important of these important essays, Guelzo makes the case for Lincoln's prudence—an utterly unromantic quality, but one considered the virtue of virtues for millennia. There is publicity to be had in sensationalistic criticisms that allege that Lincoln was a racist, or that Lincoln was a tyrant who abused his war powers as president—to name only two subjects of particular interest to Americans today, in the aftermath of the civil rights revolution and in the midst of wars and campaigns against terrorism. But such debates imply a view of politics which collapses the policies that seek to promote principles into the principles themselves, thereby defining strategy as hypocrisy and compromise as betrayal. Those who think this way, Guelzo convincingly argues, cannot understand prudent statecraft in general, much less the most prudent of American statesmen.

"In Lincoln," Guelzo writes, "we have a glimpse of prudence in a liberal democracy; but it is also our best glimpse of it, and perhaps our best hope for understanding and recovering it." To which it might be added that in the work of Allen C. Guelzo we have a glimpse of Lincoln, and perhaps our best hope for understanding and recovering him.

Abraham Lincoln

as a Man of Ideas

INTRODUCTION:
WHAT WOULD LINCOLN DO?

If there is, somewhere, a list of the top ten questions Americans ask themselves about their national life, this one has to be very near the top, or perhaps even *at* the top. In 1918, sheet music for rallying public opinion behind the American intervention in the First World War asked, "Abraham Lincoln, What Would You Do?" In 1939, Frank Capra brought Mr. Smith to Washington, and while he was there, he (in this case, Jimmy Stewart) went to the Lincoln Memorial in the search for hope and guidance, and he got it in the person of Clarissa Saunders (played by Jean Arthur):

> Jeff—listen—remember the day you got here?—what you said about Mr. Lincoln?—that he was sitting up there—watching—waiting for someone to come along? . . . Someone with a little plain, decent, uncompromising *rightness* . . . and really light up that dome for once. This country could use some of that—so could the whole drunken, cockeyed world right now—a *lot* of it!

As though Lincoln sitting in his Olympian chair were a Greek oracle, ready to dispense his eternal and abiding wisdom to Americans in their moments of crisis. In 1964, John Ford's epic Western *Cheyenne Autumn* pictured Secretary of the Interior Carl Schurz (played, improbably, by Edward G. Robinson) asking a portrait of Abraham Lincoln, "What would you do, old friend?" In the same year, when the Senate was deadlocked on the Civil Rights Act of 1964, President Lyndon Johnson appealed to Illinois's U.S. senator Everett Dirksen to break the deadlock by remembering Lincoln. "I saw your exhibit at the

World's Fair," Johnson said to Dirksen, "and it's the Land of Lincoln, so you're worthy of the Land of Lincoln. And a man from Illinois is going to pass the bill, and I'll see that you get proper attention and credit." And sure enough, when Dirksen defeated the filibuster that had blocked voting on the act, he was quick to remind the Senate that it was the same day Abraham Lincoln had been nominated for the presidency. Today, there are some 12.6 million entries on the World Wide Web which respond to the inquiry, "What would Lincoln do?" and the subject matter varies from confirming Supreme Court justices to the Iraq war. As the great Lincoln biographer David Herbert Donald once put it (quoting Dirksen), everyone wants to "get right with Lincoln."[1]

All of this makes for interesting screenplays and sometimes even interesting politics. It's worth wondering, though, whether it can possibly have any meaning. Abraham Lincoln, after all, has been dead for a century and a half, and in that century and a half both our national politics and our daily lives as Americans have changed out of all proportion to the world he inhabited. Lincoln never paid income taxes, never filled out a job application, and never had a Social Security number. My colleague at Gettysburg, Gabor Boritt, was once asked, at the height of the Boston school-bussing controversy in the 1970s, what Lincoln would have said about school bussing, and he replied, with admirable drollery, "Lincoln would have said, 'What's a bus?'" Even in Lincoln's own lifetime, permanence and steadiness seemed to be evaporating on all hands. When he was born, in 1809, Thomas Jefferson was still president of the United States (or at least would be for three more weeks) and George III was still king of England. By the time he died, in 1865, he had taken passage on a steamboat, ridden on a railroad, and communicated across the country by electrical telegraph; in fact, had his death not come at the hands of an assassin, he might have lived long enough to turn on an electrical light, hold a conversation on the telephone, and record the Gettysburg Address onto one of Thomas Edison's acoustic cylinders. Lincoln himself was conscious of how rapidly his universe had turned on its axis when he journeyed from Springfield to Washington in 1861 for his inauguration:

> We have seen great changes within the recollection of some of us who are the older. When I first came to the west, some 44 or 45 years ago, at sundown you had completed a journey of some 30 miles which you had commenced at sunrise, and thought you had done well. Now only six hours have elapsed since I left my home in Illinois where I was surrounded by a large concourse of my fellow citizens, almost all of whom I could recognize, and I find myself far from home surrounded by the thousands I now see before me, who are strangers to me.

If Lincoln's own world was faced with such startling and disruptive changes, how likely is it that he could have anything meaningful to say after more than a century of even more disruptive changes?

Certainly, some people have doubted whether "what Lincoln would do" could have any bearing on what *we* should be doing. Helen Nicolay, reflecting in 1912 on the man her father, John G. Nicolay, had served as personal secretary through the Civil War years, wrote, "The truth is that Lincoln was no prophet of a distant day. His early life was essentially of the old era. He made his career by individual effort." And the sheer scale of the war, not to mention the transformation of American industry and finance in the nineteenth century, seemed to make whatever wisdom a man of the prewar decades had acquired seem antique and useless. After the war, wrote William Dean Howells in *The Rise of Silas Lapham*, "I found that I had got back to another world. The day of small things was past, and I don't suppose it will ever come again in this country." It was in the same spirit that Richard Hofstadter, in a notorious chapter in his 1948 book, *The American Political Tradition and the Men Who Made It*, wrote that Lincoln "belonged to the age of craftsmanship rather than industrialism. . . . Had he lived to seventy, he would have seen the generation brought up on self-help come into its own, build oppressive business corporations, and begin to close off . . . treasured opportunities for the little man." In Hofstadter's view, assassination came to Lincoln as a sort of gift, because he was not compelled to watch the postwar age of the robber barons make mincemeat of the ideals which had guided his life or watch his own Republican Party become "the jackal of the vested interests."

Nor did it stop there. From the 1950s onwards, prominent African Americans whose grandparents Lincoln had freed from slavery turned their backs on him and denied that he had really freed, or even wanted to free, any black person, and claimed he was instead an old-time racist who differed comparatively little from Bull Connor or George Wallace. And more recently, civil libertarians have decided that Lincoln's wartime suspension of civil liberties probably set a bad example rather than one we should consult today. "When a President takes away a civil right, he should have to worry about explaining himself to the people," wrote Caleb Crain in a recent review in the *New Yorker*. "He should fear as well as love us."[2]

None of this questioning of the question seems to much bother professional historians and biographers; but then again, they do not ask the question, "What would Lincoln do?" but merely, "What *did* Lincoln do?" Still, even as early as 1934, James Garfield Randall felt compelled to defend the historical study of Lincoln against querulous voices which asked whether "the Lincoln theme" had become "exhausted." Randall optimistically answered *no*, and for the most part, his optimism has been justified. Although historical and biographical study of Lincoln hit a long, dry patch between the end of the Civil War centennial and the beginning of the 1990s, the last fifteen years have been the "golden age" of Lincoln scholarship. This began, in large measure, with the publication of Michael Burlingame's *The Inner World of Abraham Lincoln* in 1994, a loose-knit collection of topical essays that was built on a foundation of research so vast as to make all the Lincoln biographies since Benjamin Thomas's in 1952 look vapid and thin. This was followed in 1996 by the publication of Don and Virginia Fehrenbacher's lifetime accumulation of Lincoln quotations in *Recollected Words of Abraham Lincoln* (which, in effect, became a kind of single-volume annex to the standard *Collected Works of Abraham Lincoln*, edited by Roy Basler from 1953 to 1955) and in 1998 by the publication of Douglas L. Wilson and Rodney O. Davis's *Herndon's Informants: Letters, Interviews, and Statements about Abraham Lincoln,* which simultaneously restored the reputation of William Henry Herndon's vast archive of firsthand Lincoln reminiscence material and made it easily available between two hardcovers. Just when the overworked fields of Lincoln biographical sources seemed unable to yield anything more, Burlingame, Fehrenbacher and Fehrenbacher, and Wilson and Davis opened the gates to acres of wholly unexpected material for scholars to harvest. It has to be said, too, that the gradual revival of the Abraham Lincoln Association (which had gone dormant and nearly bankrupt after the effort it put into underwriting the Basler edition of the *Collected Works*) and the creation by Richard Gilder and Lewis Lehrman of the Lincoln Prize, both of which came about in the late 1980s, put institutional encouragement and some hefty financial incentives to work behind a Lincoln renascence.

Precious few, though, of those 12.6 million websites asking, "What would Lincoln do?" are the property of scholars. Historians, with a keen eye to cultivating a clinical aloofness toward mundane applications of history, are at best only willing to talk about how Lincoln's achievements as president still affect American life today; this is a very different enterprise, however, from looking to Lincoln as a go-to man for modern problems, and it is this that the question *What would Lincoln do?* really wants satisfied. Because, clinical or not, the vast bulk of the modern American interest in Abraham Lincoln is not punctuated by gusts of joy over finding some unlooked-at letter or reminiscence, or by sage observations on how we live still within a Union that Lincoln preserved, but by the abiding conviction that Lincoln could somehow function as our contemporary and adviser. In the face of that inquiry, the historical clinicians are inclined to gape in astonishment.

What makes this more extraordinary to the minds of history professionals is that Americans ask this question of almost no one else in American history, except perhaps Jesus (who wasn't an American but is often described as though he were) and Alan Greenspan. I have never heard anyone, gazing into the middle distance, ask what Woodrow Wilson would do, or what Millard

Fillmore would do; we only ask of Jack Kennedy what he would have *done* had he lived to see the situation in Vietnam deteriorate. Joseph Ellis, who has recently provided us with a Washington biography to add to his shelf of other books on the Revolutionary generation, actually did summon up George Washington to ask him, in the *Los Angeles Times,* what he would do about the Iraq war. But even Ellis prefaced his op-ed with the concession that this was "a ridiculous question," which largely deflates the whole purpose of asking it.[3] Washington, after all, is not really a man you ask questions of, at least not without your cap firmly gripped in both hands. The knee breeches, the cutaway waistcoat, the powdered hair all bestow on Washington a look so antique to modern sensibilities that any question of his opinions about modern affairs seems moot; and that formidable (and carefully cultivated) sense of grandeur and command does not suggest that an offhand question on current events from Oprah or Leno would be warmly received by the Father of Our Country. Washington may have been first in war and first in peace, but it has been a long time since he was first in the relaxed, informal, fast-food hearts of his countrymen.

Lincoln remains a different matter entirely. The long, black frock coat and the stovepipe hat are definitely antiques, but at least he wears trousers, and a bow tie, and no uniform. And as the late historian of American speech, Kenneth Cmiel, so aptly pinned it, Lincoln cultivated a democratic, colloquial, middling way of writing and speaking, rather than the ostentatious three-decker style of the Founders. This keeps Lincoln reasonably accessible to modern readers, so that we don't feel at all out of place when we up and ask Lincoln just what he would do, without having to take on the lacy complexities of Washington's resignation letter or his farewell orders to the Continental army.[4] We can still laugh at Lincoln's jokes; we do not know whether Washington ever told any jokes.

But if we feel no impulse to ask what Washington would do, what is it but the accident of appearances which makes us think we can ask the same thing of Lincoln? Or is it possible that Hofstadter et al. are right, and that any answers Lincoln could give us were designed for questions no longer worth asking about American life? I think this is a question worth considering seriously because it goes to the heart, not only of the standing of Abraham Lincoln, but of the function of history itself. For a great many of us, the living present recedes into the historical past too swiftly and too violently for the past ever to be more than the object of antiquarian study or genealogical ancestor-worship. History becomes a pursuit similar to stamp collecting—a silent, harmless drudgery. It is surprising, however, to discover how few history professionals think that this is what they are doing. Ever since Hegel turned history into a organic chain of developments from one historical stage to another, and especially since Karl Marx identified historical development with the very urgent issue of reconfiguring economic and political society, historical practitioners have been agog with the idea that the past is a hieroglyphic, the deciphering of which can yield all manner of insights—usually political or economic—about the present and future. So, one looks hard at the emergence of capitalist society in the Mediterranean world of Philip II for evidence that capitalism is a consciously developed evolution out of feudal aristocratic society; and one assumes that a similar scrutiny of modern capitalist society (say, since the eighteenth century) will yield evidence of how it will evolve yet again, this time into a future socialist one. Or, if such predictive crudity seems a bit much, history can at least pull back the curtain on the modern inequities of a capitalist society which only a socialist one can resolve. The idea that historical clinicians are too abstract and detached from present realities to notice the bus schedule could not be further from the mark.

What this kind of clairvoyance-history is not is *personal*. Hegel's—and Marx's—concept of historical development was a chart of great, powerful, but faceless forces. This was not because Hegel was hostile to the force of individual personality in history, but because he did not want to attribute so much force to individual personalities that they had the power to redirect or halt the onrush of historical development. The fish were fine, so long as it was clear that they could do nothing to stop the river. Abraham Lincoln might, on that reasoning, be a perfectly worthwhile object of interest, but only if it were perfectly clear from the start that he was very much a prisoner of his own times and should only be thought of as a solitary moment within the general movement of things. None of us rises above the flux of our times; none of us has answers to questions beyond those of our own short moment.

I don't want to dispute the power of impersonal forces, such as markets or climate; I think it is more questionable whether they have built-in developmental direction, if only because I am very keenly aware that at certain moments in history everything really does seem to be poised on one turn of pitch-and-toss. Had Blücher not made it to Waterloo and Napoleon won the day there and achieved a restoration of the empire, or had Halifax and not Churchill prevailed in May 1940 in offering to negotiate with Hitler, it is very hard to believe that the subsequent course of modern history would be the same; or, for that matter, if John Wilkes Booth had been stopped from entering Lincoln's box that night at Ford's Theater. Development in history requires something similar to geological time—and obeys a clock which moves very slowly, but inexorably—and is innately hostile to the possibility of Thomas Carlyle's romantic notion of the "Great Man" who changes everything by sheer force of will. My own suspicion is that development in history looks less like a clock and more like an accordion, with long periods of unsurprising somno-lence and short, compressed, and agonizing periods of frenzied and unstable activity in which the decision and ideas of one individual may actually turn a very great deal around. The romantic "Great Man" is actually, at the end of the day, no more romantic than the "Long Development"; I would prefer the "Interesting Man" theory.

One very large reason why I think this way is because of the professional at-tachment I have to American intellectual history, which is to say, the history of American ideas. The Psalmist says, *As a man thinketh in his heart, so is he*, and I am inclined to agree, not because I am a Platonic philosopher who imagines that ideal forms are the only reality, but because ideas are the only things we really know and the things which turn out to have very long innings in human affairs. I suppose I came to this conclusion on the day, when I was about ten years old, that I realized, as I sat rocking and thinking, that thinking was an extremely pleasurable activity. Ideas, to be sure, have a developmental pattern to them; but ideas are also what are shaped, articulated, and applied by very different people. They do not act on their own, but through personalities, and in the hands of certain personalities, they can be terrible, indeed. Moreover, ideas do not have a chronological limitation. They can remain the same over very long stretches of time, or mutate dramatically in the hands of one or more people; and they can carry over from generation to generation in such a way that it is not at all unreasonable to ask, given a certain collection of ideas in someone's head, what they might do with the same ideas, but in different circumstances.

This is, incidentally, how I came to spend so much time on Lincoln in the first place. My reading about Abraham Lincoln actually goes back quite far—as a boy, growing up during the years of the Civil War centennial, and as the son of a career U.S. army officer, I fell pretty easily into a boy's interest in Lincoln and the war, and very likely the first thing I had in hand to read about Lincoln was a *Classics Illustrated* comic-book biography of Lincoln, bought on a train platform in 1962 as I was about to set off on a journey by rail to Chicago. Boyish interests being what they are, my attention soon wandered off to other things, until in high school—and for reasons I cannot recall with any certainty—I wrote a senior thesis in American government class on Lincoln's nomination to the presidency (heavily dependent on the school library's copy of Sandburg's *Abraham Lincoln*) and got the ticket as the narrator in the school orchestra's performance of Aaron Copland's *A Lincoln Portrait*. The next year, I bought my first wholly owned Lincoln book in (the now long-departed) Hasting's Book Store on Walnut Street in Philadelphia, an autographed copy of Stefan Lorant's photographic biography of Lincoln, which I did everything short of completely memorizing. This did not make me a Lincolnite, though. My first year in college I was a music composition major. (That did not last longer than the first year, after I finally had to face up to the fact that I lacked any real talent for it.) I wrote my doctoral dissertation at the University of Pennsylvania, not on Lincoln, but on Jonathan Edwards and the problem of free will in American thought. And it was only when, in 1995, I was working on a follow-up volume on determinism and free will in modern American thought that I decided, more for the novelty than the history, to make some reference to Abraham Lincoln, who liked to describe himself as a "fatalist."

What I discovered, especially as I worked through the Herndon-Weik Papers, was that there was a great deal more going on in Lincoln's mind than incidental notions of politics and liberty. Lincoln had not had an extensive education to speak of, and he came by much of his knowledge through whatever books happened to fall his way in frontier Indiana. But he had the temperament of a thinker, and his reading was much more formidable in its breadth than I had ever been led to suspect. That February, I read a paper on Lincoln and his "Doctrine of Necessity" to the Abraham Lincoln Association, and shortly thereafter, Chuck Van Hof and William B. Eerdmans Publishing approached me about writing a book on Lincoln and religion. I turned them down—not once, but twice—since I knew all too well what kind of swamp-life inhabited the Lincoln-and-religion genre, and I wanted no association with it. But Mark Noll (then of Wheaton College and the most suave of all historians of American Protestant theology) prevailed on me to reconsider, and I subsequently argued with Van Hof that what was really needed was a book on "Lincoln as a man of ideas." And so emerged my first Lincoln opus, *Abraham Lincoln: Redeemer President* (1999), with a title lifted lightly from Walt Whitman.

Having once put my hand into the pot, it proved very difficult to extricate it and turn to something else. (In fact, I've never gotten back to that book on free will and determinism.) It was while I was writing *Redeemer President* that Lerone Bennett published his vast anti-Lincoln screed, *Forced into Glory*, and I was so jarred by Bennett's unlikely demand of Lincoln that he possess a full-fledged set of modern sensibilities on race that when *Redeemer President* was finished, I felt almost obliged to turn my hand to the Emancipation Proclamation. I was dumbfounded to discover, at the very outset, how very little had been written on the proclamation—dumbfounded, but at the same time, relieved, since it gave me a free hand in delving into the subject. What I found was more than a little surprising—first, that Lincoln had been contemplating a serious move toward emancipation as early as November 1861; second, that a large part of his seeming slow-footedness and penchant for gradual emancipation and colonization of blacks back to Africa was not dictated by racism, but by the forbidding legal circumstances he faced as president; third, that behind the decision for a proclamation was the fear that George McClellan was on the verge of some form of military intervention, and that a proclamation was the only way Lincoln had to wedge emancipation into public policy as quickly as possible; and fourth, that he was radical enough, even in the formulation of the proclamation, to contemplate a slave uprising behind Confederate lines. The difference between Bennett's white supremacist caricature and the actual progress of Lincoln's thought leading up to the Emancipation Proclamation turned out to be as different as a straight line is from the coast of Norway.

Even with the proclamation, you will notice, I was still dealing with the history of ideas. The particular set of ideas which dominated Lincoln's life, as so often is true in the history of ideas, had grown out of Lincoln's own experiences (and resentments) and yet was remarkably free enough to survive his own personal demise. He was, if I can capture Lincoln in a phrase, a classic nineteenth-century democratic liberal—which is to say that he took his inspiration from the economic and political ideas of the Enlightenment and built his mental universe on three classic liberal dogmas: *the desirability of economic mobility*, *social moralism* (not religion per se, but certainly a sense of universal ethical norms, based on ideas of natural law), and *national union*. "There is no permanent class of hired laborers amongst us," Lincoln said in 1859, thus neatly decapitating all theories of class warfare. "Twenty-five years ago, I was a hired laborer. The hired laborer of yesterday, labors on his own account today; and will hire others to labor for him tomorrow. Advancement—improvement of condition—is the order of things in a society of equals." Five years later, he told the soldiers of an Ohio regiment, "Nowhere in the world is presented a government of so much liberty and equality. To the humblest and poorest amongst us are held out the highest privileges and positions. The present moment finds me at the White House, yet there is as good a chance for your children as there was for my father's." Nor was Lincoln interested in identity politics, for ethnic identities (like class identities) were relics of the Old World that the American Republic had exposed as childish illusions. The Declaration of Independence, for instance, was not limited in its application to any single section, race, or nationality; it contained fundamental propositions about human nature which were true of all people everywhere. "Perhaps half our people . . . are men who have come from Europe—German, Irish, French and Scandinavian," Lincoln said in 1858.

> . . . but when they look through that old Declaration of Independence they find that those old men say that "We hold these truths to be self-evident, that all men are created equal," then they feel that that moral sentiment taught in that day evidences their relation to those men, that it is the father of all moral principle in them, and that they have a right to claim it as though they were blood of the blood, and flesh of the flesh of the men who wrote

that Declaration, and so they are. That is the electric cord in that Declaration that links the hearts of patriotic and liberty-loving men together, that will link those patriotic hearts as long as the love of freedom exists in the minds of men throughout the world.

But even a man as tightly logical as Lincoln understood that nations cannot be held together merely by abstractions. In the absence of appeals to race, ethnicity, kinship, or religion—the social glue of monarch-ridden Europe—a nation founded on a *proposition* can sometimes do the wrong thing with that proposition. It can, in the case of the slaveholding South, insist that the equality in that proposition is only an equality of white people; or it can say, in the case of Stephen A. Douglas, that everyone is entitled to pursue equality in their own way, free from anyone else's objection. Lincoln saw that, as much as politics and religion and morality don't always make a good marriage, they make for even worse divorce. For this consistently secular man, who never joined a church, there was still no way to speak in America of equality and politics in ways which did not conform to the eternal principles of right and wrong; nor did he hesitate to chart out a path for a political future he did not live to realize by reminding his audience that the future had to be seen under the dictates of the justice of God. For Lincoln, "Moral principle," in the end, "is all that unites us."

Lincoln's years as president have usually been measured against the events of the Civil War, and not without reason. But the noise and carnage of the war have frequently obscured the domestic agenda Lincoln implemented, an agenda which hefted into place legislation to encourage "the development of the industrial interests of the whole country," financing a transcontinental railroad (which would have been nearly completed by the end of Lincoln's second term as president, if he had lived that long), a national banking system, the highest protective tariff schedule the nation had yet deployed to protect American manufacturing, and homestead laws to open up the Western territories to immediate settlement. As president, Lincoln championed a domestic policy revolution almost as profound in its consequences as the Civil War itself and set the course for a Republican ascendancy that lasted (with only the minor interruption of Grover Cleveland) for the next fifty years—for a full political generation—until the election of 1912.[5] Homesteads, tariffs, and the money supply remained the three most controversial issues of postwar America, and they were fully as much the hot-button issues for the McKinley presidency as they were for Abraham Lincoln.

The ultimate guarantor of self-improvement and self-transformation was the Union, for it was the national Union, not the quarrelsome jealousy of states or regions, which gave Americans the largest stage upon which to act, plan, and speak without fear of interference from parochial conformity or small-minded provincialism. Lincoln "knew no North, no South, no East, no West, but only the Union, which held them all in its sacred circle," and he wished "to be no less than National in all the positions I may take." In Lincoln's eyes, the fundamental flaw of the states' rights palaver of the Confederates was its cynical appeal to division, diversity, localism, and special interests, and all at the expense of the liberty which only a national Union could guarantee. "On the distinct issue of Union or no Union," Lincoln told Congress in 1864, "the politicians have shown their instinctive knowledge that there is no diversity among the people." Americans were everywhere Americans—including the freed slaves—and there were no gradations in that citizenship based on state, region, race, or religion.

Looking at him across the gulf of years, I am not sure that we can extort from Abraham Lincoln specific answers to the kinds of questions that come under the general heading of *what would Lincoln do?* But I do believe that the long-term trajectory of his ideas points us in certain definite directions. He believed profoundly in the virtue of social mobility, in empowering all citizens through the creation of favorable economic circumstances to achieve as much as their talents could manage. He believed that democracy was the expression of the natural possession of rights by human beings, but he also believed that it possessed a transcendent mandate to do what is intrinsically right, morally and naturally, and not merely to act as a process for endorsing whatever a majority wanted at a given moment. And he believed in the capacity of Americans as Americans to accomplish that good—not as individuals alone, but as a united nation, dedicated to the natural-law proposition of the equality of all men. I do not think that we will really learn how to "do what Lincoln would have done" merely by trying to squeeze from him a sound-bite answer to whatever question nags us at the moment; but neither do I believe that he is lost to us on the tides of time, washed away from all sight, if only because the ideas which were his polestar remain the ideas most dear to the American imagination. Lincoln the striver—Lincoln the moralist—Lincoln the American—remains, in an age whose elites shudder with embarrassment over my embrace of these terms, if not an oracle, still yet a guide.

Notes

1. David Herbert Donald, "Getting Right with Lincoln," in *Lincoln Reconsidered: Essays on the Civil War Era* (1955; New York, 2001), 13.

2. Caleb Crain, "Bad Precedent," *New Yorker*, January 29, 2007, 84.

3. Joseph Ellis, "Washington: The Crying Game," *Los Angeles Times*, December 29, 2006.

4. Kenneth Cmiel, *Democratic Eloquence: The Fight over Popular Speech in Nineteenth-Century America* (Berkeley, CA, 1990), 59–60.

5. Or until 1932, if we are disposed to regard Wilson's victory in a three-way race in 1912, and a squeaker in 1916, as only interruptions in a Republican regime that resumed its dominance in 1920.

I

—

THE UNLIKELY INTELLECTUAL
BIOGRAPHY OF ABRAHAM LINCOLN

Whatever else we are likely to think about Abraham Lincoln, the odds are that we will not be likely to think of him as a man of ideas. The image of Lincoln which comes down to most of us casts him into a number of roles, but an intellectual is not usually one of them. It is possible, for instance, that we will see Lincoln principally as a politician; and within that view, we will find little that will incline us to argue with the dictum of William Henry Herndon, Lincoln's third law partner, that "politics were his Heaven" and that therefore "his Hades" was "metaphysics." Or else our basic picture of Lincoln will be shaped by the fact that he was a lawyer; not a legal theorist, but a basic trial lawyer, a "*nisi prius* lawyer*," who had no interest in anything more abstract than a routine trespass and assumpsit. This view will be reinforced by the comment made by his second law partner, Stephen T. Logan, who dismissed Lincoln as a competent, but mentally shallow, legal technician. "I don't think he studied much," Logan said in 1875. "I think he learned his law more in the study of cases. He would work hard and learn all there was in a case he had in hand. He got to be a pretty good lawyer though his general knowledge of law was never very formidable." As Herndon once remarked, Lincoln was the quintessentially practical man of law: "Mr. Lincoln was a very patient man generally, but if you wished to be cut off at the knee, just go at Lincoln with abstractions, glittering generalities, indefiniteness, mistiness of idea or expression."[1]

Or else, what is most predictable of all, our notion of Lincoln will be shaped by his presidency, an office where we may look for someone to possess substantial management or political skills, but where being an intellectual of any sort is not what we have come to expect, except perhaps in the case of Thomas Jefferson. And in fact, most accounts of Lincoln in the White House convey to us the picture of a man who combined political sharpness with a certain amount of cheap humor. Treasury Secretary Salmon Portland Chase was as genuinely puzzled as that owlish and pious man could be by Lincoln's affection for newspapers and joke books. Three weeks before his reelection in 1864, "in a lull of despatches," Lincoln's secretary John M. Hay noticed Lincoln "took from his pocket the Nasby Papers and read several chapters of the experiences of the saint & martyr Petroleum V. They were immensely amusing. Stanton and Dana [the secretary and assistant secretary of war] enjoyed them scarcely less than the President who read on *con amore* until 9 oclock."[2]

Nothing seems to underscore Lincoln's image as a shrewd but untutored fixer than Lincoln's own self-descriptions. In the entry he composed for a biographical dictionary of Congress, he described his early education as "defective"; in two autobiographical sketches he wrote for publicists in the 1860 presidential campaign, he maintained that he went to mere "A.B.C. schools by little" when he went at all, and he estimated that "the aggregate of all his schooling did not amount to one year." In all of this, Lincoln remembered that "there was absolutely nothing to excite ambition for education." The result was that "when I came of age I did not know much" beyond how to "read, write, and cipher to the Rule of Three."[3] From such a thinly furnished mental world, we are not surprised to find Lincoln describing himself as a politician who "never had a policy," who "simply tried to do what seemed best each day, as each day came," and who described public opinion as "everything."[4] Not that this, in Herndon's estimation, subtracted from Lincoln's greatness; for Herndon, Lincoln was great, but in a romantic, natural, rough-hewn way. A formal education would have ruined Lincoln.

> Had he gone to college and half graduated, or wholly so, and before his style was crystallized, or had he been educated in our rounded, flat, dull artistic style of expression, writing or speaking, he would have lost, and the world would have lost, his strong individuality in his speech, his style, manner, and method of utterance. He would have been a rounded man in an artistic way, would have sunk into the classic beautiful.[5]

All of this does nothing except yield greater support to Herndon's notorious comment that "Lincoln read less and thought more than any other American."[6] And what he thought about most, Herndon added, was politics and political advantage. Even as people esteemed Lincoln an honest man—"Honest Old Abe"—they still doubted whether his politics were much more than adroit (or adroitly timed) manipulations. "He had all shades of sentiments and opinions to deal with," explained his Illinois law associate, Leonard Swett, "and the consideration was always presented to his mind, How can I hold these discordant elements together? Hence in dealing with men he was a trimmer, and such a trimmer the world has never seen."[7] This reputation for intellectual mediocrity, politely dressed up as crude naturalism, was already hardening into public reputation while he was president, and at his funeral in Springfield, Illinois, in May 1865, not even the preacher of the funeral sermon, Methodist bishop Matthew Simpson, could avoid apologizing for Lincoln's meager intellectual visibility. "A few months spent in the schoolhouse gave him the elements of education," Simpson acknowledged, but since "his home was in the growing West, the heart of the republic . . . he learned lessons of self-reliance" instead of philosophy, "which sustained him in seasons of adversity."[8]

Lincoln's biographers merely picked up where his eulogists left off. In the biographies written by his onetime associates—Ward Hill Lamon in 1872 and Herndon in 1889—Lincoln appears as the offspring of a crude backcountry, whose triumph lies in his capacity to outgrow those crudities by sheer dint of natural effort. For Carl Sandburg, Lincoln is the naturally endowed lover of liberty, a Christ-figure without real intellectual antecedents, beyond (and not merely above) ideological political squabbling.

> Like something out of a picture book for children—he was. . . . He looked like an original plan for an extra-long horse or a lean tawny buffalo that a Changer had suddenly whisked into a man-shape. Or he met the eye as a clumsy, mystical giant that had walked out of a Chinese or Russian fairy story, or a bogy who had stumbled out of an ancient Saxon myth with a handkerchief full of presents he wanted to divide among all the children in the world. . . . In his way he belonged to the west country as Robert Burns belonged to Scotland or Hans Christian Anderson to North Europe.

And in the most recent versions, such as David Donald's 1995 *Lincoln*, he possesses an "essential passivity," which, while it did not exactly induce "lethargy or dissipation," certainly did not drive him to more than "a pragmatic approach to problems."[9]

Some of this picture of Lincoln as a doer rather than a thinker was Lincoln's own fault, since he was almost deliberately careless in identifying the intellectual springs of his political and professional actions. Lincoln professed to have no interest in laying out evidence of his thought processes for biographical explanation, his own or others', at all. In 1843, shortly after entering into partnership with Lincoln as the junior partner in Lincoln's law business, Herndon recommended Lincoln read a new biography of Edmund Burke, which Herndon had been greatly impressed by. "No, I don't want to read it,"

Lincoln replied. He was too suspicious that most biographies were written with something less than the ink of truth and something more of the whitewash bucket. "Biographies as written are false and misleading."

> The author of the Life of his love paints him as a perfect man, magnifies his perfections and suppresses his imperfections, describes the success of his love in glowing terms, never once hinting at his failures and his blunders. Why do not . . . book merchants and sellers have blank biographies on their shelves always ready for sale, so that, when a man dies, if his heirs, children, and friends wish to perpetuate the memory of the dead, they can purchase one already written, *but with blanks*, which they can fill up eloquently and grandly at pleasure, thus commemorating a lie, an injury to the dying and to the name of the dead.[10]

And given the rules which governed biographical writing in the nineteenth century—in fact, given what happened in Lincoln biography after his death—there were some grounds for Lincoln's skepticism. Leonard Swett warned Herndon in 1887 not to reveal too much of Lincoln's inner life in the biography Herndon was trying to complete because "history is made to perpetuate a man's virtues or hold up his vices to be shunned." It was, in other words, designed either to tell a saint's tale or a sinner's, not to offer a dispassionate rendering of events or characters. "The heroes of the world are its standards, and in time, all faults and all bad or common humanities are eliminated and they become clothed with imaginary virtues. . . . If I should say Mr. Lincoln ever swore & you were to publish it, the public would believe I lied about it. It would damage your book, and if the book were otherwise acceptable, the next edition would leave out that fact, in the publication." (One biography which tried to do exactly that, Ward Hill Lamon's *Life of Abraham Lincoln*, was a case in point, since the first volume of Lamon's 1872 tell-all biography aroused so much criticism that the projected second volume was never published, and Lamon's ghostwriter, Chauncey F. Black, believed that the publisher had deliberately sabotaged sales.) In the end, even Herndon, for all of his confidence that he could (and should) "state all the facts" concerning Lincoln's life, kept back "some *secret* and *private* things which I would let no other man have Even a sight at." Telling absolute truth was, as Herndon discovered, "a hard road to travel in this world when that truth runs square up against our ideas of what we think it *ought* to be."[11]

Lincoln had other reasons to be wary of self-revelation. Even before his nomination for the presidency in May of 1860, Republican newspapers had been picking up notices concerning the Illinois party chief who had bearded Stephen Douglas in his own political den, and Illinois Republican editors like John Locke Scripps and Charles H. Ray of the *Chicago Tribune* begged him to write out a brief autobiography, which they could use to promote his candidacy among East Coast Republicans. "Why, Scripps, it is a great piece of folly to attempt to make anything out of my early life," Lincoln replied. "It can all be condensed into a single sentence, and that sentence you will find in Gray's Elegy: 'The short and simple annals of the poor.' That's my life, and that's all you or anyone else can make of it." This was not merely an exhibition of charming humility. Newspapermen like Scripps and Ray who came to know Lincoln first in the 1850s, as his political star began to ascend in Illinois, saw only a well-respected railroad lawyer and politico who had married into an influential political family in the state, and whose legal practice on the Eighth Judicial Circuit had built for him an impressive network of political friends and supporters. "My dear Sir," wrote Ray, by way of introducing himself to Lincoln in 1858 during Lincoln's great senatorial debates with Stephen A. Douglas, "it was my suspicion that Abe Lincoln was not born with a silver spoon in his mouth," and nothing surprised Ray more than to find out this was indeed the case.[12]

The truth was that Lincoln was not at all proud of his humble, yeoman agricultural origins, and precisely because those origins seemed to yield so little in the way of intellectual respectability. Born into what might be justifiably described as the archetypal Jacksonian subsistence-farming family, Lincoln (at least from adolescence) hugely disliked farmwork and, even more, the narrow constraints of rural culture; he disliked the uncouthness, violence, and drunkenness of his neighbors; and above all, he disliked his father, whom he once characterized as knowing not much "more in the way of writing than to bunglingly sign his own name."[13] Part of this arose from the coolness and mutual incomprehension that arose between father and son, especially when Thomas Lincoln remarried after Abraham's mother died. "Thos. Lincoln never showed by his actions that he thought much of his son Abraham when a boy," recalled A. H. Chapman, the son-in-law of Lincoln's unreliable but voluble cousin, Dennis Hanks. "He treated him rather unkindly than otherwise, always appeared to think more of his stepson John D. Johnston than he did of his own son, Abraham."[14] Lincoln left his father's farm near Decatur, Illinois, soon after he turned twenty-one and was no longer obliged to work for his father, and left at once for the big city—in this case, New Orleans, where he arrived in 1831 as part of the crew of a flatboat owned by Denton Offutt, a raffish central Illinois entrepreneur. Offutt liked Lincoln so much that he hired Lincoln to work in his store in another promising entrepôt, New Salem, Illinois, and so Lincoln embarked on his first career, as a storekeeper. It was not a particularly successful career, but even so he never once considered farming as an occupation, even after two stores in New Salem failed underneath him.

Instead, he moved to Springfield in 1837, where he undertook the study of law and became the junior partner of one of the sharpest Whig lawyers in the state, John Todd Stuart. He thus joined a profession and took up a major role in a political party which were both very nearly the antithesis of Jeffersonian agrarianism, for lawyers and Whigs in the early Republic were the chief enforcers of contract, the principal agents of banks and agricultural bankruptcy statutes, and the great promoters of Henry Clay's "American System" of government sponsorship for business and industrial development.

Lincoln was ever afterward wary of people who would expose his crude frontier origins, and he was even warier of those who wanted to hunt up some of the more unconventional aspects of his life to use against him. Certainly the most unconventional part concerned his religion, or rather his lack of it. Although he was raised among the hyper-Calvinist Baptist sects of Kentucky and Indiana and from them imbibed a strong dose of determinism, Calvinism gave shape more than content to his thinking. Born at the end of the "long Enlightenment," Lincoln was captured by the "infidelity" of "[Constantin] Volney & Tom Pain[e]," and John Todd Stuart remembered that, in his twenties, Lincoln "went further against Christian beliefs—& doctrines & principles than any man I ever heard." All of Lincoln's friends from his early days in Springfield united in describing Lincoln as a religious "skeptic" or even an "infidel," and there is no evidence through the 1840s that Lincoln attended any church in Springfield. This failure to establish a recognizable religious profile had long been, as Lincoln knew, a major political liability: as early as 1837, he was aware that his political enemies were asking "an old acquaintance of mine" whether "he ever heard Lincoln say he was a deist," and in 1843 he acknowledged that "because I belonged to no church," he had suffered "a tax of a considerable per cent. upon my strength throughout the religious community." He sometimes replied, in religious self-defense, that "his parents were Baptists, and brought him up in the belief of the Baptist religion," and even offered the private opinion that adult "baptism by immersion [rather than baptizing infants by pouring or sprinkling] was the true meaning of the word." But even Noyes Miner, the minister of Springfield's First Baptist Church, who liked Lincoln and often borrowed the Lincoln family's horse and carriage for church work, could only bring himself to suggest that Lincoln "was what is termed an experimental Christian." And Lincoln frankly admitted to Thomas D. Jones, "My father was a member of the Baptist Church, but I am not." Given the cultural dominance of evangelical Protestantism in the early Republic, Lincoln had no reason to welcome any discovery of this part of his intellectual biography.[15]

And yet, despite his distaste for intellectual self-revelation, the outlines of an intellectual life kept leaking through. Halfway through the summer of 1863,

Lincoln's Brown University-educated secretary, John Milton Hay, "had a talk on philology" with Lincoln, a subject for which Lincoln turned out to have "a little indulged inclination." Herndon was equally surprised to be told that in the 1840s, Lincoln "made Geology and other sciences a special study," and that the impact made by Sir Charles Lyell's *Principles of Geology* (1830–33) and Robert Chambers's *Vestiges of the Natural History of Creation* (1844) turned Lincoln, who was already a religious skeptic, into "a firm believer in the theory of development." And when James Quay Howard interviewed Lincoln's first law partner, John Todd Stuart, for a campaign biography in 1860, Stuart caught Howard off guard by describing Lincoln's mind as being "of a metaphysical and philosophical order . . . of very general and varied knowledge." Lincoln, said Stuart, "has an inventive faculty—is always studying into the nature of things."[16]

This wide-ranging intellectual curiosity had early beginnings for Lincoln. As a young man, he was "not energetic Except in one thing," remembered his stepsister, Matilda Johnston, but "he was active & persistent in learning—read Everything he Could." As a store clerk in New Salem in the 1830s, he picked up lessons in grammar from a local schoolmaster and "also studied 'Natural Philosophy'"—possibly Thomas Brown's *Lectures on the Philosophy of the Human Mind* (1820) or the more well-known utilitarian William Paley's *Principles of Moral and Political Philosophy* (1785)—as well as "Astronomy, Chemistry," using whatever books he could find "from which he could derive information or knowledge." One New Salem neighbor remembered that "History and poetry & the newspapers constituted the most of his reading," while "[Robert] Burns seemed to be his favorite. . . . Used to sit up late of nights reading, & would recommence in the morning when he got up." And whatever he read, "he generally mastered a book quickly—as one who was simply reading—so comprehensive was his mind." Once Lincoln moved to Springfield to read law under the tutelage of John Todd Stuart, he continued to "read hard works—was philosophical—logical—mathematical—never read generally" and managed to make himself "an Educated Man in 1860—more than is generally known." His closest friend, Joshua Speed, remembered that "he read law, History, [Thomas] Browns Philosophy or [William] Paley—Burns, Byron, Milton or Shakespeare." Herndon remembered that the Lincoln-Herndon law office filled up, not only with the standard court report volumes, but also with volumes of essays by Thomas Carlyle and Ralph Waldo Emerson, sermons by Theodore Parker and Henry Ward Beecher, the philosophy of the French "common-sense" realist Victor Cousin and his English counterpart, Sir William Hamilton, the biblical criticism of D. F. Strauss and Ernst Renan, the left-Hegelianism of Ludwig Feuerbach, the materialist *History of Civilization in England* by Henry Thomas Buckle, and the evolutionary psychology of Sir Herbert Spencer. Even if Lincoln was not, as Herndon insisted, "a general reader"—someone who read anything that came to hand—he was still "a persistent thinker, and a profound analyzer of the subject which engaged his attention." Lincoln not only "frequently read parts of the volumes," but readily slipped "into a philosophic discussion, and sometimes on religious questions and sometimes on this question and on that." Even in the last few weeks of his life, the president who was better known for reading aloud from humor books reminded Noah Brooks that he "particularly liked [Bishop Joseph] Butler's Analogy of Religion, Stuart Mill on Liberty, and . . . always hoped to get at [Jonathan] Edwards on the Will."[17]

Nothing, however, captured Lincoln's intellectual fancy more than "political economy, the study of it." Shelby Cullom, who served in the Illinois legislature and then in Congress, thought that "theoretically . . . on political economy he was great." And the backbone of his reading in the 1840s and 1850s was the basic texts of classical nineteenth-century liberalism: "[John Stuart] Mill's political economy, [Henry] Carey's political economy . . . McCullough's [John Ramsay McCulloch's] political economy, [Francis] Wayland, and some others." (Herndon remembered that "Lincoln ate up, digested, and assimilated" Wayland's 1837 textbook, *The Elements of Political Economy*.) From Jeremy Bentham, he not only borrowed the standard utilitarian maxim of "the greatest good for the greatest number," but also Bentham's concept of legal punishment as rehabilitation rather than retribution, and the Benthamite axiom that all human choices are a function of selfishness and self-interest. It is against this overall context of liberal democracy that Lincoln's emergence as an antislavery activist in the 1850s must be seen, since he defined African American slavery primarily as an economic relationship—as the suppression of economic mobility and self-improvement—and was largely indifferent to its racial dimension.[18]

But the most decisive way in which Lincoln's built-up habits of mind influenced American political life was the peculiar and unpredictable way in which his ancestral Calvinism reappeared as a device for interpreting the events of the Civil War. Lincoln's rationalist skepticism on religious matters had been shifting as he entered on midlife in the 1850s; but the hammering of the war forced that shifting to accelerate, since he could find no other answer for the pointless slaughter of the war except in the activity of a mysterious Providence who had aims and ends which ordinary people had not expected. At the close of the disastrous summer of 1862, he wrote a brief memorandum "on the Divine Will" in which he reminded himself that the presumed directions of the war were, under the relentless grinding of combat, being diverted by God toward entirely different conclusions.

> The will of God prevails. . . . In the present civil war it is quite possible that
> God's purpose is something different from the purpose of either party. . . .
> By his mere quiet power, on the minds of the now contestants, He could

have either saved or destroyed the Union without a human contest. Yet the contest began. And having begun He could give the final victory to either side any day. Yet the contest proceeds.[19]

And his pledge "with malice toward none; with charity for all" at the end of the Civil War was actually a product of his fatalistic conviction (part Calvin, part Bentham) that real decisions were out of human hands, and therefore neither Northerners nor Southerners had the privilege of judging each other. This, Herndon believed, was the real spring of Lincoln's "patience" and "his charity for men and his want of malice for them everywhere." "His whole philosophy made him free from hate," Herndon remarked. "No man was to be eulogized for what he did or censured for what he did not do or did do."[20]

What the complexity of Lincoln's intellectual life shows is an Enlightenment figure who struggled to create a mediating ground between a society focused on individual rights and a society eager to affirm certain moral, philosophical, and intellectual nonnegotiables. He was a fatalist who promoted freedom; he was a classical liberal who couched liberalism's greatest deed—the emancipation of the slaves—in the highly unliberal language of divine providence and predestination; he was a religious doubter who became a national icon almost bordering on religion; and he was a rights-oriented liberal who shifted to appeals to natural law when confronting slavery. "What natural right requires Kansas and Nebraska to be opened to Slavery? Is not slavery universally granted to be, in the abstract, a gross outrage on the law of nature?" Lincoln asked in 1854. "Have not all civilized nations, our own among them, made the Slave trade capital, and classed it with piracy and murder? Is it not held to be the great wrong of the world? . . . In all these cases it is your sense of justice, and human sympathy, continually telling you, that the poor negro has some natural right to himself that those who deny it, and make mere merchandise of him, deserve kickings, contempt and death."[21]

It is said, and to the point of numbness, that Lincoln was a *pragmatist*, because he had a politician's eye for concession and compromise when they were needed. But if by *pragmatist* we mean someone who had regard only for results and not for principles, we could not be more wrong. Lincoln, wrote his friend Leonard Swett, "loved principles and such like large political & national ones, Especially when it leads to his own Ends—paths—Ambitions—Success—honor &c. &c." Even as a "trimmer," what Lincoln was looking for was a society which prized individual rights—"self-government"—but which balanced the pursuit of personal rights with the need for a national consensus about moral, philosophical, and intellectual issues.

Seen in this way, Lincoln poses a serious question to the pragmatic reading of American intellectual history; perhaps on the same grounds, he also poses a question about the role pragmatism has played as a sort of popular national philosophy. The Great Convention of American intellectual history ever since the 1930s has been that American ideas begin with Jonathan Edwards, move to the religious liberals who undermined the Puritan tradition, introduce nonreligious political secularists like Franklin and Jefferson, and then shift to Emerson, Thoreau, and the New England novelists as a way of finally introducing William James and John Dewey as the "Golden Age of American Philosophy."[22] Today, this progress has been reupholstered by the rise in reputation of Charles Sanders Peirce, but even then this is usually as means of treating Peirce as a precursor of postmodernism and the bridge over which we cross from James to Richard Rorty, who purported to speak as James's (and Dewey's) modern philosophical executor.[23]

This "pragmatic captivity" of American intellectual history shortchanges us on several fronts: First, the Great Convention, which is mostly a product of James's and Dewey's admirers, is straightforwardly a secular and antisystematic convention. It acknowledges religion only as a starting point to move away from, and its heroes (Franklin, Jefferson, Emerson) tend idiosyncratically to confirm secularists in the conviction that theirs is the only story worth telling. This might be more tolerable if the secularists under examination had been systematic thinkers in any way, but it would be hard on even the most optimistic grounds to portray Benjamin Franklin, much less Ralph Waldo Emerson, as a systematist. In fact, the intellectual genealogy which connects Franklin to Emerson is built around ill-arranged, amateurish texts and New England fiction and actually has very little internal consistency, apart from a certain common animus against Calvinism. It stands in sorry contrast to the system-building efforts of Edwards and even more to the extraordinary labors of religious systematists after him, ranging from the Edwardsean "New Divinity" to romantic confessionalists like John Williamson Nevin and the pious rationalism of the collegiate moral philosophers. A curriculum which moves from Franklin to Emerson with no station for Francis Wayland has not only revealed a certain incoherency but has neglected immense chunks of American philosophy whose only offense was that they thought epistemology was important in ways that William James did not. And it certainly has no way of recognizing the intellectual life of a public man like Lincoln, which was derived from the struggles of Calvinists, moral philosophers, and common-law lawyers to achieve systematic consistency.

Second, the Great Convention confines what intellectual biography there is worth doing to a comparative handful of individuals centered in New England and particularly within the orbit of Cambridge. This is comparable to, say, writing the history of opera in America as a function of the Saturday matinee at the Met. If such an operatic history were written that way, we would probably dismiss it as a function of New York City *hubris*—failing in the process to see how much of American intellectual history, from Emerson to Hilary Putnam, represents a Harvard *hubris,* and forgetting how much of American intellectual history *writing,* from Vernon Louis Parrington to Perry Miller, was produced by a faculty which still teaches the subject in Emerson Hall, beneath a group portrait of James, Josiah Royce, and George Herbert Palmer. There has been an American mind outside Harvard Yard—Edwards was a Yale graduate, as were Francis Wayland and Noah Porter; Hegelianism found its first homes in America in Mercersburg, Pennsylvania, and St. Louis, Missouri; Josiah Royce was a graduate of Berkeley; and Charles Peirce's one lonely full-time teaching job was in Baltimore—and one step towards reclaiming it is to shift our geographical horizons farther afield, including the fields of Lincoln's Illinois.

The admirers of pragmatism who, beginning with Ralph Barton Perry in the 1930s, attempted to redate the beginnings of American philosophy to William James did at least mark a dramatic transition in the history of American ideas. There is no doubt that James, Peirce, and Chauncey Wright signal a sea change in the foundations of American epistemology, ethics, and metaphysics; but it is the direction of a pragmatic tradition which makes the words *intellectual biography* fail on the lips; for how can one compose intellectual biographies of angry philosophers like Richard Rorty, who defiantly assures us that "for purposes of thinking about how to achieve our country, we do not need to worry about the correspondence theory of truth, the grounds of normativity, the impossibility of justice, or the infinite distance that separates us from the other. For those purposes, we can give both religion and philosophy a pass. We can just get on with trying to solve what Dewey called 'the problems of men.'"[24]

Still, acknowledging the immense shift that pragmatism represents between 1870 and 1900 should not be the same thing as saying that no worthwhile tradition in American thought existed beforehand. Not just one, but several, such intellectual traditions existed, the most dominant being the tradition of collegiate metaphysics known as "moral philosophy," and one of the most rigorously ethical being the immaterialist theology handed on by Edwards and his successors and culminating in Charles Grandison Finney. If not in the pragmatists, then certainly in these lost traditions of American intellectual life we can find more than enough occupation for American intellectual biography. And it is in those lost traditions that we first begin to discover that Abraham Lincoln, too, has an intellectual biography.

Lincoln, for all of his intellectual hobbies, "was not a speculative-minded man," admitted Herndon, and "never ran in advance of his age." Lincoln never wrote a book, or even (unlike his bête noire, Stephen A. Douglas) published an opinion piece in the *Atlantic Monthly.* But his great Cooper Union address of February 1860 was a remarkable piece of constitutional scholarship; and it is still possible to read even the apparent ephemera of Lincoln's *Collected Writings* as markers of an intellectual geography. Lincoln was a cautious and immensely private man, who rarely divulged his plans or motives to anyone, and so the tendency has been to assume ether that he had no real plans and drifted with events, or that his motives were wrapped inside a godlike shroud of virtue. But Lincoln's political plans were guided, from his earliest days as a state legislator in Illinois, by a strict loyalty to the Whig political ideology and a loathing of Jacksonian democracy, and even his domestic policies as president were, in many respects, little more than the final installation of Henry Clay's "American System" as a philosophy of government. And, as Herndon argued, much of what passes for merciful instinct was, in fact, a spin-off of Lincoln's fundamental disbelief in human freedom and human personal responsibility. His declaration of charity for all and malice toward none was not, as it is often portrayed, a testimony to Lincoln's kindliness (if so, it makes for a jarring contrast with the declaration preceding it, that every drop of blood drawn by the lash would be paid for by one drawn with the sword); it was a product of his fundamental conviction that human beings had no free will, and therefore one could hardly offer as a response anything other than charity and the withholding of malice. What Thomas Powers observed about Robert F. Kennedy can profitably be applied to Lincoln: "He was not an intellectual in the usual sense; he did not discuss, analyze, and argue with the books he was reading, but instead visited them, hunted solace in them, let them speak for him when he was overwhelmed by the imponderables of life."[25] Perhaps this is why we need to know that Lincoln thought and what he thought about.

Notes

This essay first appeared in *Transactions of the C. S. Peirce Society* 40.1 (2004), 83–106.

1. Herndon, November 24, 1882, in *The Hidden Lincoln: From the Letters and Papers of William H. Herndon*, ed. Emmanuel Hertz (New York, 1937), 90; "Conversation with Hon. S. T. Logan at Springfield, July 6, 1875," in *An Oral History of Abraham Lincoln: John G. Nicolay's Interviews and Essays*, ed. Michael Burlingame (Carbondale, IL, 1996), 37; Herndon to Jesse W. Weik, January 9, 1886, Herndon-Weik Papers, Library of Congress.

2. *Inside Lincoln's Cabinet: The Civil War Diaries of Salmon P. Chase*, ed. David H. Donald (New York, 1954), 149; *Inside Lincoln's White House: The Complete Civil War Diary of John Hay*, ed. Michael Burlingame and J. R. T. Ettlinger (Carbondale, IL, 1997), 239. "Petroleum Vesuvius Nasby" was the pen name of humorist David R. Locke.

3. Lincoln, "Brief Autobiography," June 1860, "Autobiography written for John L. Scripps," January 1860, and "To Jesse W. Fell, Enclosing Autobiography,"

December 20, 1859, in *The Collected Works of Abraham Lincoln*, ed. Roy P. Basler (New Brunswick, NJ, 1953–55), 2:459, 4:61, 3:511.

4. John M. Palmer, in *Recollected Words of Abraham Lincoln*, ed. Don Fehrenbacher and Virginia Fehrenbacher (Stanford, CA, 1996), 351; Lincoln, "First Debate with Stephen A. Douglas," August 21, 1858, in *Collected Works*, 3:27.

5. Herndon to Jesse W. Weik, January 7, 1886, in Herndon-Weik Papers, Library of Congress.

6. Herndon, "Lincoln the Individual," in Hertz, *Hidden Lincoln*, 417.

7. Leonard Swett to Herndon, January 17, 1866, in *Herndon's Informants: Letters, Interviews, and Statements about Abraham Lincoln*, ed. Douglas L. Wilson and Rodney O. Davis (Urbana, IL, 1998), 165.

8. Wayne C. Temple, *Abraham Lincoln: From Skeptic to Prophet* (Mahomet, IL, 1995), 384.

9. Carl Sandburg, *Abraham Lincoln: The Prairie Years* (New York, 1926), 2:284–85; David H. Donald, *Lincoln* (New York, 1995), 14–15.

10. Herndon to Jesse W. Weik, February 16, 1887, in Herndon-Weik Papers, Library of Congress.

11. Leonard Swett to Herndon, August 30, 1887, in Wilson and Davis, *Herndon's Informants*, 636–37; Douglas L. Wilson, "Keeping Lincoln's Secrets," *Atlantic Monthly* (May 2000), 78–88; Benjamin Thomas, *Portrait for Posterity: Lincoln and His Biographers* (New Brunswick, NJ, 1949), 74–75.

12. John L. Scripps to Herndon, June 24, 1865, in Wilson and Davis, *Herndon's Informants*, 57; Charles H. Ray to Lincoln, July 27, 1858, in *The Lincoln Papers*, ed. David C. Mearns (Garden City, NY, 1948), 1:218.

13. Lincoln, "Autobiography Written for John L. Scripps," June 1860, in *Collected Works*, 5:61.

14. A. H. Chapman to William Herndon, September 28, 1865, in Wilson and Davis, *Herndon's Informants*, 134.

15. Lincoln, "Second Reply to James Adams," October 18, 1837, and "To Martin S. Morris," March 26, 1843, in *Collected Works*, 1:106, 320; Abner Ellis to William Herndon, February 14, 1866, and interview with John Todd Stuart, March 2, 1870, in Wilson and Davis, *Herndon's Informants*, 210, 576.

16. John Hay, diary entry for July 25, 1863, in Burlingame and Ettlinger, *Inside Lincoln's White House*, 67–68; John Todd Stuart, in Mearns, *Lincoln Papers*, 159.

17. Mentor Graham, May 29, 1865, Henry McHenry, May 29, 1865, and Joshua Speed, December 6, 1866, to Herndon, in Wilson and Davis, *Herndon's Informants*, 10, 14, 499; William G. Green, in Mearns, *Lincoln Papers*, 154; Noah Brooks, "Personal Recollections of Abraham Lincoln," in *Lincoln Observed: Civil War Dispatches of Noah Brooks*, ed. Michael Burlingame (Baltimore, 1998), 219.

18. Herndon to Jesse W. Weik, January 1, 1886, in Hertz, *Hidden Lincoln*, 117; Shelby Cullom, in Walter B. Stevens, *A Reporter's Lincoln*, ed. Michael Burlingame (Lincoln, NE, 1998), 154.

19. Lincoln, "Meditation on the Divine Will," September 2, 1862?, in *Collected Works*, 5:403–4.

20. Herndon to Jesse W. Weik, February 26, 1891, in Hertz, *Hidden Lincoln*, 266.

21. Lincoln, "Speech at Springfield, Illinois," October 4, 1854, and "Speech at Peoria, Illinois," October 16, 1854, in *Collected Works*, 2:245, 265.

22. Bruce Kuklick, "Does American Philosophy Rest on a Mistake?" in *American Philosophy*, ed. Marcus G. Singer (Cambridge, 1985), 177–78.

23. William James, *Pragmatism*, ed. Bruce Kuklick (Indianapolis, 1981), 56; Cornel West, *The American Evasion of Philosophy: A Genealogy of Pragmatism* (Madison, WI, 1989), 42.

24. Richard Rorty, "The Dark Side of the Academic Left," *Chronicle of Higher Education,* April 3, 1998, B6; Simon Blackburn, "The Professor of Complacence," *London Review of Books,* August 20, 2001.

25. Thomas Powers, "The Interesting One," *New York Review of Books,* November 2, 2000, 24.

2

—

Abraham Lincoln and the Doctrine of Necessity

braham Lincoln was a fatalist. That, at least, was what he told many people over the course of his life. "I have all my life been a fatalist," Lincoln informed his Illinois congressional ally, Isaac Arnold. "Mr. Lincoln was a fatalist," remembered Henry Clay Whitney. "He believed . . . that the universe is governed by one uniform, unbroken, primordial law." His Springfield law partner, William Henry Herndon, likewise affirmed that Lincoln "believed in predestination, foreordination, that all things were fixed, doomed one way or the other, from which there was no appeal." Even Mary Todd Lincoln acknowledged that her husband had been guided by the conviction that "what is to be will be, and no cares of ours can arrest nor reverse the decree."[1] What this meant in practical terms, as Herndon discovered, was that Lincoln believed that "there was no freedom of the will," that "men had no free choice":

> things were to be, and they came, irresistibly came, doomed to come; men were made as they are made by superior conditions over which they had no control; the fates settled things as by the doom of the powers, and laws, universal, absolute, and eternal, ruled the universe of matter and mind....[Man] is simply a *simple tool*, a mere cog in the wheel, a part, a small part, of this vast iron machine, that strikes and cuts, grinds and mashes, all things, including man, that resist it.[2]

Even as president, Lincoln often described himself as "but an accidental instrument, temporary, and to serve but for a limited time."[3] He compared himself over the years to "a piece of floating driftwood." Even at the height of the Civil War, he told Canadian journalist Josiah Blackburn that he had only "drifted into the very apex of this great event."[4]

This does not strike us as a particularly cheerful or heroic way of looking at the world. Of course, fatalism—the idea that all future events have a pattern which is preestablished and unchangeable—did not always show itself negatively in Lincoln, since it sometimes seems to have given him the assurance he needed to persist in whatever course of action he believed had been thus preordained. "I feel quite sure that there was not a moment when he despaired of success in putting down the rebellion," Joseph Gillespie told Herndon in 1866, "and he came to believe that he himself was an instrument foreordained to aid in the accomplishment of this purpose as well as to emancipate the slaves." As far back as Lincoln's New Salem days, Herndon told Ward Hill Lamon in 1870, Lincoln had been confident "that he would be a great man," and Orville Browning recalled Lincoln's certainty in the 1850s that he had before him "what he considered some important predestined labor or work . . . nobler than he was for the time engaged in."[5] But more often, Lincoln's fatalism seemed to his friends to weigh him down in gloom rather than buoy him up in hope. Lincoln's private predictions of greatness were accompanied by confessions of powerlessness and passivity. In 1864, anxious over his prospects for reelection, he claimed no feeling of having "controlled events, but confess plainly that events have controlled me."[6] And those confessions were often tinged with the kind of "foreboding of his fate" which led him to put a "somewhat superstitious" value on the meaning of dreams and caused him "more than a dozen times" to tell Herndon, "I feel as if I shall meet with some terrible end."[7]

Accounting for Lincoln's "fatalism" has generally produced an uneasy shrug of the shoulders among interpreters and biographers of Lincoln.[8] For one thing, the term *fatalism* is fairly vague in its connotations; and just going as far as I have in describing Lincoln's fatalism has drawn a host of related terms and problems onto the board.[9] *Fatalism* suggests that all events are controlled by *fate*, which is to say that they are *determined* or *necessary* (and *fatalism*, in nineteenth-century philosophical discourse usually had such pejorative, anti-religious overtones that *determinism* or *necessitarianism* became the prevailing philosophical terms of choice). But who or what, then, does the determining? Lincoln frequently spoke during his presidency of "an all-wise Providence" or "the Divine Being who determines the destinies of nations" as the intelligent and self-conscious dictator of human fates, but he also told Herndon that "motives"—a significantly more secular term—"ruled the man always and everywhere under the sun."[10] And if all events are determined, and everything happens by necessity, do people really have a free will? Herndon insisted that Lincoln did not think so, and so did Henry Clay Whitney, who remembered

Lincoln declaring, "that we were impelled along in the journey of life with no freedom of the moral will."[11]

This vagueness of definition, in turn, opens doors into other questions about Lincoln. The "free will" problem, in its classic form, has been a constant feature of Western philosophy from Aristotle onwards, but free will took on an added political sharpness for Americans in the early Republic as they struggled to reconcile Jefferson's affirmation that human liberty was a self-evident political and metaphysical truth with the need to create a new republican structure of law and responsibility that would ensure order and curtail riot, chaos, and disunion.[12] "Government and law" in the United States, wrote Lincoln's contemporary and admirer, Henry Philip Tappan (the president of the University of Michigan in the 1850s), are "based upon human freedom," and the direction the mind takes in defining "reason and free will" inevitably winds up, according to Tappan, affecting "the idea of right and wrong and consequently law and responsibility."[13] In that atmosphere, Lincoln's sharp denial of free will presents a disturbing picture. To see the man who urged "work, work, work" as the formula for professional success, who lauded the Declaration of Independence as his political inspiration, and who gave political freedom to millions through the Emancipation Proclamation—to see *this* man turn and disavow any belief in the individual's freedom to choose, or create alternatives of choice, creates at best an image of a mind divided within itself, and at worst, whispers of an underlying moral cynicism about the meaning of Lincoln's most important deeds.

All of this metaphysical turning and twisting raises in its wake another major problem: Where did Lincoln get these ideas about fatalism? Herndon alternately blamed Lincoln's fatalism on "his early Baptist training," on "a defective physical organization," and even on a sort of crude genetic determinism, based on what Lincoln suspected was the possibility of his mother's illegitimate birth.[14] Lincoln himself was sometimes inclined to chalk up his fatalism to simple temperament: he told Josiah Grinnell, "You flaxen men with broad faces are born with cheer, and don't know a cloud from a star. I am of another temperament."[15] But accounting for Lincoln's fatalism in terms of something as psychologically vague as "temperament" tempts us to trivialize it; and trivializing the mind of Abraham Lincoln was exactly what David Davis and other Lincoln intimates guaranteed would land anyone foolish enough to do so with their backs in a ditch.[16] The persistence and depth of Lincoln's comments on the subject of free will and determinism are too heavy and too complex to have emerged from nothing more than the romanticized psychological ills of "melancholy" or "temperament." And, what is more, Lincoln had easier access to formal intellectual resources in theology, metaphysics, and law for his fatalism than Lincoln biographers have usually been interested in exploring. Finding that Lincoln had "a little-indulged" inclination to philology took both Joseph Gillespie in

Springfield and the young John Hay in the White House off guard; we have less excuse than Gillespie or Hay for finding that Lincoln's fatalism may have sprung from an equally recondite taste for problems in nineteenth-century American moral philosophy.[17]

Herndon is the most important source for analyzing Lincoln's fatalism, and much of the significance that this idea held for Lincoln can be seen just by how often Herndon referred back to his discussions with Lincoln about it in the years Lincoln and Herndon shared their Springfield law office. Lincoln, according to Herndon, "was a fatalist and believed that fatalism ruled the world." What Lincoln meant by this, Herndon explained, was that "the great leading law of human nature is motive."[18] All human action, in other words, begins with a reason for that action; and actions that occur seemingly without reason are just what we are wont to call irrational or even insane (and even then, most irrational persons imagine that they have "reasons" for what they are doing). These reasons for action are what Lincoln called *motives*, and he was very clear that motives did more than simply provide the occasion for action. "Motives moved the man to every voluntary act of his life," Lincoln told Herndon.[19] During the Civil War, Lincoln fastened on the connection between motives and actions in order to explain why black soldiers had to have political rights guaranteed to them as part of the inducement to enlist. "Negroes, like other people, act upon motives," Lincoln explained in terms that he plainly thought were axiomatic. "Why should they do any thing for us, if we will do nothing for them? If they stake their lives for us, they must be prompted by the strongest motive—even the promise of freedom."[20]

Motives, therefore, ruled (or, if you will, *caused*) human action, and they possessed that power because motives appealed, at the most basic level, to human self-interest. "His idea," recalled Herndon, "was that all human actions were caused by motives, and at the bottom of these motives was self."[21] Lincoln evidently had little patience with the idea that human behavior could arise spontaneously from some inherent human goodness, or even that it could be educated to guide its choices by some rule of otherworldliness, impartiality or (to use a favorite nineteenth-century term) disinterested benevolence. "At bottom," Herndon told the audiences for his controversial Springfield lectures on Lincoln in 1866, Lincoln always expected that "the snaky tongue of human selfishness will wag out."

> We often argued the question [Herndon remembered], I taking the op-
> posite view. . . . I once contended that man was free and could act without
> a motive. He smiled at my philosophy, and answered that it was impos-
> sible, because the motive was born before the man. . . . He defied me to act
> without motive and unselfishly; and when I did the act and told him of it,

he analyzed and sifted it to the last grain. After he had concluded, I could not avoid the admission that he had demonstrated the absolute selfishness of the entire act.[22]

Similarly, Lincoln found no evidence in human behavior that the process of choosing or willing could be broken down into stages that might soften or divert the attractive power of motives. He did not, for instance, believe that willing involved two separate stages, one of perception or attraction and then one of cool, quiet deliberation, in which we decide whether or not to yield to the motive which has attracted us. "He maintained that there was no conscious act of any man that was not moved by a motive, first, last, and always," Herndon wrote. Thus, "there was no freedom of the will," and "men are made by conditions that surround them, that have somewhat existed for a hundred thousand years or more."[23]

In fact, the self-interested response to motive was so regular and predictable that it amounted to the force of law, "continuous and unchangeable," and it led Lincoln to reduce a good deal of the variety of human behavior to "a calculation of the law of forces and ultimate results."[24] The key word in this was *forces*, since nowhere in Herndon's description of Lincoln's fatalism is there any inference that the causation of human action might be attributed to an intelligent Causer, to God or Divine Providence. "His idea of God was a kind of 'Sufficient Cause,'" Herndon told Lamon in 1870, and it was the simple operation of cause-and-effect, and not a supreme sovereign Creator, which "ruled both matter and mind" for Lincoln.[25] Similarly, Lincoln seems to have been unconcerned that, in attributing all action to a comparatively impersonal *cause* or *force* rather than a supernatural and reasonable being, he was subverting a moral sense of right or wrong, or any possibility of attributing blame or praise for human actions. To the contrary, Lincoln, according to Herndon, was inclined by his fatalism to soften or excuse what appeared to be the most obvious examples of human guilt or responsibility. He "quoted the case of Brutus and Caesar, arguing that the former was forced by laws and conditions over which he had no control to kill the latter, and vice versa, that the latter was specially created to be disposed of by the former."[26]

Herndon had a well-known weakness for embroidery and exaggeration in some of his memories of Lincoln, but it is not likely in this case that he was guilty of misrepresentation, since Lincoln himself provided one large piece of confirmation for Herndon's description of his fatalism. This appears, however, in a peculiar place in Lincoln's writings—the so-called "Handbill Replying to Charges of Infidelity," which Lincoln printed and distributed during his 1846 campaign for the seat of the Illinois Seventh Congressional District. Lincoln had experienced considerable anxiety about this election, first because the Seventh District was the only one then in Illinois where a Whig had a clear opportunity of winning (and Lincoln had taken no small amount of trouble to persuade a potential Whig rival, John J. Hardin, to leave Lincoln a clear field), and second, because the Democratic nominee for the Seventh District seat, Peter Cartwright, was a popular and brass-lunged Methodist preacher who would be certain to play his religious cards for all they were worth.[27] Lincoln's own failure to establish a recognizable religious profile had long been, as he well knew, a major political liability: as early as 1837, he was aware that his political enemies were asking "an old acquaintance of mine" whether "he ever heard Lincoln say he was a deist," and in 1843 he acknowledged that "because I belonged to no church," he had suffered "a tax of a considerable per cent. upon my strength throughout the religious community."[28] Now, in addition to that liability, he was dealing with a representative of one Protestant Christian community—the Methodists—for whom free will was a nonnegotiable fundamental of religious faith.

Worried by rumors that Cartwright had instigated a "whispering campaign" that urged pious Whigs to vote their piety and not their politics, Lincoln drew up on July 31, 1846, a formal statement for inclusion in several central Illinois newspapers. This "handbill" has been intensively studied ever since its rediscovery by Harry E. Pratt in 1942 in the back files of the *Illinois Gazette* for its somewhat disingenuous statement of Lincoln's religious preferences: that he was not a member of any Christian church, but that he had never actually denied the truth of Christianity or spoken with "intentional disrespect of religion in general," and that he would never himself contemplate supporting any politician who did.[29] What is usually missed is the central part of the document, where Lincoln turns, without any warning, to an explanation of his belief in the "Doctrine of Necessity." Lincoln defined this "doctrine" in terms very close to those used by Herndon in describing Lincoln's idea of *motives*: "that is, that the human mind is impelled to action, or held in rest by some power, over which the mind itself has no control."[30] Presumably, Cartwright must have added (or else Lincoln believed that he had added) to his accusation of Lincoln's general distaste for churchgoing the charge that Lincoln was guilty of a particularly nasty form of "infidelity," the notion that all human conduct is the forced result of physical laws, with the possible implication that Lincoln believed that there was no such thing as right or wrong human actions, only actions compelled by faceless and impersonal motives. To a nineteenth-century audience, grilled on evangelical Protestant notions of moral responsibility and the natural-law moralisms of Francis Wayland, Francis Bowen, Mark Hopkins, Eliphalet Nott, Thomas Upham, and Joseph Haven, this was negative campaigning at its worst.

It is important to note, however, that Lincoln carefully sidestepped the accusation in the "Handbill" rather than denying it. It is true, he conceded, "I have sometimes (with one, two or three, but never publicly) tried to maintain this argument," but he did not repudiate his "Doctrine of Necessity"; to the contrary, he struck back at Cartwright by reminding his readers that some form of "this same opinion" was held by several of the Methodists' rivals among "the Christian denominations."[31] If Lincoln's "necessity" horrified Methodists like Cartwright, then by way of reply, Lincoln was indirectly suggesting that Cartwright's free-willism horrified a good many righteous Presbyterians and Congregationalists. Likewise, it is also important to underscore the basic similarity between Lincoln's protestation in the "Handbill" and Herndon's account of his discussions with Lincoln on necessity and free will: Lincoln believed that human choice is caused, and caused in such a way that the human mind is compelled, without the countervailing power of deliberation or free will, to cooperate with the cause.

This now raises the second question about Lincoln's fatalism, and that concerns the possible sources for this "Doctrine of Necessity," especially since the rather well-developed vocabulary he deployed in arguing it with Herndon and "with one, two or three" others like Whitney, Lamon, and Arnold lifts it above the level of law office chit-chat. Herndon supplied part of the answer when he claimed that Lincoln's fatalism stemmed in some measure from "his early Baptist training," although he muddled what that "training" could have amounted to by identifying Thomas Lincoln as a "Free-will Baptist," which would have been the very antithesis of "necessity."[32] Thomas and Nancy Lincoln, in fact, were members in Kentucky of the Little Mount Separate Baptist Church, a congregation linked to a rigidly predestinarian Baptist subgroup, and Thomas Lincoln declined to join the Pigeon Creek Baptist Church in Indiana for seven years until, in 1823, it affiliated with the Separates (Sarah Bush Lincoln was received into membership by the Separates on the same day "by experience," and Lincoln's sister, Sarah, was admitted to the Separates' fellowship in 1826).[33] The Separate Baptists, who were also known as the "Anti-Mission" or "Hard-Shell" Baptists, and who amounted to almost 20 percent of all American Baptists by the 1840s, prided themselves on a radical Calvinism which had "no Mission Boards for converting the heathen, or for evangelizing the world," since God had already determined "from before the foundation of the world" who, in his wisdom, he would have evangelized and who not.[34] The Pigeon Creek Church, for example, established as part of its articles of faith that "we believe in one god the father, the word & holly gost who haith created all things that are created by the word of his power for his pleasure" and that "we believe in Election by grace given us in Christ Jesus Before the world began & that God Cawls, regenerates and sanctifies all who are made meat [meet, i.e., fit] for Glory by his special grace."[35] Add to this the fact that Thomas Lincoln was "one of the five or six most important men" among the

Indiana Separates, and it becomes clear that, for all effective purposes, Abraham Lincoln's life in Indiana was lived in an atmosphere of what William Barton called "a Calvinism that would have out-Calvined Calvin."[36]

Abraham Lincoln never became a Baptist, although in the 1846 congressional campaign his friends noticed that he did not hesitate to point out, in religious self-defense, that "his parents were Baptists, and brought him up in the belief of the Baptist religion."[37] But what Barton called "the ultra Calvinism of his boyhood" did stay with him, most obviously in the sense that it laid the groundwork for his later argument that all events were necessarily predetermined. "Mr. Lincoln seldom said anything on the subject of religion," recalled Joseph Gillespie in 1882, but the one theological opinion Gillespie did remember hearing from him was that he "could never reconcile the 'prescience of Deity with the uncertainty of events.'"[38] Separate Calvinism also stayed with Lincoln in the way that it allowed him, as the case required, to switch rhetorical gears between talking about a divinely ordered necessity and a cause-and-effect necessity.[39] The same Lincoln who in 1846 could write about the "Doctrine of Necessity" without any reference to supernatural causality could just as easily, less than five years later, compose a farewell letter to his stepbrother John D. Johnston for his dying father, assuring Thomas Lincoln in predestinarian terms Thomas would have been much more comfortable with, that "He who notes the fall of the sparrow, and numbers the hairs of our heads . . . will not forget the dying man, who puts his Trust in him."[40] A year later, Lincoln eulogized Henry Clay as "a man the times have demanded, and such, in the providence of God was given us."[41]

And it is well-known that during his embattled presidency, Lincoln's allusions to "the Divine Being who determines the destinies of nations," to "an all-wise Providence," and to "Divine assistance" without which "all must fail," multiplied.[42] He repeatedly described himself as nothing more than "a humble instrument in the hands of the Almighty," and expanded that on at least one occasion to claim that "we are all agents and instruments of Divine Providence."[43] *Providence*, in time, became a term of convenience for Lincoln: without committing him to any specific form of theism, it allowed him the psychological comfort of referring all events to an unseen control, a control which might also enjoy at least some form of recognizability as the God of his parents.

These invocations of *providence* were too oft repeated and the powers he ascribed to providence too absolute to be mere political window-dressing. The purposes of that Providence were, as he informed Eliza Gurney in 1864, "perfect and must prevail"—meaning that they were completely formed and irresistible—and on those occasions when Lincoln derived some measure of confidence from this, he chided those of little faith, like Congressman James Wilson and his Iowa delegation in 1862, with the assertion that "my faith is greater than yours" because "I also believe He will compel us to do right in order that He may do these things, not so much because we desire them as that they accord with His plans of dealing with this nation.[44] However, when the war news turned disastrous, he frequently surrendered to a sense of helplessness in the face of an inscrutable cosmic will. In a private memorandum during the dark September of 1862, Lincoln admitted that "the will of God prevails," but that God's purpose in doing so was deeply puzzling, "something different from the purpose of either party." In 1864, he pointed out that "Now at the end of three years' struggle the nation's condition is not what either party, or any man devised, or expected" and that "God alone can claim it." More dramatically, he "moaned and groaned in anguish" to Pennsylvania governor Andrew Curtin, "saying over and over again: 'What has God put me in this place for.'"[45] Whether or not this meant that Lincoln actually believed in a personal God (and Herndon was quite explicit in stating that Lincoln did not) or merely that Lincoln habitually personalized with the term *God* the gigantic fate that he believed relentlessly ruled and judged all human events is almost beside the point. What is clear is that, even if we grant Herndon's skeptical conclusion that the Johnston letter was "merely a message of consolation from a dutiful son to his dying father," or heed Charles H. Ray's warning to Ward Hill Lamon not to give "Calvinistic theology a chance to claim him as one of its saints and martyrs," Lincoln remained gripped all through his life by the same sense of things that the Separate Baptists of his youth preached: of a universe whose order eluded human control.[46]

These Calvinistic origins and overtones, however, do not go very far in explaining the specific shape of Lincoln's fatalism, with its intricate vocabulary of motives, necessity, and self-interest, all of which were foreign to the discourse of the Separate Baptists. It would be easier to trace the subsequent development of this fatalism if we had a clearer idea of what Lincoln was reading once he left his father's new farm in Illinois in 1831 and struck out on his own. One thing that we do know is that as early as the mid-1830s, Lincoln had repudiated what little he might have earlier embraced of Separate Baptist theology beyond that looming sense of "necessity."[47] Some of the fuel for that repudiation came from Lincoln's reading of arguments for deism and "infidelity" in the form of Thomas Paine's *Age of Reason*, Constantin-François Volney's *The Ruins; or, A Survey of the Revolution of Empires*, and by the mid-1840s, Robert Chambers's proto-Darwinian *Vestiges of the Natural History of Creation*.[48] All of these books would have confirmed a basic skepticism about Christian dogma, and based on what a number of Herndon's informants told him, Lincoln may have even written a small essay of his own in the mid-1830s on "infidelity" which "denied the miraculous conception of Christ, ridiculed the Trinity, and denied that the Bible was the divine special revelation of God."[49]

Another thing, quite incidentally, which all of these would have confirmed was a thoroughgoing secular determinism. Virtually all of the major deistic or "infidel" literature published in America in the late eighteenth and early nineteenth centuries incorporated some form of determinism, largely as a way of accounting for order in the universe without invoking a personal God to create and provide for it. Paine, for instance, mocked predestination as a theological doctrine, but he just as quickly described the operation of the universe as a "vast machinery" which "still goes on . . . whether we wake or sleep," and his favorite model for explaining universal motion was a mechanical orrery.[50] Robert Chambers, whose *Vestiges* went through eleven editions between 1844 and 1860 (including a cheap, fifty-cent American paperback), believed in a universal order so all-encompassing that "man is now seen to be an enigma only as an individual; in the mass he is a mathematical problem," and all "mental action, being proved to be under law, passes at once into the category of natural things."[51] Free will, fatalism, and determinism left their tracks throughout Lincoln's reading in the two middle decades of his life in Springfield, and the imprint they made on him was deep enough that he appeared in 1849 to Springfield Presbyterian pastor James Smith to be "very depressed and downcast" and "perplexed and unsettled by the fundamentals of religion, by speculative difficulties, connected with Providence."[52]

But the determinism of Chambers, Volney, and Paine had little of the sophistication and none of the specific vocabulary of *motive* and *self-interest* which Lincoln's fatalism possessed, and while they may have helped to denature Lincoln's youthful Calvinism and re-dress it in secularized garb, they certainly could not have given it the configuration it assumed in Lincoln's 1846 "Handbill." Instead, the rhetorical clues in Lincoln's fatalism point to a source which may lie unsuspectingly close at hand, in the debates among American lawyers in the early Republic over the shape of a republican jurisprudence.

Lincoln began the practice of law in Springfield in 1837, and like most lawyers in the United States outside major urban centers, he acquired his legal education more or less on the job as a junior partner in an already established law practice (in this case, that of John T. Stuart), and through reading a list of basic texts which began with the *Commentaries* of the English jurist Sir William Blackstone and later included Supreme Court Justice Joseph Story's *Commentaries*.[53] Given the recognition that Blackstone's name manages to command even among nonlawyers, it is ironic that his was actually the most embattled figure on that list, for Blackstone was an English Tory whose principal labor had been to establish the supremacy of king and common law over natural law and religious dissent, and to secure the protection and preservation of property ownership as the supreme duty of the law.[54] Blackstone encoded, in effect, many of the notions of sovereignty and property that the American revolutionaries had fought to resist, and much of the history of American law in the early Republic is the story of how American jurists, led by Story and John Marshall, sought to Americanize and domesticate Blackstone and the English common law; and on the other hand, how a pugnacious minority, under the inspiration of the English Utilitarians James Mill and Jeremy Bentham, struggled to repel the imposition of common law and instead make law a matter of positive legislative statute that served in the interest, not of property holding, but (in Bentham's phrase) of "the greatest happiness for the greatest number."[55]

Although Bentham recruited the support of only a comparatively small portion of the American legal profession before the Civil War—only Louisiana, which had no previous experience of English common law, adopted a Benthamite law code—his attractions were not limited to legal theory, for Bentham had also written on metaphysics, and his comments on free will and necessity have what will by now seem a familiar ring. In general, Bentham professed to be irritated by the need to talk about free will and necessity, although he admitted that any jurisprudence worth its salt had to come to terms with these problems if only to have a clear notion of what responsibility before the law meant. Bentham's irritation grew from his insistence that the entire problem was really quite simple:

> On every occasion, *conduct*—the *course* taken by a man's conduct—is at the absolute command of—is the never-failing result of—the *motives*. . . . It is an acknowledged truth, that every kind of act whatever, and consequently every kind of offence, is apt to assume a different character, and to be attended with different effects, according to the nature of the *motive* which gives birth to it. This makes it requisite to take a view of the several motives by which human conduct is liable to be influenced.[56]

What gave these *motives* their power over human willing was, precisely as it had been for Lincoln, the self-interest to which they appealed. "On every occasion, [an act] is at the absolute command of *motives* and corresponding *interest*." Thus, every choice—and neither Bentham nor Lincoln made any exceptions—was a motivated one, and the fundamental characteristic of human nature to which motives played was a plain, bleak concern for one's own self-interest. "No human act ever has been or ever can be *disinterested*," wrote Bentham. "For there exists not ever any voluntary action, which is not the result of the operation of some *motive* or *motives*, nor any motive, which has not for its accompaniment a corresponding *interest*, real or imagined."[57]

It is hard to miss the extraordinary resemblance between Lincoln's and Bentham's descriptions of the operation of motives and self-interest, and all that is lacking to seal the identification of Benthamite Utilitarianism as the ultimate source of Lincoln's fatalism would be a cameo appearance by Bentham on the streets of Springfield in, say, about 1846. Unhappily, Bentham died in 1832, and although Bentham gave John Quincy Adams twenty-five copies of each of his principal writings in 1817 to distribute to "strategic repositories" in the United States, there is no evidence that Lincoln read them, and no direct citation of Bentham occurs anywhere in Lincoln's writings. Still, Lincoln need not have studied Bentham to have absorbed him, for Bentham's ideas were available through other American lawyers and legal reformers, including Richard Hildreth, William Beach Lawrence, Edward Livingston (the author of the Benthamite Louisiana law code), the Philadelphia lawyer John Allyn, and the Louisiana Supreme Court jurist Henry Carleton.[58] The latter two, not coincidentally, also published treatises on free will, frankly hawking the Benthamite line on necessity. "Necessity varies with motive," wrote Carleton, and "when once the motive is fixed, it is no less certain in its effects than the forces of physical necessity."[59]

Lincoln was much too committed to the defense of property rights and land tenure to have become an outright Utilitarian like Allyn, Carleton, or Hildreth; in fact, the only political theorist we know Lincoln studied in detail was the moral philosopher Francis Wayland, who was the mortal enemy of both moral and political Utilitarianism, and Lincoln's recommended legal reading was anchored to both Blackstone and Story.[60] But the presence of a mediating Utilitarian discourse within the American legal profession does remove the obstacle of remoteness from Lincoln's recognition of Bentham's musings on free will (being a lawyer, in fact, placed Lincoln more directly in the track of Bentham than had he been part of any other professional community). And certainly one has to say that Lincoln also gave a Utilitarian twist to the ultimate purpose of property jurisprudence. "The democracy of today hold the *liberty* of one man to be absolutely nothing, when in conflict with another man's right of *property*," wrote Lincoln in 1859. "Republicans, on the contrary, are for both the *man* and the *dollar*; but in cases of conflict, the man *before* the dollar."[61] And even if Benthamite Utilitarianism gets no explicit credit from Lincoln in his arguments with "one, two or three" about "fatalism," we cannot dismiss lightly the striking similarity of vocabulary and meaning on free will between the Springfield lawyer and the London jurist.

Lincoln's speculations on fatalism indicate that he burrowed deeper into the mazes of Anglo-American intellectual life in the nineteenth century—through the competing Springfield lyceums, through the religious conflicts of predestination and perfection, through the distribution networks of books and the culture of print in the trans-Appalachia before 1860—than his interpreters have given him credit. Lincoln's speculations on fatalism and necessity also throw a different light on one of Lincoln's most-admired attributes, his "charity for all" and his "malice toward none," from the defeated Confederate leadership down to the sentry caught asleep on duty. Lincoln interpreters have been tempted to ascribe this "charity" to a mysterious, godlike reservoir of virtue in Lincoln; but Herndon knew better and knew that it was closely linked to Lincoln's fatalism. Since Lincoln was a "thorough fatalist" and "believed that what was to be would be, and no prayers of ours could arrest or reverse the decree," then "men were but simple tools of fate, of conditions, and of laws," and no one "was responsible for what he was, thought, or did, because he was a child of conditions."[62]

This does not, at first blush, seem like a very congenial attitude for a case-lawyer like Lincoln to adopt, but it is worth noting that this was a problem that Bentham and the Utilitarians had addressed by redefining the connection between responsibility and punishment by abandoning all idea of legal punishment for crimes as retributive justice and reconceiving imprisonment as an opportunity for moral exhortation and rehabilitation.[63] Punishment, wrote the American Benthamite John Allyn, should not be "an expression of hatred, but a means of exciting in the mind of the delinquent a motive to do right, and thereby . . . remedying his deficient moral state."[64] Laws should therefore be "remedial" rather than retributive, according to the Utilitarians, and Bentham's most well-known proposals for legal reform addressed the reconstruction of the English penal system, including the architecture of prisons, to promote penitence rather than to inflict pain.[65] Not surprisingly, Lincoln often took the same line of argument in asking for the revision of sentences for wartime criminals. "Five years at hard labor in the Penitentiary is not at all necessary to prevent the repetition of the crime by himself and others," wrote Lincoln in remitting the sentence of William Yocum in 1864, and the pertinent thing to note in that judgment was Lincoln's conviction that the purpose of punishment was not to even scores but, in good Utilitarian fashion, to present a sufficient motive to deter repetition or imitation.[66]

Otherwise, Lincoln shrank from objective assessments of responsibility, because, to the extent that necessity was irresistible, human efforts to oppose it or flee from it were fruitless. In 1854, he had remarked that Southern slave-holders "were neither better, nor worse than we of the North" because "if we were situated as they are, we should act and feel as they do; and if they were situated as we are, they should act and feel as we do; and we never ought to lose sight of this fact in discussing the subject."[67] Later, when reviewing the appeals of deserters, Lincoln liked to discover necessity in a case, rather than the sentimental application of pity, as the grounds for granting a pardon. "Well, after all, Judge, I think I must put this with my leg cases," Lincoln remarked on one occasion to Judge Advocate General Joseph Holt:

> They are the cases that you call by that long title, "cowardice in the face of the enemy," but I call them for short, my "leg cases." But I put it to you, and I leave it for you to decide for yourself: if Almighty God gives a man a cowardly pair of legs how can he help their running away with him?[68]

"This philosophy as a whole will account for much of the facts and laws of his splendid life," promised Herndon, and that promise may also include Lincoln's most eloquent statement on the meaning of responsibility, in the third paragraph of the Second Inaugural.

Almost by custom, the attention commentators devote to the Second Inaugural is drawn largely to the final paragraph, with its benediction-like exhortation to end the Civil War "with malice toward none; with charity for all; with firmness in the right, as God gives us to see the right." What is frequently missed is how, in the preceding paragraph, Lincoln had expressed grave reservations about how much of the right God had actually given people to see. Even though the Confederate cause had been dedicated to a palpable injustice—that of "wringing their bread from the sweat of other men's faces"—even this injustice had been part of "the Almighty's purposes," and Lincoln was loath to pass too severe a judgment of his own on Southerners when it was those purposes which were the ultimate cause of their misdoings. Much as he might pray "that this mighty scourge of war might pass away," Lincoln could not escape the sense of necessity in the four years of bloodshed that the war was something which "God wills to continue." Faced with the inscrutability of that necessity, Lincoln warned, "let us judge not that we be not judged" in dealing with each other; and let us not judge God, whose mysterious purposes are still, above any human willing or judgment, "true and righteous altogether." This is not so much a declaration of forgiveness as it is acquiescence in the face of a "necessity" which forbids the imputation of too much praise or blame. Even at the end, Lincoln's fatalism had managed to have the last word.

And yet, Lincoln the "fatalist," who had no assurance that the will of any person was free, is also the great giver of liberty, the emancipator of millions and the rebuilder of a sundered Republic. There is no greater paradox in Lincoln's life than the one arising from the juxtaposition of these two images, for there seems no easy way to reconcile the man who believed that all human action was decided by powers beyond human control, and the president who reiterated his faith in the capacity of individuals to improve themselves via a free-labor system which "gives hope to all, and energy, and progress, and improvement of condition to all."[69] Unhappily, paradoxes tempt the curious to resolve them into their separate parts; in Lincoln's case, the paradox of the Great Emancipator and the Fatalist has more significance for us if we leave it standing and ask what purpose the paradox might have served. In the most general sense, the paradox of Lincoln's fatalism falls into a pattern that has reappeared throughout modern Western history, and it arises from the peculiar tendency of determinists, from Oliver Cromwell to Karl Marx, to preach divine or material inevitability at one moment and then turn into the most avowed revolutionary activists at the next. The significance of Lincoln's paradox may, in that light, be that doctrines of necessity possess a strange psychological dynamic of their own, one that ironically promotes action rather than passivity, construction rather than indolence, persistence rather than hopelessness. And in Lincoln's American context, the need to preserve a sense of paradox about necessity and choice was, as Jon Pahl and Michael Kammen have suggested, a necessary part of the building of "a new and distinctive culture or ethos" in America.[70] Kammen notes that Americans, faced with the overwhelming challenge of subduing a new continent and establishing a new republic, could find the resolve to confront that challenge only by simultaneously asserting a divine providence which would assure their triumph *and* a "hope in human striving" which would give them the incentive to strive in the first place. In that context, it was precisely Lincoln's embrace of paradox—of both "necessity" and the "right to rise"—which granted him both the deterministic stability and the self-willed initiative to save the Republic from the greatest challenge it would face.

But the paradox of Lincoln's fatalism may also be linked, and in a more paradoxical way, to a subtler change in Western consciousness in the nineteenth century. Rice University historian Thomas Haskell, in a celebrated debate in 1985 and 1987 with David Brion Davis and John Ashworth, asked his readers to see a linkage between the rise of market capitalism in the Atlantic world in the nineteenth century and the simultaneous rise of humanitarianism, especially in the form of antislavery. Haskell reasoned that capitalism taught people, for the first time in Western history, to look beyond short-term gains and losses and "attend to the remote consequences of their actions." Capitalism, in other words, expanded the horizons of trade, and with it forced the traders to widen their mental horizons, in terms of both geography (treating the world as the market rather than just the village down the lane) and time (calculating long-term gains and long-term patterns in marketing); this, in turn, created an extraordinary expansion of what people conceived themselves capable of doing and "inspired people's confidence in their power to intervene in the course of events."[71] In Haskell's view, this expansion of possibilities had particular application to the antislavery movement, since it was precisely this new confidence of power, and the new awareness of a larger world of problems to use that power on, which explained for Haskell why no one before 1760 seemed to have felt that slavery was a problem they could or should address, and why after 1760 so many people abruptly changed that opinion.

By that reckoning, no one ought to emerge as a better example of this consciousness than Lincoln, especially since his career as a Whig lawyer so often served the interests of an expanding American market system. But Lincoln's fatalism points toward exactly the opposite form of consciousness, toward a sense of increased restraint and futility in the face of invisible powers over which one has no meaningful control. To an observer like Lincoln, the dramatically expanding commercial economy, with its impersonal connections, with strangers bidding prices on distant markets, with railroads bringing goods and immigrants from heretofore unimaginable distances, was just as likely to be a reminder of how little could be ascribed to individual human willing, and how much to the power of "interest." In Lincoln's case, the expansion of horizons described by Haskell could not dispel a contradictory sense of inability, of what could *not* be achieved; even the preoccupation of "promise-keeping," which Haskell selected as a prime characteristic of the new market consciousness (and which is incarnated in Lincoln's fabulous reputation for scrupulous honesty) has to sit uneasily beside Lincoln's effacement of moral responsibility in the face of "motives."

So once again Lincoln presents us with a paradox. For Lincoln, the expansion of America and the abolition of slavery would certainly give "hope to all." But as Americans rose to meet the moral challenge of slavery, they would have to learn the humbling lesson of fatalism: that moralism does not come unmixed with motives and self-interest; and as America grew in commercial power and strength across the continent, that growth would sooner or later bring Americans to the kind of conceptual and economic boundaries on growth which no one can supersede. Not for Lincoln would there be the straightforward acceptance of a world of new horizons, but rather a complex struggle to assimilate the expansion of what could be accomplished with the diminution of what one could be responsible for. His antislavery convictions may have had less to do with embracing the new consciousness of the market than with an ambivalent effort to contain it. He did not live to see how futile that effort would have been in the Gilded Age, but perhaps that would not, in the end, have greatly shocked a "fatalist" like Lincoln. *Why should the spirit of mortal be proud*, Lincoln asked, in reciting his favorite poem; and why should it expect to accomplish more than the purposes the Almighty had laid down for it? Perhaps that realization, more than any other single factor, left him no other explanation for human action but the "Doctrine of Necessity."

Notes

This essay first appeared in *Journal of the Abraham Lincoln Association*, Winter 1997.

1. Isaac Arnold, *The Life of Abraham Lincoln* (1884; repr., Lincoln, NE, 1994), 81; Henry Whitney, *Life on the Circuit with Lincoln* (Boston, 1892), 267, 276;

Herndon to Jesse Weik, February 6, 1887, in Herndon-Weik Papers, Group 4, reel 10, #2031-34, Library of Congress; Herndon, "Lincoln's Philosophy and Religion," in *The Hidden Lincoln: From the Letters and Papers of William H. Herndon*, ed. Emmanuel Hertz (New York, 1937), 406.

2. Herndon to Weik, February 25, 1887, in Herndon-Weik Papers, Group 4, reel 9, #1893-96.

3. Lincoln, "Reply to Oliver P. Morton at Indianapolis, Indiana," February 2, 1861, in *The Collected Works of Abraham Lincoln*, ed. Roy P. Basler (New Brunswick, NJ, 1953–55), 4:194.

4. William H. Herndon and Jesse W. Weik, *Abraham Lincoln: The True Story of a Great Life* (New York, 1917), 1:70; Josiah Blackburn, in *Conversations with Lincoln*, ed. Charles M. Segal (New York, 1961), 336.

5. Joseph Gillespie to Herndon, December 8, 1866, in Hertz, *Hidden Lincoln*, 322-23; Michael Burlingame, *The Inner World of Abraham Lincoln* (Urbana, IL, 1994), 237, 239.

6. Lincoln, "To Albert Hodges," April 4, 1864, in *Collected Works*, 7:282.

7. Herndon to Weik, February 6, 1887, in Herndon-Weik Papers, Group 4, reel 10, #2031-34; see also Herndon to Weik [no date], Group 4, reel 11, #2906.

8. J. G. Randall led the way in dismissing Lincoln's "fatalism" as simply a function of his "melancholy"—and therefore impervious to explanation—in *Lincoln the President: Springfield to Gettysburg* (New York, 1945), 2:28, 48; Carl Sandburg, in similar fashion, wrote it off as an expression of Lincoln's "mysticism," in *Abraham Lincoln: The War Years* (New York, 1939), 3:370-82, as did one of the early attempts at Lincoln psychobiography, L. Pierce Clark's *Lincoln: A Psycho-Biography* (New York, 1933), 531-32, 540-42. Stephen B. Oates deals with it as an expression of Lincoln's depression over the deaths, first of Ann Rutledge, and then of William Wallace Lincoln, in *With Malice toward None: The Life of Abraham Lincoln* (New York, 1977), 29, 293.

9. For surveys of the problem of "fatalism" and "free will," see Vernon K. Bourke, *The Will in Western Thought: An Historico-Critical Survey* (New York, 1964); Bernard Berofsky, ed., *Free Will and Determinism* (New York, 1966); Sidney Hook, ed., *Determinism and Freedom in the Age of Modern Science* (New York, 1958); Maurice Mandelbaum, *Purpose and Necessity in Social Theory* (Baltimore, 1987); Gary Watson, ed., *Free Will* (New York, 1982); and Linda Zagzebski, *The Dilemma of Freedom and Foreknowledge* (New York, 1991).

10. Lincoln, "Response to Evangelical Lutherans," May 13, 1862, in *Collected Works*, 5:212-13; Herndon, "Lincoln's Philosophy and Religion," 407-8.

11. Henry Whitney, *A Life of Lincoln*, ed. M. M. Miller (New York, 1908), 1:105-6.

12. See Jon Pahl, *Paradox Lost: Free Will and Political Liberty in American Culture, 1630-1760* (Baltimore, 1992), 163-76; and Jay Fliegelman, *Prodigals and Pilgrims: The American Revolution against Patriarchal Authority* (New York, 1982), 98-106, 169-70.

13. Tappan, "A Course of Moral Philosophy," in Henry Philip Tappan Papers, Bentley Historical Library, University of Michigan—Ann Arbor.

14. Herndon to C. O. Poole, January 5, 1886, in Herndon-Weik Papers, Group 4, reel 9, #1885; Jesse Weik, *The Real Lincoln: A Portrait* (New York, 1922), 112.

15. Burlingame, *Inner World of Abraham Lincoln*, 106.

16. David Davis, in Weik, *Real Lincoln*, 129.

17. John Hay, diary entry for July 25, 1863, in *Inside Lincoln's White House: The Complete Civil War Diary of John Hay*, ed. Michael Burlingame and J. R. T. Ettlinger (Carbondale, IL, 1997), 67-68; Gillespie to Herndon, December 8, 1866, in Herndon-Weik Papers, Group 4, reel 8.

18. Herndon to Weik, February 25, 1887, in Herndon-Weik Papers, Group 4, reel 9, #1893-96; Herndon and Weik, *Abraham Lincoln*, 2:306.

19. Herndon to Weik, February 25, 1887, in Herndon-Weik Papers, Group 4, reel 9, #1893-96.

20. Lincoln, "To James Conkling," August 26, 1863, in *Collected Works*, 4:409.

21. William Herndon, "Analysis of the Character of Abraham Lincoln," in *Abraham Lincoln Quarterly* 1 (September 1941): 371-72; Herndon and Weik, *Abraham Lincoln*, 2:306.

22. William Herndon, "Analysis of the Character of Abraham Lincoln," *Abraham Lincoln Quarterly* 1 (December 1941): 411; Herndon and Weik, *Abraham Lincoln*, 2:148, 306. For a similar description, probably also retailed by Herndon, see Josiah G. Holland, *The Life of Abraham Lincoln* (Springfield, MA, 1866), 79.

23. Herndon to Senator Fowler, February 18, 1886, in Hertz, *Hidden Lincoln*, 141-42; Herndon to Weik, February 6, 1887, in Herndon-Weik Papers, Group 4, reel 10, #2031-34.

24. Herndon, "Analysis of the Character of Abraham Lincoln," *Abraham Lincoln Quarterly* 1 (September 1941): 366.

25. Herndon, in David H. Donald, *Lincoln's Herndon: A Biography* (New York, 1948), 291.

26. Herndon and Weik, *Abraham Lincoln*, 2:146.

27. Donald W. Riddle, *Lincoln Runs for Congress* (New Brunswick, NJ, 1948), 51, 58. On Lincoln's rivalry with Cartwright, as far back as the 1830s, see Robert Bray, "The Power to Hurt: Lincoln's Early Use of Satire and Invective," *Journal of the Abraham Lincoln Association* 16 (Winter 1995): 43-50.

28. Lincoln, "Second Reply to James Adams," October 18, 1837, and "To Martin S. Morris," March 26, 1843, in *Collected Works*, 1:106, 320.

29. See the original republication of this text in "Abraham Lincoln's Religion: His Own Statement," *Abraham Lincoln Quarterly* (March 1942): 1-4.

30. Lincoln, "Handbill Replying to Charges of Infidelity," in *Collected Works*, 1:382.

31. Ibid.

32. Herndon and Weik, *Abraham Lincoln*, 1:8.

33. William J. Wolf, *The Almost Chosen People: A Study of the Religion of Abraham Lincoln* (Garden City, NY, 1959), 34-37; William E. Barton, *The Soul of Abraham Lincoln* (New York, 1920), 36-41; J. G. Nicolay and John Hay, *Abraham Lincoln: A History* (New York, 1890), 1:32-33; Louis A. Warren, *Lincoln's Youth: Indiana Years*

Seven to Twenty-One, 1816-1830 (New York, 1959), 11, 13, 114-15, 206, and "Pigeon Creek Church," in *Lincoln Lore* 661 (December 8, 1941); Francis Marion Van Natter, *Lincoln's Boyhood: A Chronicle of His Indiana Years* (Washington, DC, 1963), 12.

34. R. H. Pittman, *Biographical History of Primitive or Old School Baptist Ministers of the United States* (Anderson, IN, 1870), 30; Bertram Wyatt-Brown, "The Antimission Movement in the Jacksonian South," *Journal of Southern History* (November 1970), 501-29; M. L. Houser, "Some Religious Influences Which Surrounded Lincoln," in *Lincoln Group Papers: Twelve Addresses Delivered before the Lincoln Group of Chicago*, 2nd series (Chicago, 1945), 16-20; "Primitive Baptists," in *Encyclopedia of Southern Baptists* (Nashville, TN, 1958), 1114-15; "Primitive or Old School Baptists," in *The Baptist Encyclopedia*, ed. William Cathcart (Philadelphia, 1883), 77-78.

35. D. Raymond Taggart, *The Faith of Abraham Lincoln* (Topeka, KS, 1943), 278.

36. Ida Tarbell, *In the Footsteps of the Lincolns* (New York, 1924), 143-44; Charles Garnett Vannest, *Lincoln the Hoosier: Abraham Lincoln's Life in Indiana* (St. Louis, MO, 1928), 7-8; William Barton, *Life of Abraham Lincoln* (Indianapolis, IN, 1925), 2:460.

37. Thomas Mostiller to B. F. Irwin, 1874, in B. F. Irwin, *Lincoln's Religious Belief* (Springfield, IL, 1919), 7.

38. Joseph Gillespie, in *The Lincoln Memorial: Album-Immortelles*, ed. Osborn H. Oldroyd (New York, 1883), 457.

39. Barton, *Soul of Abraham Lincoln*, 271-72; Richard N. Current, *The Lincoln Nobody Knows* (Westport, CT, 1980), 71.

40. Lincoln, "To John D. Johnston," January 12, 1851, in *Collected Works*, 2:97.

41. Lincoln, "Eulogy on Henry Clay," April 6, 1852, in *Collected Works*, 2:132.

42. Lincoln, "Response to Evangelical Lutherans," May 13, 1862, "To Baltimore Methodists," May 1862, "Annual Message to Congress," December 3, 1861, "Remarks to Baltimore Presbyterian Synod," October 24, 1863, and "Remarks to a Delegation of Progressive Friends," June 20, 1862, in *Collected Works*, 5:53, 212-13, 215-16, 279, 6:535-36.

43. Lincoln, "Reply to Eliza P. Gurney," October 26, 1862, and "Address to the New Jersey Senate at Trenton, New Jersey," February 21, 1861, in *Collected Works*, 4:236, 5:279. See also Barton, *Soul of Abraham Lincoln*, 332.

44. Lincoln, "To Eliza P. Gurney," September 4, 1864, in *Collected Works*, 7:535; Wolf, *Almost Chosen People*, 146. See also Lucius Eugene Crittenden, *Recollections of President Lincoln and His Administration* (New York, 1891), 448-50.

45. Lincoln, "Meditation on the Divine Will," September 2, 1862?, and "To Albert G. Hodges," April 4, 1864, in *Collected Works*, 5:403-4, 7:282; Burlingame, *Inner World of Abraham Lincoln*, 105.

46. *Herndon's Life of Lincoln*, ed. Paul Angle (New York, 1949), 352-53; Herndon to Weik, November 24, 1882, in Hertz, *Hidden Lincoln*, 87; C. H. Ray, in Ward Hill Lamon, *The Life of Abraham Lincoln from His Birth to His Inauguration as President* (Boston, 1872), 489-90. There were, of course, other brands of Calvinism on offer

in the early Republic which might have exercised influence on the young Lincoln. Jonathan Edwards, the most formidable of early American Calvinist divines, laid the groundwork for a major reconciliation of absolute predestination and a thinly defined version of free will in his great treatise *Freedom of the Will* (1754), which was easily the most carefully read American philosophical work before 1850 and which also described human actions as a response to *motives*. But in Lincoln there is no sign of any reconciliation between necessity and free will, or at least nothing resembling Edwards's formulas; and nothing in Lincoln's use of the term *motives* which shares any ground with Edwards's. Moreover, Lincoln told Noah Brooks in 1865 that "Edwards on the Will" was one of the books he wanted to read at some point—hence, Edwards was not a thinker he had previously worked through.

47. Herndon to Lamon, February 25, 1870, in Hertz, *Hidden Lincoln*, 64-65; Isaac Cogdal to B. F. Irwin, in Irwin, *Lincoln's Religious Belief*, 8; James H. Matheny to Lamon, in Lamon, *Life of Abraham Lincoln*, 487-88, 495; Joshua Speed, *Reminiscences of Abraham Lincoln; and Notes of a Visit to California* (Louisville, KY, 1884), 32-33; Henry B. Rankin, *Personal Recollections of Abraham Lincoln* (New York, 1916), 324-25.

48. Angle, *Herndon's Life of Lincoln*, 347; Herndon, "Lincoln's Philosophy and Religion," 407; John Hill to Herndon, June 6, 1865, in Herndon-Weik Papers, Group 4, reel 7, #118; William Eleroy Curtis, *The True Abraham Lincoln* (Philadelphia, 1903), 376; Kunigunde Duncan and D. F. Nickols, *Mentor Graham: The Man Who Taught Lincoln* (Chicago, 1944), 143; Barton, *Life of Abraham Lincoln*, 2:459; Albert J. Beveridge, *Abraham Lincoln, 1809-1858* (New York, 1928), 1:138-40.

49. Herndon to Bartlett, October 1887, in Hertz, *Hidden Lincoln*, 209. See also John Hill's letter to Herndon, June 6, 1865, which includes Hill's February 15, 1862, article in a Petersburg, Illinois, newspaper, describing Lincoln's "dissertation," in Herndon-Weik Papers, Group 4, reel 7, #118.

50. Thomas Paine, "Predestination" and "The Age of Reason," in *The Writings of Thomas Paine*, ed. M. D. Conway (New York, 1896), 4:31, 193, 424-27.

51. Robert Chambers, *Vestiges of the Natural History of Creation* (1844), ed. James A. Secord (Chicago, 1994), 331. Lincoln also acquired a taste for poetry, especially Burns and Shakespeare; and it is worth remembering in this context that Burns was read in the early nineteenth century as a religious skeptic, while the work of Shakespeare Lincoln liked best had a strong whiff of "fatalism" to it. Lincoln's comment to the actor James Hackett in 1863 that he preferred the king of Denmark's "soliloquy in Hamlet commencing 'O, my offence is rank'" to the more celebrated "To be, or not to be" is usually treated as an embarrassing but amiable example of an amateur's enthusiasm. Not enough interpreters of Lincoln have taken the trouble to read the soliloquy (Act 3, scene 3) and notice that it speaks in agonizing tones about the inability of human beings to choose, on their own, even the most desirable ends:

> O, my offense is rank, it smells to heaven . . .
> . . . what then? what rests?
> Try what repentance can: what can it not?

Yet what can it when one can not repent?
O wretched state! O bosom black as death!
O limned soul, that struggling to be free
Art more engaged!

52. James Smith, in Taggart, *Faith of Abraham Lincoln*, 51; Barton, *Soul of Abraham Lincoln*, 162-63. Another possible "infidel" influence on Lincoln may have come in the form of Robert Owen, whose communal experiment at New Harmony, Indiana, lay about fifty miles from the Lincolns' Pigeon Creek settlement and only ten miles from a parcel of land which Thomas Lincoln bought for speculative purposes in 1827. Owen was a Paine-like determinist who staged a sensational debate with Alexander Campbell in Cincinnati in 1829 in which Owen frankly and skillfully defended a nontheistic, determinist position. Years after Lincoln's death, Dennis Hanks claimed that Lincoln had visited and admired New Harmony. See Owen, *Debate on the Evidences of Christianity* (Cincinnati, 1829), 1:22-24; E. H. and D. W. Madden, "The Great Debate: Alexander Campbell vs. Robert Owen," *Transactions of the Charles S. Peirce Society* 18 (Summer 1982): 207-26; Warren, *Lincoln's Youth*, 124, 171-72; Van Natter, *Lincoln's Boyhood*, 118-24.

53. Lincoln composed a sample reading list in a letter to James T. Thornton, December 2, 1858 (*Collected Works*, 3:344), which included, beyond Blackstone, Joseph Chitty's *Treatise on Pleading and Parties to Actions . . . Containing Precedents of Pleadings, and an Appendix of Forms*, 3 vols. (Springfield, MA, 1844), Simon Greenleaf's *A Treatise on the Law of Evidence*, 3 vols. (Boston, 1842-53), and Joseph Story's *Commentaries on Equity Jurisprudence as Administered in England and America*, 2 vols. (Boston, 1836), and *Commentaries on Equity Pleadings, and the Incidents Thereof, according to the Practice of the Courts of Equity, of England and America*, 2nd ed.(Boston, 1840).

54. J. C. D. Clark, *The Language of Liberty, 1660-1832: Political Discourse and Social Dynamics in the Anglo-American World* (Cambridge, 1994), 5, 83, 110, 140.

55. On Blackstone and the struggle to incorporate English common law into American jurisprudence, see Gregory S. Alexander, "Time and Property in the American Republican Legal Culture," *New York University Law Review* 66 (May 1991): 273-352; Morton J. Horwitz, *The Transformation of American Law, 1780-1860* (Cambridge, MA, 1977), 9-15; R. Kent Newmyer, *Supreme Court Justice Joseph Story: Statesman of the Old Republic* (Chapel Hill, NC, 1985), 272-73, 280; and G. Edward White, *The Marshall Court and Cultural Change, 1815-1835* (New York, 1991), 68-71, 95, 119, 151-52, 489-91, 493, 676-77. On Bentham, see D. B. Crook, "The United States in Bentham's Thought," *Australian Journal of Politics and History* 10 (1964): 196-204; John Dinwiddy, *Bentham* (New York, 1989), 55, 85; H. L. A. Hart, "The United States of America," in *Essays on Bentham: Studies in the Jurisprudence and Political Theory* (Oxford, 1982), 53-78; and Rogers M. Smith, *Liberalism and American Constitutional Law* (Cambridge, MA, 1985), 39. On the "greatest happiness" formula, see Jeremy Bentham, *Deontology; together with A Table of the Springs of Moral Action*, ed. Amnon Goldworth (Oxford, 1983), 60.

56. Bentham, *Deontology*, 112; Jeremy Bentham, *An Introduction to the Principles of Morals and Legislation*, ed. J. H. Burns and H. L. A. Hart (London, 1982), 96; Douglas E. Long, *Bentham on Liberty: Jeremy Bentham's Idea of Liberty in Relation to His Utilitarianism* (Toronto, 1977), 41, 231.

57. Bentham, *Deontology*, 19, 99-100.

58. Merle Curti, *The Growth of American Thought* (New York, 1943), 373-75.

59. Henry Carleton, *Liberty and Necessity; in which are considered the Laws of Association of Ideas, the meaning of the word Will, and the true intent of punishment* (Philadelphia, 1857), 148; John Allyn, *The Philosophy of Mind in Volition; or, An Essay on the Will* (Oberlin, OH, 1851), 30, 32, 50, 53-54, 61, 64.

60. Olivier Frayssé, *Lincoln, Land and Labor, 1809-1860*, trans. Sylvia Neely (Urbana, IL, 1994), 91-92; Gabor Boritt, *Lincoln and the Economics of the American Dream* (1978; repr., Urbana, IL, 1994), 121-52; D. H. Meyer, *The Instructed Conscience: The Shaping of the American National Ethic* (Philadelphia, 1972), 46-49.

61. Lincoln, "To Henry L. Pierce and Others," April 6, 1859, in *Collected Works*, 3:375; Frayseé, *Lincoln, Land, and Labor*, 170-71.

62. Herndon to Weik, February 25, 1887, in Herndon-Weik Papers, Group 4, reel 9, #1893-96; Herndon to Fowler, February 18, 1886, and Herndon to Weik, February 26, 1891, in Hertz, *Hidden Lincoln*, 141-42, 266-67.

63. Richard Double, *The Non-Reality of Free-Will* (New York, 1991), 134-37; Christopher Lasch, "Guilt," *Intellectual History Newsletter* 16 (December 1994): 15-17.

64. Allyn, *Philosophy of Mind*, 99.

65. Carleton, *Liberty and Necessity*, 161; William Holdsworth, *The History of English Law* (London, 1935), 11:137; Melvin I. Urofsky, *A March of Liberty: A Constitutional History of the United States* (New York, 1988), 308, 313.

66. Lincoln, "To Edwin M. Stanton," March 18, 1864, in *Collected Works*, 7:257.

67. Lincoln, "Speech at Bloomington, Illinois," September 12, 1854, in *Collected Works*, 3:230.

68. Current, *Lincoln Nobody Knows*, 165-66.

69. Gabor S. Boritt, "The Right to Rise," in *The Public and Private Lincoln: Contemporary Perspectives*, ed. Cullom Davis et al. (Carbondale, IL, 1979), 57-70; Lincoln, "Address before the Wisconsin State Agricultural Society, Milwaukee, Wisconsin," September 30, 1859, in *Collected Works*, 3:478-79.

70. Pahl, *Paradox Lost*, 167-70; Michael Kammen, *People of Paradox: An Inquiry concerning the Origins of American Civilization* (New York, 1973), 32-47.

71. Thomas Haskell, "Capitalism and Humanitarian Sensibility, 2," in *The Antislavery Debate: Capitalism and Abolitionism as a Problem in Historical Interpretation*, ed. Thomas Bender (Berkeley, CA, 1992), 141, 148.

3

COME-OUTERS AND COMMUNITY-MEN:
ABRAHAM LINCOLN AND THE IDEA OF COMMUNITY
IN NINETEENTH-CENTURY AMERICA

The most eloquent and moving words Abraham Lincoln ever uttered about any community were those "few and simple words" he spoke on the rear platform of the railroad car that lay waiting on the morning of February 11, 1861, to take him to Washington, to the presidency, and ultimately to his death. As his "own breast heaved with emotion" so that "he could scarcely command his feelings sufficiently to commence" (in the description of James C. Conkling), Lincoln declared that "No one, not in my situation, can appreciate my feeling of sadness at this parting."[1] To leave Springfield was to leave the only real home he had ever known. His professional life had been bound up in Springfield; he had married, raised a family, and been elected to Congress from Springfield; he had even refused offers to relocate in Chicago and (so it was rumored later) even in New York City to stay in Springfield.[2] "To this place, and the kindness of these people, I owe everything," Lincoln said. "Here I have lived a quarter of a century, and have passed from a young to an old man. Here my children have been born, and one is buried. I now leave, not knowing when, or whether ever, I may return, with a task before me greater than that which rested upon Washington."

But well-known as these kindly and affectionate words are, it is often overlooked that Lincoln said them in a very peculiar context—the moment he was leaving Springfield, never to return alive. Nor was this the first time that Lincoln expressed his sense of debt to communities after he had left those communities behind him for good. In the brief autobiographical sketch he composed for John Locke Scripps in 1860, he recalled harder times in his youth in New Salem, how he had been beaten in his first run for the state legislature and had been beaten down even more sorely by the business failure of his employer, Denton Offutt. Nevertheless, even though "he was now without means and out of business," Lincoln "was anxious to remain with his friends who had treated him with so much generosity."[3] And he did—but for only two and a half years, until the opportunity of learning and practicing law in Springfield beckoned. Lincoln's departures from the two communities which had nurtured him were framed in soft words—but he still left them. In fact, Lincoln seems to have had the most admiring things to say about communities when he was just at the point of severing his ties to them.

The odd context of Lincoln's comments about Springfield and New Salem situates Abraham Lincoln in a peculiar position within one of the most unsettling cultural dilemmas of American life, and that is the way we define, exalt, and (alternately) mourn the idea of community in American life. With the rise of what has frequently been called the "new communitarianism," the tone in which we have discussed this dilemma has increasingly become one of mourning, because it is widely suggested in the popular work of sociologists, political theorists, and philosophers as widely dispersed as Amitai Etzione, Robert Bellah, Alasdair MacIntyre, Charles Taylor, and Michael Sandel that American society has lost any meaningful sense of community, and with it, any sense of genuine human relationships, of social health, of cultural sanity. We have become a nation of utterly self-centered, self-seeking individualists, a heartless society that wrecks every nontangible, nonfinancial human connection. Neighborhoods are accidental throw-togethers of strangers who hardly know each other and who will probably not live there long enough to get that knowledge; education, welfare, even old-age care, are fobbed off onto 401K plans and faceless government agencies and bureaucrats; our single most distinguishing feature is not our names, our families, the place we were born, but a set of integers—our Social Security numbers. We have lost a sense of "we-ness," Etzione charged, and exchanged the restraints and supports of community for a model of society which more resembles a "den of thieves." Modern society, complained MacIntyre, appears like nothing so much as "a collection of citizens of nowhere." "We Americans tend to think that all we need are energetic individuals and a few impersonal rules to guarantee fairness," Bellah sighed. "Anything more is not only superfluous but dangerous—corrupt, oppressive, or both." But the price for the decay of community, Bellah warned, has been staggering: "Our institutions today—from the family to the school to the corporation to the public arena—do not challenge us to use all our capacities so that we have a sense of enjoyable achievement and of contributing to the welfare of others. . . . And the malaise is palpable: a loss of meaning in family and job, a distrust of politics, a disillusion with organized religion." What we need, Bellah argued, is "a dramatically new level of democratic institutional-ization, not only in America but in the world."[4]

But the jeremiads of Etzione, Bellah, and other "new communitarians" were not actually all that new. The nineteenth-century founders of scientific sociol-ogy—Auguste Comte, Max Weber, Emil Durkheim, and especially Ferdinand Tonnies—all contrasted the new industrial nation-states of the late 1800s with their medieval and traditional predecessors, and usually to the disadvantage of the former. Tonnies gave this contrast its classic (and ominously bipolar) form in 1887 by speaking of the precapitalist, preindustrial, preurbanized world as a *Gemeinschaft* (a "community" dominated by folkways, religion, and consensus) and the new industrial Europe as a *Gesellschaft* (a "society" typified by indi-vidualism, formal law, and a concern with rights).[5] And the dread of losing a sense of community is already apparent from the very first Anglo-American settlements in North America, where colonists who had been uprooted from traditional societies full of traditional geographical and cultural markers were now jumbled together in a hostile and unfamiliar landscape where it was no longer possible to assume that the conventional rules of social interchange could be practiced or enforced. Governor John Winthrop had not even gotten his boatloads of Puritan colonists into Massachusetts Bay before he felt it neces-sary to warn his contentious and theologically opinionated charges that "we must be knit together in this work as one man, we must entertain each other in brotherly affection, we must be willing to abridge ourselves of our superflui-ties, for the supply of others' necessities, we must uphold a familiar commerce together in all meekness, gentleness, patience, and liberality . . . always having before our eyes . . . our Community as members of the same body."[6]

And of course they didn't. They disobeyed Winthrop's injunction to be a single settlement—"a city on a hill"—and scattered over the landscape; and far from agreeing to live in communities, govern themselves by some form of common consensus, and subordinate private interests to the good of the whole, Winthrop's settlers displayed an extraordinary penchant for mobility, debate, and entrepreneurial land-development. In fact, from the 1970s onward, no question has bedeviled early American historians more often or more loudly than whether pre-Revolutionary America was predominantly a system of local, consensus-based, agrarian communities based on self-contained systems of sub-sistence agriculture and yeoman farmers, or a socially fluid field of self-seeking entrepreneurs and cash-crop farmers, each seeking a place of advantage in the new international commercial capitalist markets of the British empire.[7]

Nowhere has the complaint over the disappearance of American commu-nity generated more fury among historians than among those whose scholarly bailiwick is Lincoln's own lifetime. In his monumental 1991 survey, *The Market*

Revolution: Jacksonian America, 1815–1846, Charles G. Sellers painted a picture of the American Republic at the close of the War of 1812 as a society divided, in large measure, by its transportation: out beyond the immediate environs of the large East Coast port towns, America had developed rural communities of yeoman republicanism, where farmers took advantage of the cheapness of Western land and the near-absence of serious taxation to set themselves up as independent patriarchs, growing on as little as twenty acres everything a family could need in terms of food for themselves and their animals and the raw materials for clothing and shelter, dealing in barter for whatever else was needed and in cash money and interest not at all, and "abundantly meeting human needs for security, sociability, and trust" through neighborly reciprocity and sexually-segregated participation in male honor-sports and in female supervision of domestic production and child-bearing. These communities came at a price, as Sellers admits, "in patriarchy, conformity, and circumscribed horizons," and they were terrifically vulnerable whenever land came up short or children numerous, or whenever the blandishments of market exchange could find ways to invade the trans-Appalachian interior, as it did by the introduction of steamboats, canals, and finally railroads, all of them bearing the gifts of the market and tempting yeoman farmers to abandon self-sufficiency to develop single-crop cash agriculture and buy manufactured store goods rather than making their own. The serpent in Sellers's garden is industrial capitalism, and as if echoing the new communitarians' concern for the atomization and alienation of modern American society, Sellers frankly depicted the Whig program of "internal improvements" and market development as the first step toward the current crisis of community, where "competitive stress intensifies, the fruits of free-enterprise autonomy sour with job flight and social breakdown, environmental disaster looms, politics gridlocks, and huckster-driven media increasingly dominate public consciousness."[8]

The most obvious antidote then available lay in a network of what Nathaniel Hawthorne (in *The House of Seven Gables*) called "community-men and come-outers"—"reformers, temperance-lecturers, and all manner of cross-looking philanthropists"—who arose to re-create precapitalist communities through experiments which would be proof against the market's temptations, from Robert Owen's experiment in Lincoln's own southwestern Indiana at New Harmony in the mid-1820s to George Ripley's Brook Farm in 1841, the Northampton Association for Education and Industry in 1842, and 116 others before 1859, dedicated more or less generally (as the Northampton Association was) to making "ourselves and friends happier—to get rid of the competition so omnipresent and oppressive" in American society.[9]

But in the case of Abraham Lincoln, there is no sense that a need for any such antidotes was at all felt, no sense in fact that Lincoln felt any abiding or supervening loyalties to agrarian communities or any particular dread of competitive individualism; unlike the communitarians, Lincoln viewed wage labor and cash exchange as symbols of freedom, and he defined slavery, not so much as a system of racial injustice, but as an economic arrangement whose object was to compel men to labor without wages. "I used to be a slave," Lincoln remarked in 1856, "we were all slaves at one time or another," but "now I am so free that they let me practice law." Above all, he repeatedly cast social relations, not in terms of community, but in terms of competition, as "the race of life."[10] If what the new communitarians—and the old ones, too—feared was the emergence of a society which looked like Oliver Stone's Wall Street, Lincoln feared a society which looked like Sinclair Lewis's Main Street, a society in which established elites played on the populist resentments of an agrarian proletariat—white or black, it made no difference—in order to repress the dynamism and mobility of a market-driven middle class. In all the major works of the new communitarians—Etzione, Taylor, Bellah—the name of Abraham Lincoln makes no appearance. There is good reason for that.

Abraham Lincoln diverges from the communitarian ideal in American life on four major levels—the personal, the ideological, the practical, and the professional—and all of them in fact made him a much more controversial political figure in his own time than he is often understood to be. At the most personal level, though, Lincoln was a poor candidate for communitarianism simply because he fit so poorly the temperamental model of a person willing to be restrained by communal standards or to encourage the predominance of community in social life. The twenty-two-year-old Lincoln who in 1831 planted himself in New Salem as Denton Offutt's clerk had, at least at first, all the makings of a fun-loving, high-spirited member of the local "b'hoys": he made himself popular with his remarkable memory for rollicking stories and his sheer physical strength, and although he was "as ruff a specimen of humanity as could be found," he was easily remembered for being "full of Highlarity and fun, which made him companionable, and rather Conspicuous among his associates."[11]

And yet, even in his New Salem days, while Lincoln "never Seemed to be rude," he also "Seemed to have a liking for Solitude." He already seems to have had the sense that "he was the superior of all" and allowed himself to be "governed by his intellectual superiority," and that fueled both a single-minded concentration on self-improvement and the peculiar conviction that (as Orville Hickman Browning observed) "there was a predestined work for him in the world . . . that he was destined for something nobler than he was for the time engaged in." Consequently, whatever reputation Lincoln won for frontier "familiarity"—John Mack Faragher's phrase for the essential ingredient of egalitarian community in early Illinois—he also developed a strain of aloofness and separateness as New Salem failed to live up to the expectations of its founders that it would become the principal commercial entrepôt of central Illinois. "While he was down there at New Salem I think his time was mainly given to fun and social enjoyment and in the amusements of the people he came daily in contact with," recalled Stephen T. Logan, but "after he came here to Springfield however he got rid to a great degree of this disposition."[12]

Lincoln did not, of course, get rid of all of that "disposition" for "familiarity" when he came up to Springfield in 1837. Lincoln possessed, even at the beginning of his professional career, a surprising charm, a transparency of expression and intention which inspired trust and encouraged sponsorship. "Lincoln was the favorite of everybody—man, woman, and child—where he lived and was known," Herndon recalled. "Lincoln was a pet, faithful and an honest pet in this city." So even though Lincoln "was a poor man and must work his way up," Herndon recollected that Springfielders tripped over each other to help Lincoln. "He never saw the minute, the hour, nor the day that he did not have many financial friends to aid him, to assist him, and to help him in all ways. His friends vied with each other for the pleasure of the honor of assisting him . . . they almost fought each other for the privilege of assisting Lincoln." From the moment he walked into Abner Ellis's store and struck up an immediate friendship with what turned out to be another ambitious Kentucky-born store clerk, Joshua Speed, Lincoln became the magnet for "eight or ten choice spirits" among Springfield's budding community of lawyers and civil servants—James Matheny, Milton Hay, Evan Butler, James Conkling, "and other habitues of the court-house"—who met either in Ellis's store or Matheny's office "once and sometimes twice a month." Springfield became, in effect, the college that Lincoln never attended. "There was scarcely a day or an hour when a knot of men might not have been seen near the door of some leading store, or about the steps of the court house eagerly [discussing] a current political topic—not as a question of news for news . . . but rather in the nature of debate or discussion," Milton Hay recalled forty years later, and Hay particularly remembered that "it was always a great treat when Lincoln got amongst us—we would always be sure to have some of those stories of his for which he had already got a reputation."[13]

But none of that "familiarity" translated into a secure place in the Springfield community for Lincoln. "Mr. Lincoln was not a social man by any means," warned Judge David Davis, "his Stories—jokes &c. which were done to whistle off sadness are no evidences of sociality." Herndon agreed: "Mr. Lincoln was not a social being . . . he was rather cold—too abstracted—and too gloomy. . . . Mr. Lincoln only revealed his soul to but few beings—*if any*, and then he kept a corner of that soul from his bosom friends." The same man with the reputation for the outrageously funny (and occasionally outrageously lewd) stories was simultaneously "a man of quite infinite silences," who held even his closest associates at arm's length, who "was thoroughly and deeply secretive, uncommunicative, and close-minded as to his plans, wishes, hopes, and fears." Herndon was inclined to attribute this to Lincoln's political ambitions.

> His ambition was never satisfied; in him it was [a] consuming fire which smothered his feelings. . . . Mr. Lincoln never stopped in the street to have a social chat with anyone; he was not a social man, too reflective, too abstracted; he never attended political gatherings till the thing was organized, and then he was ready to make a speech, willing and ready to reap any advantage that grew out of it, ready and anxious for the office it afforded, if any in the political world.[14]

Others attributed Lincoln's personal remoteness to simple temperament. James Matheny believed that "Mr. Lincoln's fancy—Emotion, & Imagination dwindled" during his Springfield years, "that is to Say his reason & his Logic—swallowed up all his being . . . became dominant. . . . Mr. Lincoln grew more abstracted—Contemplative—&c. as he grew older." There was no question (as Milton Hay put it) that Lincoln's mind "ran to mathematical exactness about things." "Did Mr. Lincoln rule himself by the *head* or heart?" Herndon asked. "He was great in the *head* and ruled & lived there." And Lincoln himself left little room for doubt that reason and logic, rather than communal habits of the heart, were his polestars in his 1842 address to the short-lived Washington Temperance Society chapter in Springfield: "Happy day, when, all appetites controlled, all passions subdued, all matters subjected, *mind*, all conquering *mind*, shall live and move the monarch of the world. Glorious consummation! Hail fall of fury! Reign of Reason, all hail!" But Elizabeth Todd Edwards, his sister-in-law, put Lincoln's withdrawnness in simpler terms. "I knew Mr. L[incoln] well," she told Herndon bluntly, "he was a cold Man—had no affection—was not Social—was abstracted—thoughtful."[15]

Lincoln's withdrawnness made him the opposite of what might be expected of a "community-man." Herndon declared that "Mr. Lincoln was a riddle and a puzzle to his friends and neighbors among whom he lived and moved. . . . The man was hard, very difficult to understand, even by his bosom friends and his close and intimate neighbors among whom he associated."[16] It was, in fact, Lincoln's friends who were most baffled by the shield he erected behind the seeming sociability. David Davis was nettled by how Lincoln "never asked my advice on any question" except "about money affairs and how to put out his money," and "never thanked me for any thing I did." Ninian Edwards, Lincoln's brother-in-law, agreed that "Lincoln was not a warm-hearted man" and often "Seemed to be ungrateful" even if he really "was not." Jesse Dubois, who had served as a fellow Whig with Lincoln in the state legislature in the 1830s, who promised Lincoln that "I am for you against the world" in 1854, and who managed Lincoln's nomination in Chicago in 1860, was furious when Lincoln refused to listen to his patronage nominations and even more pointedly refused to help Dubois obtain either the Illinois Republican gubernatorial nomination in May 1864 or the Department of the Interior secretariat. "Lincoln is a singular man and I must Confess I never Knew him," Dubois wrote angrily to Henry Clay Whitney a week before Lincoln's death: "He has for 30 years past just used me as a plaything to accomplish his own ends: but the moment he was elevated to his proud position he seemed all at once to have entirely changed his whole nature and become altogether a new being—Knows no one and the road to his favor is always open to his Enemies whilst the door is hymetically [hermetically] sealed to his old friends." This might, in Dubois's case, have been written off to simple political disappointment, since Lincoln did in fact reward a large number of his political backers with patronage plums (including Whitney, who obtained an army paymastership). But many of those backers were not necessarily his friends. John Todd Stuart agreed that Lincoln "did forget his friends—That there was no part of his nature which drew him to do acts of gratitude to his friends." And even David Davis, who was eventually singled out by Lincoln to fill Justice John McLean's seat on the U.S. Supreme Court, complained that Lincoln used "men as a tool—a thing to satisfy him—to feed his desires &c."[17]

There is at least one particular sense in which Lincoln could not have been "a very social man" even if he had been inclined to it, and that concerned the most intimate community he belonged to: his marriage with Mary Todd Lincoln. Although the Lincoln marriage was suspected almost from the start of being "a policy Match all around," the fact is that all of Lincoln's attempts at marriage were, in more than a few respects, policy matches, in that his sadly aborted love match with Ann Rutledge as well as his rebound proposal to Mary Owens were, whatever the quotient of affection in them, both potential marriages up for Lincoln—Ann Rutledge, of course, belonged to the first family of New Salem (and while that may not have been very much of a social climb from Lincoln's later perspective, it certainly was from New Salem's), and Mary Owens was not only "jovial" and "social" but "had a liberal English education & was considered wealthy." His marriage to Mary Todd was also a match with a deeply emotionally troubled woman, whose "spells of mental depression" and mental instability drove her into shrieking fits and physical abuse of her husband and children and turned the Lincoln marriage into what Herndon called "a domestic hell on earth." The difficulties of that "hell" have usually been described in terms of the private agonies Lincoln suffered; what is often missed is how much of a liability Mary could be to Lincoln's standing in the

Springfield political and social community. Neither David Davis nor John Todd Stuart could ever remember when they had been "asked to dinner" at the Lincoln home, and Herndon believed that "Lincoln as a general rule dared not invite anyone to his house, because he did not know what moment she would kick Lincoln and his friend out of the house." Herndon exaggerates this, since the Lincolns did do a substantial amount of political entertaining; but what is true is that Lincoln spent inordinate amounts of time appeasing outraged domestic help (and their parents) and irritated storekeepers who had been the victims of Mary's temper and penuriousness, and even in the White House, Lincoln was "constantly under great apprehension lest his wife should do something which would bring him into disgrace."[18]

The result was that, outside of the circle of his immediate friends, Lincoln was by no means Springfield's most admired citizen. In the legislative elections which followed the great debates of 1858, Douglas Democrats easily defeated Lincoln Republicans in both Springfield and Sangamon Counties, and Lincoln's losses there and in neighboring Morgan County are what tipped the scale against him in the senatorial election that followed in January 1859; in the 1860 presidential election, Lincoln outdistanced Douglas by only sixty-nine votes in Springfield, while losing Sangamon County by over four hundred; Springfield voters rejected Lincoln's policies and party by giving big majorities to Democratic legislative candidates in the by-election of 1862; and in the 1864 presidential race, Lincoln carried Springfield over McClellan by only ten votes, while McClellan took all of Sangamon County by almost four hundred votes.[19] "Mr. Lincoln was not appreciated in this city, nor was he at all times the most popular man among us," Herndon wrote. Part of this was political, in that Lincoln "had the courage of his convictions and the valor of their expression" in a state where he was, all of his life, a spokesman for a minority party; but another part was that Lincoln "was not a social man, not being 'hail fellow well met.'"[20] What Lincoln loved was not individuals or communities but ideas, especially political ideas. "He had no idea—no proper notion or conception of particular men & women," Herndon wrote. "He scarcely could distinguish the individual."[21] "In dealing with men, he was a trimmer, and such a trimmer as the world has never seen," Leonard Swett told Herndon. "Yet Lincoln never trimmed in principles—it was only in his conduct with men." Lincoln "felt no special interest in any man or thing—Save & Except politics," recalled John Todd Stuart. He "loved principles and such like large political & national ones, Especially when it leads to his own Ends—paths—Ambitions—Success—honor &c. &c."[22]

It was those ideas, fully as much as his temperamental remoteness, which decisively distanced Abraham Lincoln from the glorification of community life and communal values, especially when they came in the form of the local agrarian community so beloved of Jeffersonian and Jacksonian Democrats. It was "the cultivators of the earth," the freeholding yeomen who supplied their own needs and wants and controlled their means of production apart from dependence on markets and cash exchange, who were looked upon by the Jacksonians "as the great and perennial foundation of that Republican spirit which is to maintain and perpetuate our free institutions." And consequently, the *Democratic Review* declared in 1839 that

> The farmer is naturally a Democrat—the citizen may be so, but it is in spite of many obstacles. . . . In the city men move in masses . . . in the country, on the other hand, man enjoys an existence of a healthier and truer happiness, a nobler mental freedom, a higher native dignity. . . . And to live he must labor: all the various modes by which, in great congregations of men, certain classes are ingeniously able to appropriate to themselves the fruits of the general toil of the rest, being to him alike unknown and impracticable. Hence does he better appreciate the true worth and dignity of labor, and knows how to respect, with a more manly and Christian sympathy of universal brotherhood, those oppressed masses of the laboring poor. . . . And hence, as we have said above, the farmer is naturally a democrat.

And it would have been difficult to find a better example of the Jacksonian yeoman farmer than Thomas Lincoln. Although Thomas Lincoln was hardly the "ne'er-do-well" or "poor white trash" that Lincoln's first biographers painted him as being in order to greater magnify his son's achievements, what is true is that he was a classic subsistence farmer who was ambitious mostly to produce by himself no more than what his household required. One of his neighbors remarked simply that Thomas Lincoln "was satisfied to live in the good *old* fashioned way; his shack kept out the rain; there was plenty of wood to burn . . . the old ways were good enough for him," while other neighbors explained that Thomas Lincoln "never planted more than a few acres" because "they wasn't no market for nothing unless you took it across two or three states. The people raised just what they needed."[23]

Thomas Lincoln evidently saw no reason why his son would not follow him in these classic agrarian patterns. "I was raised to farm work," Lincoln remembered in 1859, which meant (as he explained to John Scripps a year later) that "A. though very young . . . had an axe out into his hands at once; and from that till within his twentythird year, he was almost constantly handling that most useful instrument—less, of course, in plowing and harvesting seasons." It also meant that as Lincoln grew into adolescence, Thomas loaned his son out to neighboring farmers as part of the incessant borrowing-and-swapping of rural subsistence networks of exchange, and pocketed for his own use whatever

small change Abraham had been paid (which was not much, given the paucity
of cash in circulation on the frontier). But instead of inuring his son to the
traditional patterns of Jeffersonian yeoman agriculture, the experience only
alienated young Abraham. Lincoln often remarked in later years that "his father
taught him to work but never learned him to love it"—or at least not the kind
of work his father intended for him. What he did cherish was a memory of a
very different sort of work, of two men hurrying down to the ferry landing
on the Ohio River where Lincoln kept a small cockboat, dragooning him into
rowing them out midstream to intercept an oncoming steamboat, and each
rewarding him with "a silver half-dollar" which they "threw . . . on the floor
of my boat. . . . Gentlemen, you may think it was a very little thing, and in
these days it seems to me a trifle; but it was a most important incident in my
life. I could scarcely credit that I, a poor boy, had earned a dollar in less than
a day. . . . The world seemed wider and fairer before me."[24] Abraham Lincoln
had met the cash economy.

Once having met it, Lincoln saw it at once as his ticket to advancement
and status. He never entertained any romantic affection for landholding and
agriculture—his address to the Wisconsin State Agricultural Society in 1859
was frankly dismissive of any reverence for farmers and traditional farming
methods—and he indulged very little in the mania for land speculation that
made so many of his friends, like David Davis, so wealthy. He left his father's
farm to enter on the life of what he hoped would become a great commercial
town in New Salem, and moved again to become part of the professional life
of what became a great city. In what really amounts to his most savage criticism
of yeoman agrarianism in favor of a wage labor economy, Lincoln chided his
stepbrother, John D. Johnston, for not producing cash crops "merely because it
does not seem to you that you could get much for it." Lincoln's recommenda-
tion to Johnston was, in effect, to abandon subsistence agriculture and enter
himself into the cash-labor market: "You are in need of some ready money;
and what I propose is, that you shall go to work, 'tooth and nails' for some
body who will give you money [for] it. Let father and your boys take charge
of things at home—prepare for a crop, and make the crop; and you go to
work for the best money wages, or in discharge of any debt you owe, that you
can get." As a state legislator, Lincoln regularly voted against the granting of
preemption rights to squatters, supported to its dying breath the Illinois State
Bank and the agricultural liquidations it executed after the Panic of 1837, and
struggled to ensure that the sale of federally owned lands in Illinois would
support commercial and transportation projects. As Olivier Fraysse remarks,
"The small landowner threatened with seizure, the squatter who sold his clothes
to keep his rights of pre-emption from falling into the hands of speculators,
had trouble recognizing one of their own kind in Lincoln."[25]

Lincoln's indifference to yeoman agrarianism was rooted in his distaste for what he regarded as the claustrophobia of agrarian communities. "Individuals held the sacred right to regulate their own family affairs," Lincoln reminded his hearers in 1854; and "the legitimate object of government" is only "to do for a community of people, whatever they need to have done, but can not do, *at all*, or can not, *so well do*, for themselves. . . . In all that the people can individually do as well for themselves, government"—and one might as well also say, *community*—"ought not to interfere." And in contrast to the static nature of social relations in rural communities, Lincoln praised the competitiveness which characterized market relations, especially when they involved the use of wage labor. "I am glad to see that a system of labor prevails in New England under which laborers CAN strike when they want to," Lincoln told a crowd in New Haven during the 1860 shoemakers' strike.

> What is the true condition of the laborer? I take it that it is best for all to leave each man free to acquire property as fast as he can. Some will get wealthy. I don't believe in a law to prevent a man from getting rich; it would do more harm than good. So while we do not propose any war upon capital, we do wish to allow the humblest man an equal chance to get rich with everybody else. . . . Then you can better your condition, and so it may go on and on in one ceaseless round so long as man exists on the face of the earth!

Lincoln was, in the largest sense, a classical nineteenth-century liberal and shared classical liberalism's cultural commitments to rationality, individualism, personal rights, and progress. He tempered this with a strong overlay of moral principle, but then again, the Whig Party itself embodied a unique compromise of evangelical Protestant moralism with opportunism; Lincoln, in that respect, was the perfect Whig.[26]

It was this embrace of the transformation of the American economy into a cash-based market economy which brought Lincoln into opposition to the Democrats as early as his first political stirrings in 1832 and into the forefront of the Whig Party once Henry Clay had begun reorganizing his "national Republican" schism from the Democrats as a national party in 1834. Where the Democrats thought of the yeoman farmer as the bulwark of republican independence, the Whigs, prompted by the disastrous example of the War of 1812, were convinced that a nation of subsistence farmers and unprotected manufacturing was a sitting duck for the great industrial capitalist powers of Europe, beginning with Great Britain. "Our republican system demands and requires protection to our republican laborers," cried the *American Whig Review* in 1851, and by *protection* the Whigs meant Henry Clay's "American System" of national bank finance, tariff-protected industry, commercial (rather than subsistence) farming, railroads, and free wage labor. Lincoln found in Clay his "beau ideal of a statesman," his "favorite of all the great men of the Nation," and even as late as his own presidency, he still described himself as an "old-line Henry Clay Whig."[27] Stephen Logan found Lincoln "as stiff as a man could be in his Whig doctrines," and Joseph Gillespie, his longtime political ally, described him as an advocate "for a National Currency, Internal Improvements by the general government, and the encouragement of home manufactures. On this latter subject I have heard him make arguments greatly more powerful and convincing than anything I have ever heard or read." His highest ambition, as he told Joshua Speed, "was to become the De Witt Clinton of Ills."—to imitate, in other words, the New York canal pioneer who opened up the rural hinterlands of New York to the competitive forces of the international markets. And even with the threat of secession and civil war hanging over him in 1860, Lincoln still insisted that "the question of Slavery" should not serve as a distraction from "the old question of tariff—a matter that will remain one of the chief affairs of national housekeeping to all time—the question of the management of financial affairs; the question of the disposition of the public domain"—in short, the entire Whig domestic agenda. He was, as he once described himself, "always a Whig in politics," and that committed him ideologically to a nationalist political mentality, rather than to the localism and diversity so beloved of Democratic agrarianism, and later on, the clamor for "popular sovereignty" and "states' rights," both of which were, so to speak, the nineteenth century's ultimate expressions of Democratic communitarianism. What Lincoln praised "Harry of the West" for in his 1852 eulogy of Clay was precisely Clay's placing of the principles of the republican ideology above the demands of local, and even national, community:

> He loved his country partly because it was his own country, but mostly because it was a free country; and he burned with a zeal for its advancement, prosperity and glory, of human liberty, human right and human nature. He desired the prosperity of his countrymen partly because they were his countrymen, but chiefly to show to the world that freemen could be prosperous.[28]

It was not that Lincoln pulled shy only of agrarian community; that much might be explained purely in terms of his Whiggism and his sympathies for a commercial and industrial economy. Even in Springfield, Lincoln showed little enthusiasm for entering into the broad variety of community-based societies and activities that the Illinois capital afforded. He was, of course, instrumental in engineering the transfer of the state capital from Vandalia to Springfield in the first place and served briefly on the Springfield town board in 1839 and 1840, largely (one suspects) to oversee the smooth completion of the transition he had done so much in the legislature to produce. He also shows up occasionally on the organizing committees of receptions and cotillions, serving as guest of honor and toastmaster at a dinner for a neighboring fire company in 1858, commemorating the centenary of the birth of Robert Burns at a gala dinner (at which a large number of "mysterious-looking bottles" circulated freely), and serving as one of the eleven managers of the state Colonization Society in 1857 and as a featured speaker at the Colonization Society's annual January meetings throughout the 1850s.[29]

But the Colonization Society was, in large measure, an adjunct of Lincoln's Whig political activities, and Paul Simon's study of Lincoln's state legislative career has warned us not to overvalue Lincoln's role in the transfer of the state capital above those of the other Sangamon County legislators. And what is significantly missing in Lincoln's life in Springfield is any but the most tangential involvement in the most obvious forms of community organization. He never ran for any town office once Springfield was duly incorporated in 1840. And although he addressed the Washington Temperance Society chapter in 1842, and was clearly proud enough of it to mention it twice in letters to Joshua Speed, it is not clear just how Lincoln was involved with the Washingtonians, if at all. A petition Lincoln signed for use of the Hall of Representatives for a temperance lecturer in 1845 makes it clear that the event was being sponsored by "private contribution," not by a society; an inquiry from a temperance society member in 1860 received only the answer that he had "never held the 'cup' to the lips of my friends," and made no mention of having belonged to a temperance society. Certainly by the later 1850s Lincoln retained no memberships in temperance societies, since he responded to teasing from Stephen Douglas about alcohol by insisting that "No, I am not a member of any temperance society; but I am temperate in this that I don't drink anything." He also declined to join any of Springfield's churches, despite his reasonably cordial but distant relations with the Springfield clergy, and although he paid for a pew rental for his family at Springfield's First Presbyterian Church, the Reverend George W. Pendleton wrote with ill-disguised irritation that Lincoln "often goes to the railroad shop and spends the sabbath in reading Newspapers, and telling stories to the workmen, but not to the house of God."

> He went to the old school church [wrote Charles Ray, speaking of First Presbyterian's "Old School" theological affiliation]; but in spite of that outward sign of assent to the horrible dogmas of the sect, I have reason from himself to know that his "vital piety," if that means belief in the impossible, was of the negative sort. I think that orthodoxy, if that means the Presbyterian doxy, was regarded by him as a huge joke; but he was far too kindly and cautious to challenge any man's faith without cause.

He also declined to join fraternal societies such as the Masons, despite the fact that Masonic membership offered important political advantages. "Mr.

Lincoln I do not think belonged to any Secret Society," recalled Abner Ellis, "neither Masonic or Oddfellows. I once heard Judge Denney ask him if he was Not a Mason And his answer Was I do not belong to any society except it be for the Good of my Country."[30]

But even the good of his country did not draw Lincoln into the one community organization where he could actually have brought some valuable experience, and which had already proven its political usefulness to him, and that was the local militia. Springfield's first militia company was organized in 1835, and another was recruited the following year by Lincoln's close political friend and ally, Edward Dickinson Baker. But despite Lincoln's own service in the Black Hawk War (which brought him for the first time into contact with influential Illinois anti-Jacksonians like John Todd Stuart and Orville Hickman Browning), and despite his willingness to give "warm, thrilling, and effective" speeches at recruitment rallies for the Mexican War in 1846, there is no record of Lincoln's ongoing involvement in any of Springfield's military companies. To the contrary, Lincoln was more likely to lampoon them:

> We remember one of these parades ourselves here, at the head of which, on horseback, figured our old friend Gordon Abrams, with a pine wood sword, about nine feet long, and a paste-board cocked hat, from front to rear about the length of an ox yoke, and very much the shape of one turned bottom upwards; and with spurs having rowels as large as the bottom of a teacup, and shanks a foot and a half long. That was the last militia muster here. Among the rules and regulations, no man is to wear more than five pounds of cod-fish for epaulets, or more than thirty yards of bologna sausages for a sash; and no two men are to dress alike, and if any should dress alike the one that dresses most alike is to be fined, (I forget how much). Flags they had too, with devices and mottoes, one of which latter is, "We'll fight till we run, and we'll run till we die."

To be sure, Lincoln had political reasons for shunning the Masons, the militia, and a number of the churches. Masonry, as a "secret Society," was publicly deplored by the Whigs as an example of dark Democratic conspiracy-mongering, and Illinois Masons like Stephen Douglas gave the Masons a definite Democratic flavor; and Lincoln later claimed that most state militias were political instruction schools for the Democrats. "Antislavery men, being generally much akin to peace," he told John F. Seymour, brother of Horatio Seymour, New York's Democratic governor, in 1863, "had never interested themselves in military matters and in getting up companies, as Democrats had." He also tended to judge the clergy by their political affiliations, and even George W. Pendleton admitted that one reason why Lincoln skipped out on services at First Presbyterian in 1860 was that "the pastor is afflicted with Douglas proclivities."[31] Even so, it cut Lincoln off from three of the most important community organizations in Springfield.

There were, however, at least two communities in which Lincoln did obtain an important place, one of which was the Illinois Whig Party, and the other the professional brotherhood of his fellow lawyers on the Eighth Judicial Circuit. He began his political life in Illinois almost at the same time as the Whig Party was being organized, was five times a successful Whig candidate for the state legislature, a Whig presidential elector, a Whig congressman, and almost a Whig senator in 1855. In addition to his place on numerous Whig tickets, Lincoln also was heavily involved in the construction of local Whig clubs and the organization and mobilization of Whig political cadres "to organize the whole State so that every Whig can be brought to the polls." He labored self-lessly as a stump speaker and campaign manager, not only for the Whigs, but after 1856, for the new Republicans, managing congressional campaigns for Richard Yates and Archibald Williams, brokering the nomination of William Bissell for governor, and pacifying intraparty quarrels between Norman Judd and "Long John" Wentworth in Chicago, and between Chicago and downstate Republicans (like David Davis). One reason why Lincoln wielded so much heft within party organizations was the visibility and name-recognition he had purchased on the long swings through the Eighth Judicial Circuit he had taken as a trial lawyer from the organization of the Eighth Circuit in 1841 until the great senatorial debates of 1858. "In my opinion I think Mr. Lincoln was happy—as happy as *he* could be, when on this Circuit—and happy no other place," David Davis recalled. "This was his place of enjoyment." And among the "fraternity of the bar," Lincoln developed some of the most satisfying personal relationships he ever enjoyed in his life: Ward Hill Lamon, Leonard Swett, Henry Clay Whitney, Lawrence Weldon, and of course the rotund David Davis himself. "Following the court around on the circuit was, no doubt, one of the greatest pleasures Lincoln enjoyed."[32]

But to reach for Lincoln's party work as a Whig, or his legal business around the circuit, as the last evidence of communitarian longings on Lincoln's part is quite a stretch indeed. After all, the Whig Party represented the triumph of nationalism over local community, of rationalism and commerce over passion and agrarianism; and in practical terms, it actually netted Lincoln compara-tively little in hard results. His term in Congress, which he might have hoped would be the prelude either to major national office holding under a Whig president, Zachary Taylor, or to the Senate, fizzled under layers of party indif-ference. "In 1840 we fought a fierce and laborious battle in Illinois, many of us spending almost the entire year in the contest," Lincoln complained. "The general victory came, and with it, the appointment of a set of drones . . . who had never spent a dollar or lifted a finger in the fight." He found himself with so little leverage at the national level that he was forced to tell an office seeker who wanted his endorsement, "You overrate my capacity to serve you. Not one man recommended by me has yet been appointed to any thing, little or big, except a few who had no opposition."[33]

It would also be difficult to cast the Eighth Circuit as a kind of surrogate community for Lincoln. Whatever good fellowship Lincoln enjoyed in David Davis's traveling court, the fact was that it was *traveling*—it was rootless, professional, and so careless of commitment that lawyers on the circuit (including Lincoln) regularly combined and opposed each other in case after case and in place after place. Above all, the legal profession came to be, in the same years that Lincoln was coming to maturity as a lawyer, the principal enforcement of abstract contract, of national commerce, and of market relations—becoming, in the wickedly accurate phrase of Charles Sellers, "the shock troops of capitalism." Although the romantic legend of Lincoln as a lawyer offers us a vision of a community counselor—defending Duff Armstrong *pro bono* for the sake of his father's memory, "skinning" Erastus Wright for mulcting a Revolutionary War widow, browbeating Judge E. Y. Rice into unwillingly admitting testimony to acquit Peachy Harrison—the bulk of Lincoln's law practice, not to mention its most profitable aspects, had moved by 1856 into the state supreme court and the federal courts and was devoted to the service of precisely those agents of the markets which were most lethal to rural and local communities: the railroad corporations, the banks and insurance companies of Sangamon, McLean, and Morgan Counties, and even at least one St. Louis venture capital firm. Lincoln's single greatest fee was won by the verdict he obtained for the Illinois Central Railroad, denying the power of a local community—in this case, McLean County—to tax the railroad's property. He took no fee for freeing Duff Armstrong, but by the same token, Henry Clay Whitney "never found him unwilling to appear in behalf of a great 'soulless corporation.'"[34]

On every important level of his life, Abraham Lincoln showed only the thinnest interest in the protection or encouragement of communitarian attitudes or values. To the contrary, he resented the deadening hand of localism as a restraint on independence, reason, ambition, and talent. Even the word *community* turns up comparatively infrequently in Lincoln's surviving writings—less than a hundred times in the eight volumes of his *Collected Works*—and usually in only the most conventional and unspecific usage. It would be a caricature to suggest that Lincoln's Whiggish individualism meant that he had *no* recognition of the interdependence with others or of the validity of community norms. In fact, when Peter Cartwright challenged Lincoln's fitness for office in 1846 on the grounds of religious infidelity, Lincoln deftly sidestepped the infidelity charge and averred that "I still do not think any man has the right thus to insult the feeling, and injure the morals, of the community in which he may live." By the same token, Lincoln's liberalism did not consist of indifference to people or to people's beliefs—as he demonstrated repeatedly in pressing on Stephen Douglas the immorality, rather than merely the inutility, of slavery. Lincoln's opposition to slavery always contained substantive moral judgment. "I have always hated slavery," he declared in his great debates with Douglas in 1858; and in 1854, he explained, "I object to it because it assumes that there CAN be MORAL RIGHT in the enslaving of one man by another."[35] Douglasite Democrats, ironically, set tremendous store by community decision-making but then denied that there were any necessary moral underpinnings to that process.

If Lincoln considered himself, like Henry Clay, a nationalist, it was not because he believed national government was a better communitarian agency than local government but because nationalism provided him with a court of appeal and a stage of opportunity beyond the constraints and confinements of localities and regions. Lincoln did not see himself the way Michael Sandel defines the communitarian self, as someone who is "always embedded in the story of those communities from which I derive my identity." In contrast to the organic rhetoric of romantic or postmodern communitarianism, Lincoln believed that the universalist premises of American politics were intended to help Americans transcend the pettiness of their local origins. "Half our people . . . have come from Europe—German, Irish, French, and Scandinavian," Lincoln argued in 1858. "But when they look through that old declaration of independence," they find principles that transcend the communities of one's birth, whether another country or another state of the Union. "They find that those old men say that 'We hold these truths to be self-evident, that all men are created equal,' and then they feel that that moral sentiment taught in that day evidences their relation to those men . . . and that they have a right to claim it as though they were . . . flesh of the flesh of the men who wrote that Declaration."[36] For Lincoln, political and civil rights, not considerations of the general good, were central to the protection of a republican society.

But why, then, as he stood on the rear platform of his train in the drizzle and slush of that February morning, did he believe that he owed Springfield "every thing"? Paul Angle once answered that question with a series of questions of his own. "Could Lincoln . . . have attained high standing at the bar if he had not resided at the one city in the state where the high courts sat?" In all likelihood, *no*, since Springfield and the Eighth Circuit sat athwart all the major commercial development of the 1850s in Illinois. "Could he have become a power in Illinois politics if the legislature and the courts had not drawn the political leaders to his home at regular and frequent intervals?" Only possibly, since so much of his political work was coterminous with his circuit work. "Could he have held to his faith in political democracy if he had not lived in a city where economic opportunity was a fact?" Plainly, *no*, but this was to define Springfield in something other than communitarian terms; to define it, in fact, as something other than a community or a village and more like a springboard for Lincoln's ambitions. It was no exaggeration, therefore, for Lincoln to express his sadness at departing from Springfield, because unlike other communities he had known—Little Pigeon Creek, New Salem—Springfield had not swaddled him with communitarian demands. Springfield, in that respect, suited Lincoln because it was so much like Lincoln himself, unburdened with expectations for a collective life and eager for growth and opportunity. It had stood back, sometimes all too willingly, and allowed him the room he craved to grow and to strive. "Lincoln was not a very social man," Herndon wrote in 1874. "He was not spontaneous in his feelings; was, as some said, rather cold." But it was the coldness of God's lonely man, "rather reflective, not cold." For all the coldness, "take him all in all, he was as near a perfect man as God generally makes."[37] All Lincoln wanted from his community was the opportunity to test that perfection to its limits.

Notes

This essay first appeared in the *Journal of the Abraham Lincoln Association* 21.1 (Winter 2000): 1–30.

1. James C. Conkling to Clinton Conkling, February 12, 1861, in *Concerning Mr. Lincoln: In Which Abraham Lincoln Is Pictured as He Appeared to Letter Writers of His Time*, ed. Harry E. Pratt (Springfield, IL, 1944), 50; Lincoln, "Farewell Address at Springfield, Illinois," in *The Collected Works of Abraham Lincoln*, ed. Roy P. Basler (New Brunswick, NJ, 1953–55), 4:190.

2. According to David Davis, in 1849, Grant Goodrich proposed that Lincoln join his law firm in Chicago, but Lincoln declined; after the Cooper Union address in February 1860, Erastus Corning, one of the directors of the New York Central Railroad, was rumored to have offered Lincoln the position of general counsel for the NYCR. See David Davis to William Henry Herndon, September 19, 1866, in *Herndon's Informants: Letters, Interviews, and Statements about Abraham Lincoln*, ed. Douglas L. Wilson and Rodney O. Davis (Urbana, IL, 1998), 349; and John W. Starr, *Lincoln and the Railroads* (New York, 1927), 126–31.

3. Lincoln, "Farewell Address at Springfield, Illinois," and "Autobiography Written for John L. Scripps," in *Collected Works*, 4:190, 64–65.

4. Amitai Etzione, *The Spirit of Community: Rights, Responsibilities and the Communitarian Agenda* (New York, 1993), 118–19; Alasdair MacIntyre, *After Virtue: A Study in Moral Theory* (London, 1981), 147; Robert Bellah et al., *The Good Society* (New York, 1991), 6, 49, 51.

5. Ferdinand Tonnies, *Fundamental Concepts of Sociology*, trans. C. P. Loomis (New York, 1940), 53–73.

6. "A Modell of Christian Charity," in *The Puritans: A Sourcebook of Their Writings* (1938; repr., New York, 1963), 1:198.

7. Darrett B. Rutman, *Winthrop's Boston: Portrait of a Puritan Town, 1630–1649* (New York, 1965), 96–97; John Frederick Martin, *Profits in the Wilderness: Entrepreneurship and the Founding of the New England Towns in the Seventeenth Century* (Chapel Hill, NC, 1991), 3–5; James A. Henretta, "Families and Farms: Mentalite in Pre-Industrial America," *William and Mary Quarterly* 35 (April 1978): 3–32; Allan Kulikoff, "The Transition to Capitalism in Rural America," *William and Mary Quarterly* 46 (April 1989): 120–44, and "The American Revolution, Capitalism, and the Formation of the Yeoman Classes," in *Beyond the American Revolution: Explorations in the History of American Radicalism*, ed. Alfred F. Young (DeKalb, IL, 1993), 81–119; Winifred B. Rothenberg, "The Market and Massachusetts Farmers, 1750–1855," *Journal of Economic History* 4 (October 1981): 283–314; Michael Merrill, "Cash Is Good to Eat: Self-Sufficiency and Exchange in the Rural Economy of the United States," *Radical History Review* 4 (Winter 1977): 42–71; Christopher Clark, *The Roots of Rural Capitalism: Western Massachusetts, 1780–1860* (Ithaca, NY, 1990), 8–11.

8. Charles G. Sellers, *The Market Revolution: Jacksonian America, 1815–1846* (New York, 1991), 12–21. Sellers's portrait of yeoman republicanism is echoed in Harry Watson, *Liberty and Power: The Politics of Jacksonian America* (New York, 1990); Sellers, "Capitalism and Democracy in American Historical Mythology," in *The Market Revolution in America: Social, Political, and Religious Expressions, 1800–1880*, ed. Melvyn Stokes and Stephen Conway (Charlottesville, VA, 1996), 314.

9. Nathaniel Hawthorne, *The House of the Seven Gables*, ed. Allan Lloyd Smith (London, 1995), 73; Daniel Feller, *The Jacksonian Promise: America, 1815–1840* (Baltimore, 1995), 77–83; Christopher Clark, *The Communitarian Moment: The Radical Challenge of the Northampton Association* (Ithaca, NY, 1995), 1–38.

10. John E. Roll, in *Recollected Words of Abraham Lincoln*, ed. Don Fehrenbacher and Virginia Fehrenbacher (Stanford, CA, 1996), 383; Michael Burlingame, *The Inner World of Abraham Lincoln* (Urbana, IL, 1994), 35–36; Lincoln, "Speech in Independence Hall, Philadelphia, Pennsylvania," February 22, 1861, and "Message to Congress in Special Session," July 4, 1861, in *Collected Works*, 4:240, 438.

11. Erastus Wright interview, July 10, 1865, in Josiah G. Holland Papers, New York Public Library, New York; William Butler, interview with James Q. Howard, May 1860, in *The Lincoln Papers*, ed. David C. Mearns (Garden City, NY, 1948), 1:151.

12. E. R. Burba to William Henry Herndon, March 31, 1866, in Wilson and Davis, *Herndon's Informants*, 241; Herndon to Jesse Weik, April 4, 1890, in *The Hidden Lincoln: From the Letters and Papers of William H. Herndon*, ed. Emmanuel Hertz (New York, 1937), 251; John Mack Faragher, *Sugar Creek: Life on the Illinois Prairie* (New Haven, CT, 1986), 153–55; O. H. Browning interview, June 17, 1875, and S. T. Logan interview, July 6, 1875, in *An Oral History of Abraham Lincoln: John G. Nicolay's Interviews and Essays*, ed. Michael Burlingame (Carbondale, IL, 1996), 7, 37–38.

13. Herndon to C. O. Poole, January 5, 1886, in Herndon-Weik Papers, Library of Congress, Group 4, reel 9, #1885; Herndon to Jesse Weik, January 15, 1886, in

Hertz, *Hidden Lincoln*, 134; Milton Hay interview, July 4, 1875, in Burlingame, *Oral History of Abraham Lincoln*, 26–27.

14. David Davis interview, September 20, 1866, in Wilson and Davis, *Herndon's Informants*, 348; William Henry Herndon, "Analysis of the Character of Abraham Lincoln," *Abraham Lincoln Quarterly* 1 (December 1941): 413, 419; Herndon to Jesse Weik, November 24, 1882, in Hertz, *Hidden Lincoln*, 88, 177; Herndon to Jesse Weik, February 24, 1887, in Herndon-Weik Papers, Group 4, reel 10, #2113–16.

15. James H. Matheny interview, November 1866, and Elizabeth Todd Edwards interview, 1865–66, in Wilson and Davis, *Herndon's Informants*, 432, 443; William H. Herndon, "Analysis of the Character of Abraham Lincoln," *Abraham Lincoln Quarterly* 1 (September 1941): 347; Lincoln, "Temperance Address," February 22, 1842, in *Collected Works*, 1:279.

16. Herndon to C. O. Poole, January 5, 1886, in Herndon-Weik Papers, Group 4, reel 9, #1880.

17. John T. Stuart interview, June 1865, Ninian Edwards interview 1865–66, David Davis interviews, September 19 and 20, 1866, and Jesse Dubois to Henry Whitney, April 6, 1865, in Wilson and Davis, *Herndon's Informants*, 63–65, 346–47, 351, 446, 620; Harry J. Carman and Reinhard H. Luthin, *Lincoln and the Patronage* (New York, 1943), 309.

18. John Todd Stuart interview, June 1865, and L. M. Greene interview, May 3, 1866, in Wilson and Davis, *Herndon's Informants*, 63–65, 250; Herndon to C. O. Poole, January 5, 1886, and Herndon to Jesse Weik, January 9, 1886, in Herndon-Weik Papers, Group 4, reel 9, #1885, 1923–26; O. H. Browning interview, June 17, 1875, in Burlingame, *Oral History of Abraham Lincoln*, 1, 3; Stephen Berry, *House of Abraham: Lincoln and the Todds, a Family Divided by War* (New York, 2007), 36–37, 99–100; Michael Burlingame, *Inner World of Abraham Lincoln*, 268–355, and "Mary Todd Lincoln's Unethical Conduct as First Lady," in *At Lincoln's Side: John Hay's Civil War Correspondence and Selected Writings*, ed. Burlingame (Carbondale, 2000), 185–203.

19. Illinois Election Returns, State Senate and State House, 1858, Illinois State Archives, 216–19, 220–25 (Microfilm roll no. 30-45); Paul M. Angle, *"Here I Have Lived": A History of Lincoln's Springfield, 1821–1865* (Chicago, 1971), 234, 253, 274, 286–87; Bruce Collins, "The Lincoln-Douglas Contest of 1858 and Illinois' Electorate," *Journal of American Studies* 20 (1986): 419.

20. Herndon to James Keys, April 14, 1886, Herndon to Jesse Weik, February 11, 1887, and Herndon's essay, "Lincoln in Springfield," in Hertz, *Hidden Lincoln*, 144, 171, 424.

21. Herndon, "Analysis of the Character of Abraham Lincoln," *Abraham Lincoln Quarterly* 1 (September 1941): 372.

22. Leonard Swett to Herndon, January 17, 1866, and John T. Stuart interview, June 1865, in Wilson and Davis, *Herndon's Informants*, 64–65, 165.

23. John Ashworth, *Slavery, Capitalism, and Politics in the Antebellum Republic*, vol. 1, *Commerce and Compromise, 1820–1850* (Cambridge, Eng., 1995), 303–6; *Democratic Review* 6 (1839): 500–502; John Ashworth, *Agrarians and Aristocrats:*

Party Political Ideology in the United States, 1837–1846 (London, 1983), 22; Burlingame, *Inner World of Abraham Lincoln*, 40; Arthur E. Morgan, "New Light on Lincoln's Boyhood," *Atlantic Monthly*, February 1920, 213.

24. Lincoln, "To Jesse W. Fell, Enclosing Autobiography," and "Autobiography Written for John L. Scripps," in *Collected Works*, 3:511, 4:62; John Romine interview, September 14, 1865, in Wilson and Davis, *Herndon's Informants*, 118; William D. Kelley, in *Reminiscences of Abraham Lincoln by Distinguished Men of His Time*, ed. A. T. Rice (New York, 1886), 280.

25. Lincoln, "Address before the Wisconsin State Agricultural Society, Milwaukee, Wisconsin," September 20, 1859, in *Collected Works*, 3:472–73: "I presume I am not expected to employ the time assigned me, in the mere flattery of farmers, as a class," Lincoln began. "My opinion of them is that, in proportion to numbers, they are neither better nor worse than other people. In the nature of things they are more numerous than any other class; and I believe there really are more attempts at flattering them than any other; the reason of which I cannot perceive, unless it be that they can cast more votes than any other." See also Lincoln, "To Thomas Lincoln and John D. Johnston," December 24, 1848, in *Collected Works*, 2:16; Gabor Boritt, *Lincoln and the Economics of the American Dream* (Memphis, TN, 1978), 80–81; Olivier Fraysse, *Lincoln, Land, and Labor, 1809–1860*, trans. Sylvia Neely (Urbana, IL, 1994), 31, 76–77, 78. See Lincoln's "Opinion on Preemption of Public Land" for the Illinois Central Railroad in 1856, in *Collected Works*, 2:334–35.

26. Lincoln, "Speech at New Haven, Connecticut," March 6, 1860, "Fragment on Government," July 1, 1854, and "Speech at Bloomington, Illinois," September 26, 1854, in *Collected Works* 2:220, 239, 4:225. See also Lincoln's replies to delegation of striking shipyard workers in November 1863, as reported in the *New York Times*, December 5, 1863, in Fehrenbacher and Fehrenbacher, *Recollected Words*, 12; Herndon to Jesse Weik, January 1, 1886, in Hertz, *Hidden Lincoln*, 116–17; J. David Greenstone, *The Lincoln Persuasion: Remaking American Liberalism* (Princeton, NJ, 1993), 18–26.

27. "Unity of the Whigs: Their Principles and Measures," *American Whig Review* 8 (September 1851): 18; J. Rowan Herndon interview, May 28, 1865, in Wilson and Davis, *Herndon's Informants*, 8; John Minor Botts, in Fehrenbacher and Fehrenbacher, *Recollected Words*, 37.

28. Logan interview, July 6, 1875, in Burlingame, *Oral History of Abraham Lincoln*, 36; Gillespie interview, January 31, 1866, and Joshua F. Speed to Herndon, 1865–66, in Wilson and Davis, *Herndon's Informants*, 188, 476; Lincoln, "Eulogy on Henry Clay," July 6, 1852, and "Speech at New Haven, Connecticut," March 6, 1860, in *Collected Works*, 2:126, 4:14.

29. Angle, "*Here I Have Lived*," 182, 189–90; *Lincoln Day-by-Day: A Chronology*, ed. E. S. Miers (1960; repr., Dayton, OH, 1991), 1:113, 114, 116, 134, 135, 2:188, 220, 241.

30. Paul Simon, *Lincoln's Preparation for Greatness: The Illinois Legislative Years* (Norman, OK, 1965), 102. Lincoln's 1842 eulogy for Benjamin Ferguson, a "much-

respected member" of the Washingtonians, suggests that he may have been a member at least up to the time the Springfield Washingtonians were dissolved and absorbed into the Sons of Temperance in 1845; see "Eulogy on Benjamin Ferguson," "Request for Use of Hall of Representatives for a Temperance Lecture," January 25, 1845, and "To J. Mason Haight," June 11, 1860, in *Collected Works*, 1:343, 2:268, 4:75; James Ewing, in *Abraham Lincoln, by Some Men Who Knew Him*, ed. Isaac N. Phillips (Bloomington, IL, 1910), 55; Helen Nicolay, *Personal Traits of Abraham Lincoln* (New York, 1912), 219; Lawrence Weldon, in Rice, *Reminiscences of Abraham Lincoln*, 198; Rev. George W. Pendleton, in Burlingame, *Oral History of Abraham Lincoln*, 155 n.29; Charles H. Ray to Herndon, February 11, 1866, and Abner Y. Ellis to Herndon, January 30, 1866, in Wilson and Davis, *Herndon's Informants*, 178, 209.

31. Donald W. Riddle, *Congressman Abraham Lincoln* (Urbana, IL, 1957), 11. While still in New Salem, Lincoln received a second commission in the Illinois militia from Governor John Reynolds in December 1832, but no record survives of any service under this commission, and it may have quietly expired in 1834. See Wayne C. Temple, "Lincoln's Military Service after the Black Hawk War," *Lincoln Herald* 72 (Fall 1970): 87–89; Lincoln, "Speech to the Springfield Scott Club," August 14, 1852, in *Collected Works*, 2:149–50; John F. Seymour to Horatio Seymour, January 19, 1863, in Alexander J. Wall, *A Sketch of the Life of Horatio Seymour, 1810–1886* (New York, 1929), 30; George W. Pendleton, in Burlingame, *Oral History of Abraham Lincoln*, 155 n.29.

32. Lincoln, "Campaign Circular from Whig Committee," January 31, 1840, in *Collected Works*, 1:201; Joel Silbey, "Always a Whig in Politics: The Partisan Life of Abraham Lincoln," *Papers of the Abraham Lincoln Association* 8 (1986): 21–42; Don E. Fehrenbacher, "Lincoln and the Mayor of Chicago," in *Lincoln in Text and Context: Collected Essays* (Stanford, CA, 1987), 39–42; David Davis interview, September 20, 1866, in Wilson and Davis, *Herndon's Informants*, 349; Jesse Weik, *The Real Lincoln: A Portrait* (Boston, 1922), 189.

33. Lincoln, "To William B. Preston," May 16, 1849, and "To George W. Rives," May 7, 1849, in *Collected Works*, 2:46, 49.

34. Feller, *Jacksonian Promise*, 33–39; Sellers, *Market Revolution*, 119; Albert A. Woldman, *Lawyer Lincoln* (Boston, 1936), 161; Henry C. Whitney to Jesse Weik, 1887–89, in Wilson and Davis, *Herndon's Informants*, 733. Mark E. Steiner argues, in *An Honest Calling: The Law Practice of Abraham Lincoln* (DeKalb, IL, 2006), that Lincoln's legal practice was so broadly spread that he cannot be characterized as promoting a "market revolution." "Contrary to what earlier scholars have said, Lincoln was neither a saint nor a consistent advocate for corporate interests, economic development, or even railroad interests. Lincoln instead possessed a service mentality; he was ready to represent any client" (4). This much, however, was true of nearly every antebellum lawyer who hoped to survive by his fees in the highly competitive civil litigation environment of central and southern Illinois; it also begs the question of Lincoln's high-profile affiliations in the 1850s with Illinois railroad corporations, both as counsel and lobbyist with the Bissell

administration. Steiner's book is, nevertheless, the best survey of Lincoln's legal practice available.

35. Michael Sandel, *Democracy's Discontents: America in Search of a Public Philosophy* (Cambridge, MA, 1996), 21–23; Lincoln, "Handbill Replying to Charges of Infidelity," July 31, 1846, and "Speech at Peoria, Illinois," October 16, 1854, in *Collected Works,* 1:382, 2:274.

36. Michael Sandel, introduction to *Liberalism and Its Critics*, ed. Sandel (Oxford, 1984), 5–6; Lincoln, "Speech at Indianapolis, Indiana," September 19, 1859, in *Collected Works,* 3:468–69.

37. Angle, *"Here I Have Lived,"* xiv; Herndon, January 15, 1874, in Hertz, *Hidden Lincoln*, 83.

4

LINCOLN AND NATURAL LAW

On the day in August 1612 when Galileo wrote his second letter on the nature of sunspots, something in the nature of *nature* itself changed. "I seem to have observed that physical bodies have physical inclination to some motion . . . whenever they are not impeded by some obstacle," Galileo wrote, "and therefore, all external impediments removed, a heavy body on a spherical surface concentric with the earth will be indifferent to rest and to movements toward any part of the horizon."[1]

There was a good deal more Galileo had to say about sunspots and about gravity, motion, the solar system, and religion. But they were really only a practical coda to that single basic idea. In it, Galileo overturned with one heave the assumption which had governed Western physics since Aristotle, that all of physical reality moved by laws which were inherent (or which constituted an object's *nature*) in objects and creatures themselves, and substituted for it the assumption which has governed us ever since, that nature is simply a description of what happens when certain forces act upon inert matter. In the first view of nature, nature has a reality unto itself—or at least, it is comprised of hard-wired laws within each individual item in creation, which each individual strives to follow, sensibly or insensibly. "To obey natural law was to discern the order of one's being," writes John Habgood, "and to espouse its moral significance in the light of reason."[2] In the second view of nature, there are no laws at all, merely descriptions of repeatable phenomena. Insensible or material objects merely respond to the physical circumstances of being moved. "Sensible" creatures are creative enough to respond to their external environments by confecting conventions to govern their behavior. But these, too, are responses, and they can vary considerably from environment to environment. There is no internal law that ineluctably guides or impels individuals to certain ends.

For Galileo to challenge successfully an age-old consensus required two things, both of which fell neatly into the hands of his intellectual heirs and successors in the seventeenth and eighteenth centuries. The first was a vast internal shock to the self-confidence of Aristotelian natural law—something which was provided in spades by a century of resultless religious warfare in Europe which beggared the very notion of law. But Europeans had survived shocks to the Aristotelian consensus before—most notably in that age of skeptical nominalism which followed the Great Plague and a century later in the Protestant Reformation. What brought down the entire edifice of Aristotelian natural law in the seventeenth century was the astounding mathematical and theoretical triumphs of Galileo and Newton, laying down a whole new platform of observable and confirmable data which made the Aristotelian physics look pedantic and absurd. It followed in due course that as Aristotle's physics collapsed into silliness, it dragged down with it every other notion—religious and political—which taught that human belief and human society ought to be an effort to discover the appropriate ends and relationships designed for every being.[3]

Or at least it threatened to. It might not feel all that disturbing to sign over inanimate nature to the rule of external forces and toss away the notion that rocks obeyed some innate tendency to baseness when they fell in favor of explaining the fall of the rock by the force of gravity. It was much dicier applying the same notion to human beings or to politics. Not that Thomas Hobbes was afraid to draw that conclusion. "There is no such *Finis ultimis*, (utmost ayme,) nor *Summum Bonum*, (greatest Good,) as is spoken of in the Books of the old Morall Philosophers," Hobbes wrote in 1651. The only real goal anyone seeks is self-preservation, and in that struggle, "there is nothing he can make use of, that may not be a help unto him, in preserving his life against his enemyes." Yet, even that was more of an instinct than the pursuit of a reasonable goal; at the end of the day, Hobbes had no confidence that morality was anything else but an artifice of society, or that human choice had any intelligent purpose, because even the act of choice was merely the last stage of desire. In the face of such a terrifying and unstable prospect, even those who were happiest to embrace a physical universe governed only by force kept creeping back to notions of politics governed by inherent inclinations to some form of good society. "Justice," wrote Montesquieu, "is the proper relationship actually existing between two things" and is "eternal and independent of human conventions." Cesare Beccaria faulted Hobbes for mistaking "social conventions" as "contrary either to natural law or revelation"; human society only appeared to be a chaotic scramble for self-preservation because "natural virtue" has been "obscured by the stupidities and passions of men."[4] And so, even as the physics of the Scientific Revolution in the seventeenth century whirled material substance farther and farther away from any law but force, the politics of the Enlightenment struggled to locate social order back within human nature. It did not always succeed. But in the case of Abraham Lincoln, it did.

The Declaration of Independence makes a surprisingly explicit appeal to natural law, and indeed, it had to, since the actions of the American revolutionaries not only defied the laws of their king and empire but in fact questioned the most indulgent and least oppressive form of monarchy in the eighteenth century. It was not enough for Thomas Jefferson to compose a lawyer's declaration of grievances; precisely because it was a revolution against a comparatively limited monarchy he was justifying, he had to appeal over the head of king and empire to a more fundamental form of law, that of "Nature and Nature's God," in which certain inalienable rights are naturally "endowed" upon "all men" at their creation. The twenty-year-old Alexander Hamilton "supposed that the Deity . . . has constituted an eternal and immutable law, which is indispensably obligatory upon all mankind, prior to any human institution whatsoever," and that "upon this law depend the natural rights of mankind." When the Massachusetts Supreme Judicial Court handed down its decision in *Walker v. Jennison* in 1780, denying that Quok Walker could be held as a slave, the court asked: "Is it not a law of nature that all men are created equal? . . . [Are] not the laws of nature the laws of God? Is not the law of God then against slavery?" And the Union which emerged from the Revolution was formed, according to James Madison, "to the transcendent law of nature and of nature's God, which declares that the safety and happiness of society, are the objects at which all political institutions aim." It was the example of the Founders' appeal to natural law which led Judge Andrew Judson to order the release of the *Amistad* mutineers in 1839, and John Quincy Adams built his defense of the mutineers before the Supreme Court by appealing to the Declaration's invocation of natural law: "I know of no law . . . no code, no treaty, applicable to the proceedings of the Executive or the Judiciary, except that law, two copies of which are ever before the eyes of your Honors. I know of no other law that reaches the case of my clients, but the law of Nature and of Nature's God on which our fathers placed our own national existence. . . . That law . . . I trust will be the law on which the case will be decided by this court." And yet, it was not clear that the Founders of the American Republic, including Madison, had much more in view on other occasions when they talked about natural law than simply "the eternal laws of self-preservation," which was to speak about a very attenuated notion of natural law indeed.[5] The Constitution made no reference to either nature or Nature's God, and the politics of the new Republic rapidly took on the appearance, not of a natural political order, but of a fiercely contested struggle of interest groups. And American legal theory found it difficult to disentangle notions of natural law from those of British common law, both of which suggested a concept of social hierarchy that sat very ill indeed beside the Revolutionary generation.

That, in turn, raised the specter that the American Republic might degenerate into a squabble for power, and *power*, as the generation of the Founders believed with the earnestness of theological dogma, was the enemy of liberty. All that could keep *power* at bay was the intervening action of *virtue*; but from what quarter was the Republic to receive the necessary infusion of virtue? George Washington, whose last years as president were clouded by insurrection, sectional and ideological partisanship, and opposition mud-slinging, warned that "religion and morality are indispensable supports" of "political prosperity." But whose religion, and whose morality? One source might have been the evangelical religion of the Great Awakening, which provided one major revival of religious interest in America in the 1740s and another in the 1820s. But the religion of the Awakeners veered, in the hands of its most prominent leaders, toward separatism—toward shifting religious practice to the sphere of the private and the individual, where it could be kept pure, rather than shaping it as a method for instilling direct public virtue—and anyway, evangelicalism was itself at an ebb in the critical decade of the 1790s.

A much likelier source was natural law, which became the basis of the moral philosophy curriculums and textbooks of the colleges of the new Republic. Although much of the natural law teaching of the collegiate moral philosophers was done by evangelicals—Francis Wayland of Brown, Mark Hopkins of Williams, Archibald Alexander of Princeton Theological Seminary, James Harris Fairchild of Oberlin—the actual content of their teaching and writing was consciously vetted to eliminate any suggestion that they were promoting an explicitly religious or denominational agenda. Instead, based on the presentational realism honed by the eighteenth-century Scottish moralists, they located an objective moral purpose in both the internal intuitions of a "moral sense" and in certain moral relations.[6]

But did this turn toward natural law in the American colleges reach sufficiently far to turn the political life of the Republic in the direction of virtue? There is not much evidence that it did. To the contrary, the most embarrassing failure of the moral philosophers' construction of natural law concerned slavery, since Northern and Southern philosophers divided so completely in their conclusions concerning slavery that confident appeals to natural law ended up making natural law appear confused and hollow. Joseph Haven (of Amherst College) believed that "slavery is a wrong, inasmuch as it not only deprives the slave of his natural right to self-disposal and control, but subjects him to the lawless will of a master." But Francis Wayland flinched at the thought of taking this idea to the point of actual resistance to slavery. "As citizens of the United States, we have no power whatever either to abolish slavery in the Southern States; or to do any thing, of which the direct intention is to abolish it. . . . Whether slavery be good or bad, we wash our hands of it, inasmuch as it is a matter which the providence of God has never placed within our jurisdiction." And Southerners treated the notion that natural law militated against slavery as preposterous. Thomas Smyth argued that Providence had "established . . . certain relations"—including race-based slavery—and Providence invariably trumped natural law. "Duty . . . requires us to accept God's arrangements, to acquiesce in them, to act in harmony with them, and not to fall behind or go beyond them." James Henry Hammond, in his two public "letters" to Thomas Clarkson in 1845, finally waved away natural law as a pointless abstraction. Hammond "did not like to deal in abstractions" since "it seldom leads to any useful ends." And he doubted whether there were much in the way of "universal truths." He did not "now remember any single moral truth universally acknowledged."[7]

Similarly, evangelical religion came flooding back to a high tide of cultural hegemony between 1820 and 1850, but at every point where it attempted to shape policy, it was rebuffed. At exactly the same time as evangelical revivals were saving American souls, American state legislatures were terminating public support for churches, curtailing Sabbatarian laws, and ending religious tests for office holding. The 1810 post office law, which required federal post offices to open on Sundays to process incoming mail, was vigorously opposed, even to the point of excommunicating postmasters who obeyed the regulations; but after fifteen years of continuous opposition, Congress only passed new regulations to enforce Sunday mail delivery. In 1844, in the landmark case of *Vidal v. Girard's executors*, Justice Joseph Story evenhandedly acknowledged Christianity to be an integral part of English-speaking common law—and then struck down the attempt by the City of Philadelphia to overturn the will of the atheist Stephen Girard, which forbade clergymen from venturing onto the grounds of the orphan school Girard had built for Philadelphia.[8]

"Statesmanship," grumbled Daniel Barnard in "The Social System" (1848), "is very much employed of late in teaching mankind that political government . . . instead of being something ordained of God . . . is little else any where than a stupendous fraud on human rights and human liberty, devised and practiced by cunning and wicked men for their own purposes of oppression and profit." One entire political party, Jefferson's Democrats, was not only dedicated to a "perfect free trade in religion," but denied that "any tribunal on earth or any other institution" can settle moral questions for the political community. In the mind of John C. Calhoun—like Hammond, a South Carolinian—the law which governed human political associations was physical, based on race, and historical, based on the attainment of certain levels of culture, rather than an inherent direction implanted within each person's consciousness. "Instead, then, of all men having the same right to liberty and equality," these rights are social conventions which are to be handed out as "high prizes to be won" by those races "in their most perfect state." *Nature* had returned to being what external forces made it be (with race and history substituted for gravity), not what an inherent direction led it toward fulfilling. "All men are not created equal," Calhoun announced, and with that, the idea that a natural law existed to govern all men went onto the shelf.[9]

For Calhoun, the denial of an equality which placed everyone equally under a natural *law* was mostly and obviously designed to deny certain people—American blacks—natural *rights* and thus justify their enslavement. But Calhoun was by no means the most effective or the most crudely popular promoter of that denial. That honor belonged, oddly enough, to a Northern Democrat, born in Vermont but politically born-again as an ardent disciple of Andrew Jackson in Illinois, Stephen Arnold Douglas. As the construction supervisor of the Compromise of 1850 and the architect of the Kansas-Nebraska Act of 1854, Douglas struck down the two principal restrictions on the spread of slavery in the United States, *first* by introducing the idea that the territories acquired through the Mexican Cession should be allowed on the basis of "popular sovereignty" to come to their own conclusions about slavery, and then *second*, by expanding the principle of "popular sovereignty" to include all the rest of the Western territories—and by implication every other inch of American territory except the free states.[10]

It is one mark of just how little dent the collegiate natural law philosophers made in American political thought that the doctrine of popular sovereignty nearly carried Stephen A. Douglas into the White House. The premises of popular sovereignty could be reduced without too much effort to a Hobbesian caricature of republican democracy—as indeed Hobbes himself had intended to caricature republics in *Leviathan*. And there were more than a few moments in the 1850s when Douglas's preaching of the gospel of popular sovereignty sounded exactly like a majoritarian version of Hobbes. Popular sovereignty "leaves the people to do just as they please, and to shape their institutions according to what they may conceive to be their interests both for the present and the future." If those interests included enslaving other human beings, so be it; if they differed from the interests of other states, that carried no weight whatsoever. "I claim that Illinois has the sovereign right to prohibit slavery, a right as undeniable as that of the sovereignty of Virginia may authorize its existence," Douglas declared. In the case of Kansas, which became the center of the firestorm set off by the Kansas-Nebraska Act, Douglas frankly stated, "You have no more right to force a free-State constitution on Kansas than a slave-State constitution. If Kansas wants a slave-State constitution she has a right to it. It is none of my business which way the slavery clause is decided. I care not whether it is voted down or voted up." Of course, it did not impress Douglas at all that the slaves themselves might have rights which were being violated by the institution of slavery, very largely because Douglas had no clear sense that blacks were human in the same way white people were: "We do not believe in the equality of the negro, socially or politically with the white man. . . . Our people are a white people; our State is a white State; and we mean to preserve the race pure, without any mixture with the Negro."[11]

But Douglas's larger aim in turning the territories over to popular sover-eignty for a resolution of the slavery question was neither to extend nor to restrain slavery, but to get the whole question off the floor of Congress and out of Washington, as a problem which did nothing but cause needless politi-cal havoc. If there was any sense in which "the people" could ever be found guilty of violating a natural law—or even a divine one—it was not readily apparent in Douglas. Morality—assuming that the slavery question had any moral aspects—was not a proper subject for discussion in the halls of Congress. When Douglas was presented with one petition from three thousand New England clergymen and another from twenty-five Chicago clergy, protesting the Kansas-Nebraska Bill, Douglas attacked their presumption "to pronounce an authoritative judgment upon a political question pending before the Con-gress of the United States. Our fathers held that the people were the only true source of all political powers; but what avails this position, if the constituted authorities established by the people are to be controlled and directed . . . not by the will of their constituents, but by the divinely-constituted power of the clergy." There was no point, Douglas insisted, "in "stopping to inquire into the sinfulness of slavery as a religious question." The law of God—or even the law of nature—"as revealed to us, is intended to operate on our consciences, and insure the performance of our duties as individuals and Christians." But it has nothing to say about "the form of government under which we live, and the character of our political civil institutions."[12]

There was little in the thinking of Abraham Lincoln before the 1850s which indicates that he had any serious disagreement with Douglas about the sover-eignty of the popular will. Although Lincoln's early allegiance to the Whigs allied him with a party which saw itself as the voice of "the orderly, quiet and thrifty," and characterized by "intelligent opinion and virtuous sentiment," rather than "the dangerous elements" of "the multitude," he certainly displayed none of the panic over "popular sovereignty," as a principle, seen in Orestes

Brownson, whose response to popular sovereignty was to conclude that it was no principle at all, but a "great humbug" which could only be resolved by abandoning both positive law and natural law as an independent source of moral authority and substituting the explicit authority of the Church. Lincoln was raised in a strict and passionately individualistic Calvinist Baptist home on the Indiana frontier and made his chief display of Calvinist individualism by rejecting his family's religious allegiance outright. His formal education was limited and certainly never brought him within the direct orbit of the collegiate moral philosophers. If it seemed he had a religion at all, it was the "political religion" of law-and-order. "Let every American, every lover of liberty, every well wisher to his posterity," he said in his oration on "The Perpetuation of Our Political Institutions" in 1838, "swear by the blood of the Revolution, never to violate in the least particular, the laws of the country; and never to tolerate their violation by others."[13]

But what was to happen when the laws ran contrary to something which could be called *right*, or gave support to that which Lincoln considered *wrong*? And if there was anything which in Lincoln's mind was preeminently qualified for consideration as *wrong*, it was human slavery. "I am naturally anti-slavery," he wrote years later. "If slavery is not wrong, nothing is wrong. I can not remember when I did not so think, and feel." One of his earliest votes as an Illinois state legislator was against a resolution affirming the right of the Southern states to legalize slavery, which he branded as "injustice and bad policy." But an injustice on what grounds? Merely "bad policy"? For that, Lincoln had no ready answer, because so much of his hatred of slavery was in fact subjective and rooted in his rebellion against his father's authority (which he characterized as *slavery*) and his resentment at the way aristocratic slaveholders looked down their noses at whites—like Lincoln—who had to work for their own living. Much as he criticized slavery as a "great & crying injustice" and "an enormous national crime," so long as Southern slavery was contained by the Missouri Compromise and by treaty arrangements which penned slavery into a limited area where it would, over time, die out, Lincoln stayed aloof from movements that clamored for abolishing slavery outright. "Whether this feeling accords with justice and sound judgment," Lincoln admitted, was an open question. But since the containment of slavery promised the eventual end of slavery without endangering the rule of law, it was enough to let slavery die out on its own. This was enough of a recognition of the "wrong" of slavery to satisfy Lincoln.[14]

But in 1854, the passage of the Kansas-Nebraska Act simultaneously "aroused" and stymied Lincoln—*aroused*, because Kansas-Nebraska suddenly overturned the policy of containment and effectively unlocked the gates of the Western territories (including both the old Louisiana Purchase lands and the Mexican Cession) to the legal expansion of slavery; and *stymied*, because its champion, Stephen A. Douglas, based it all on a doctrine Lincoln did not necessarily disagree with in the abstract, that of popular sovereignty. "The doctrine of self government is right—absolutely and eternally right," Lincoln believed. But he also wanted to say that "it has no just application, as here attempted." *And why not?* any Douglasite could have asked. Because one thing which majority-will cannot repeal is human nature, which included the humanity of the black man; and the equality all human beings share precludes dehumanizing any of them to the point of enslaving them. "Whether" popular sovereignty "has such just application depends upon whether a negro is not or is a man. . . . If the negro is a man, is it not to that extent, a total destruction of self-government, to say that he too shall not govern himself?" *Not*, returned the Douglasite, if you understand that the black man is, whether by law or by physical nature, something less than a part of the political community white men belong to. And arrayed behind that argument was a phalanx of nineteenth-century phrenological pseudoscience, a majoritarian political process, and the most bilious forms of white racial supremacism, all insisting that black men had neither part nor lot with whites in the public life of the nation. "I believe this government was made on the white basis," Douglas announced. "I believe it was made by white men, for the benefit of white men and their posterity for ever."[15]

Flushed out of his complacent confidence that everyone agreed that slavery was wrong and needed to be contained, Lincoln now had to make explicit the intellectual premises of antislavery which he had so long taken for granted, and in the 1850s, those premises took the form of an argument from natural law. Partly this grew from his sense that the American Republic had been founded around "something more than common . . . something even more than National Independence." But partly it was because majoritarian democracy alone offered him no other way out of slavery's box. Like Solomon of old, who asked the sluggard to consider the ant, Lincoln asked whether anything people could observe in nature suggested that slavery was a natural condition for any creature:

> The ant, who has toiled and dragged a crumb to his nest, will furiously defend the fruit of his labor, against whatever robber assails him. So plain, that the most dumb and stupid slave that ever toiled for a master, does constantly know that he is wronged. So plain that no one, high or low, ever does mistake it, except in a plainly selfish way; for although volume upon volume is written to prove slavery a very good thing, we never hear of the man who wishes to take the good of it, by being a slave himself.

The appeal to a natural instinct opposing slavery became Lincoln's strategy for outflanking Douglas's demand that whatever the electorate is, is right, and from 1854 onwards, natural law became the principal weapon Lincoln used to batter down the protecting walls of popular sovereignty and, after *Dred Scott* in 1857, the dictum of the Supreme Court in behalf of slavery. "Is not slavery universally granted to be, in the abstract, a gross outrage on the law of nature?" Lincoln asked. "Have not all civilized nations, our own among them, made the Slave trade capital, and classed it with piracy and murder? Is it not held to be the great wrong of the world?"[16]

Lincoln has frequently—and with increasing frequency in the last half-century—been criticized for his failure to move beyond natural law and natural rights to an affirmation of civil equality and civil rights. When he finally challenged Stephen A. Douglas to a face-to-face showdown in the great campaign he and Douglas waged for Illinois's U.S. Senate seat in 1858, he was quick to say that he saw nothing in the Constitution which authorized him to advocate the uprooting of the Southern states' slavery statutes and no "purpose to introduce political or social equality between the black and white races." And so it has been asked with increasing puzzlement just what Lincoln thought he was affirming when he limited himself to talking about a *natural* equality of blacks and whites. But this puzzlement only underscores how feeble and attenuated modern understandings of natural law have become, and how natural rights have been collapsed along with civil rights into a generalized, and for-the-most-part shapeless, concept of "human rights." Lincoln's affirmation of natural law was a determined step outside the increasing movement toward pure majoritarian process and toward an affirmation that American democracy was built around a transcendent core of universal truths. (That affirmation, as Lincoln enjoyed saying, had been originally crafted by Thomas Jefferson in the Declaration of Independence, thus trumping not only Jefferson's practical failure to live up to his own propositions, but Douglas's failure to live up to the standards of the founder of his own party.) Douglas's arguments had no other direction than toward the diminishment of those truths and the unmooring of American democracy from the architecture of its Founders, "pressing out of view, the Questions of Liberty" and "restoring those of classification, caste, and legitimacy."[17]

To oppose slavery on the grounds of natural law, however, was not only to sign slavery's death warrant but to put all Americans on the same footing of equality, after which all questions of civil rights could be settled by means of the ordinary political process. "Advancement," Lincoln reminded an audience of Ohioans in 1859, "is the order of things in a society of equals," and that advancement recognized no firewall between natural and civil rights. Then, as Lincoln explained in 1860, "every man" could have "the chance" for self-improvement in whatever sphere, "and I believe a black man is entitled to it."[18]

But if it was remarkable that the inadequacies of mere majoritarianism in a democracy could drive Lincoln back to a natural law defense, it is even more remarkable that the war he was eventually called upon to wage on slavery pushed him to link natural law with divine religious purpose. He invoked "universal law" as a witness to deny the legitimacy of secession in his first inaugural address, but even at that penultimate moment he did not expect that he would be making war on slavery or the South. He did expect, having the levers of the national government in Republican hands, that slavery could once again be confined by statute to the Southern states, and that there would be a variety of indirect ways that slavery in those states could be chivied out of their grasp. And he made no secret that his "personal wish" was that "all men every where could be free." But the sheer brutality and carnage of the Civil War, along with its seemingly endless prolongation through 1862, convinced Lincoln that another purpose, more than ordinary, was at work, forcing the issue of the war toward the total and outright destruction of slavery. He had come to believe that "freedom is the natural condition of the human in which the Almighty"—and not just natural law—"intended men to live," and when he finally issued the proclamation which freed the slaves on January 1, 1863, he added to it the notation that emancipation was "an act of justice" worthy of "the gracious favor of Almighty God." He did not mean to say that Southern slaveholders alone labored under some unique load of guilt that God had excused Northerner non-slaveholders from; the war was a judgment "that He gives to both North and South" for their mutual complicity in exacting "two hundred and fifty years of unrequited toil" from the "bond-man." But that mutual guilt did not erase the fact that slavery was an "offense." To do less than acknowledge slavery as an "offense" was "to deny that there is a God governing the world."[19]

It would, I think, be a mistake to attempt a description of Lincoln as a natural law *philosopher*, or a philosopher at all. He was, after all, a man of practical intellectual application; just as he once remarked about his fund of jokes and stories, that he was a wholesaler, not a retailer, so he was as a thinker. At the same time, though, no one recognized more clearly than Abraham Lincoln that the practical crisis posed by the slavery question could not be solved by practical means alone, and that "whenever this question shall be settled, it must be settled on some philosophical basis." Lincoln did not believe that politics was about the avoidance of moral judgment but about its discernment and expression. Although he never embraced the romantic absolutism of either the abolitionists or the evangelicals, he also never saw moral neutrality as a health-giving alternative. "Is it not a false statesmanship that undertakes to build up a system of policy upon the basis of caring nothing about *the very thing that every body does care the most about?*" he asked Douglas in the last of the great debates of 1858. His alternative to the Douglasite positivists, who knew no law but the *vox populi*, was to find a ground of natural law, to work out from the existence of natural law an ontological foundation for speaking about natural rights, and to link it all to the direction of Providence, so that he could speak in religious terms without binding himself to any organized religious movement. That he was able to do this and bring about the abolition of the great wrong of slavery, and at the same moment preserve the Union without damaging its constitutional order, is Lincoln's greatest achievement.[20]

Whether that has translated into a permanent legacy is another matter. The same generation which produced a Lincoln also shaped William James and Oliver Wendell Holmes, and the impress which the Civil War made on them was not about the nobility of moral purpose in a democracy but about the horrors of the carnage that men, committed to moral verities, are capable of committing. It is their legacy, more than Lincoln's, which has ruled our political culture. Lincoln's monument, a temple to the Union he preserved, stands at one end of the Mall in Washington; Stephen A. Douglas's stands at the other.

Notes

1. Galileo, "Letters on Sunspots," in Stillman Drake, ed., *Discoveries and Opinions of Galileo* (New York, 1957), 113. See also Drake, "Uniform Acceleration, Space and Time," *British Journal for the History of Science* 5 (1970): 21–43.

2. John Habgood, *The Concept of Nature* (London, 2002), 88; Robert P. George, *In Defense of Natural Law* (Oxford, 1999), 102–3.

3. Richard Westfall, *Science and Religion in Seventeenth-Century England* (New Haven, 1958), 72–73.

4. Thomas Hobbes, *Leviathan*, ed. W. G. Pogson Smith (Oxford, 1909), 75, 99; Montesquieu, *The Persian Letters*, ed. G. R. Healy (1964; repr., Indianapolis, 1977), 140; Cesare Beccaria, *On Crime and Punishment*, ed. Henry Paolucci (1963; repr., Indianapolis, 1977), 5.

5. Michael Zuckert, *The Natural Rights Republic: Studies in the Foundation of the American Political Tradition* (Notre Dame, IN, 1996), 81–87; Alexander Hamilton, "The Farmer Refuted," February 5, 1775, in *The Basic Ideas of Alexander Hamilton*, ed. Richard B. Morris (New York, 1957), 6; Gary B. Nash, *The Unknown American Revolution: The Unruly Birth of Democracy and the Struggle to Create America* (New York, 2005), 408; James Madison, "No. 43," in *The Federalist*, ed. George W. Carey and James McClellan (Indianapolis, 2001), 229; David Brion Davis, *Inhuman Bondage: The Rise and Fall of Slavery in the New World* (New York, 2006), 20–21; Pauline Maier, *American Scripture: Making the Declaration of Independence* (New York, 1987), 87; Daniel Walker Howe, *Making the American Self: Jonathan Edwards to Abraham Lincoln* (Cambridge, MA, 1997), 98–99; *Argument of John Quincy Adams before the Supreme Court of the United States in the Case of the United States, Appellants, vs. Cinque, and Others, Africans* (New York, 1841), 9.

6. George Washington, "Farewell Address," September 17, 1796, in *A Compilation of the Messages and Papers of the Presidents, 1789–1897*, ed. J. D. Richardson (Washington, DC, 1896), 1:220; D. H. Meyer, *The Instructed Conscience: The Shaping of the American National Ethic* (Philadelphia, 1972), 15–22; J. David Hoeveler, *Creating the American Mind: Intellect and Politics in the Colonial Colleges* (Lanham, MD, 2002), 123–27; Theodore Dwight Bozeman, *Protestants in an Age of Science: The Baconian Ideal and Antebellum American Religious Thought* (Chapel Hill, NC, 1977), 22.

7. Joseph Haven, *Moral Philosophy: Including Theoretical and Practical Ethics* (Boston, 1859), 122–23; Francis Wayland, *The Limitations of Human Responsibility* (New York, 1838), 173; Thomas Smyth, in E. Brooks Holifield, *The Gentleman Theologians: American Theology in Southern Culture, 1795–1860* (Durham, NC, 1978), 152; J. H. Hammond, in Michael O'Brien, *Conjectures of Order: Intellectual Life and the American South, 1810–1860* (Chapel Hill, NC, 2004), 956; Mark A. Noll, *The Civil War as a Theological Crisis* (Chapel Hill, NC, 2006), 37.

8. Fred J. Hood, *Reformed America: The Middle and Southern States, 1783–1837* (University, AL, 1980), 92, 96, 97–101.

9. Daniel Barnard, "The Social System: An Address Pronounced before the House of Convocation of Trinity College" (1848), in *The American Whigs: An Anthology*, ed. D. W. Howe (New York, 1973), 106–7; William Leggett, "Thanksgiving Day," December 3, 1836, in *Democratick Editorials: Essays in Jacksonian Political Economy*, ed. L. H. White (Indianapolis, 1984), 329; Jean Baker, *Affairs of Party: The Political Culture of Northern Democrats in the Mid-Nineteenth Century* (1983; repr., New York, 1998), 192; J. C. Calhoun, "Speech on the Oregon Bill," in *Union and Liberty: The Political Philosophy of John C. Calhoun*, ed. R. M. Lence (Indianapolis, 1992), 566, 568–69; Harry V. Jaffa, *A New Birth of Freedom: Abraham Lincoln and the Coming of the Civil War* (Lanham, MD, 2000), 431.

10. O'Brien, *Conjectures of Order*, 799–816. Douglas did not invent "popular sovereignty" as a political slogan. As a program for dealing with the territorial problem, it was proposed by Lewis Cass as part of a plan for dealing with the Mexican Cession; but as an idea, it had practical roots in the Dorr Rebellion of 1841–42, which saw Democrats line up behind the Dorrites on the grounds that the "People's Constitution" represented a majority of the voters of Rhode Island. See Patrick T. Conley, "Popular Sovereignty or Public Anarchy? America Debates the Dorr Rebellion," *Rhode Island History* 60 (Summer 2002): 72–73.

11. Stephen A. Douglas, "Speech in the Senate on the Lecompton Constitution," March 22, 1857, in Clark E. Carr, *Stephen A. Douglas: His Life, Public Services, Speeches and Patriotism* (Chicago, 1909), 231; James W. Sheahan, *The Life of Stephen A. Douglas* (New York, 1860), 144; Stephen A. Douglas, "The President's Message," *Congressional Globe*, December 9, 1857, 35th Cong., 1st sess., 18; Douglas, in Robert W. Johannsen, *Stephen A. Douglas* (Urbana, IL, 1973), 501.

12. Stephen A. Douglas, "To Twenty-Five Chicago Clergymen," April 6, 1854, in *The Letters of Stephen A. Douglas*, ed. Robert W. Johannsen (Urbana, IL, 1961), 300–313, and "Clerical Protest," *Congressional Globe*, March 14, 1854, 33rd Cong.,

1st sess., 617–23; Douglas, in Sheahan, *Life of Stephen A. Douglas*, 184, 267; J. David Greenstone, *The Lincoln Persuasion: Remaking American Liberalism* (Princeton, NJ, 1993), 149–51; Stewart Winger, *Lincoln, Religion, and Romantic Cultural Politics* (DeKalb, IL, 2003), 29–34.

13. "Political Responsibilities," *American Whig Review* 83 (November 1851): 362, 364–65; Orestes Brownson, "Democracy and Liberty," *Democratic Review* 12 (April 1843): 374–80; Lincoln, "Address before the Young Men's Lyceum of Springfield, Illinois," January 27, 1838, in *The Collected Works of Abraham Lincoln*, ed. Roy P. Basler (New Brunswick, NJ, 1953–55), 1:112.

14. Lincoln, "Protest in Illinois Legislature on Slavery," March 3, 1837, "Speech at Peoria, Illinois," October 16, 1854, and "To Albert G. Hodges," April 4, 1864, in *Collected Works*, 1:75, 2:254, 7:281.

15. Lincoln, "Speech at Peoria, Illinois," October 16, 1854, and "To Jesse W. Fell, Enclosing Autobiography," December 20, 1859, in *Collected Works*, 2:265–66, 3:512; "Mr. Douglas' Speech" in "The Ottawa Debate," in *The Lincoln-Douglas Debates of 1858*, ed. Edwin Erle Sparks (Springfield, IL, 1908), 95.

16. Lincoln, "Speech at Springfield, Illinois," October 4, 1854, "Fragment on Slavery," July 1, 1854, and "Address to the New Jersey Senate at Trenton, New Jersey," February 21, 1861, in *Collected Works*, 2:222, 245, 4:236; Joseph R. Fornieri, *Abraham Lincoln's Political Faith* (DeKalb, IL, 2003), 49–50. On Southern responses to other natural law arguments against slavery, see Elizabeth Fox-Genovese and Eugene D. Genovese, *The Mind of the Master Class: History and Faith in the Southern Slaveholders' Worldview* (Cambridge, Eng., 2005), 624–30.

17. "Mr. Lincoln's Reply," in "The Ottawa Debate," and "Mr. Lincoln's Reply," in "The Galesburg Debate," Sparks, *Lincoln-Douglas Debates*, 102, 353; David Potter, *The Impending Crisis, 1848–1861* (New York, 1976), 345, 352; Lincoln, "To Henry L. Pierce," April 6, 1859, in *Collected Works*, 3:374; Paul Berman, *Terror and Liberalism* (New York, 2003), 166–71.

18. Lincoln, "Speech at Cincinnati, Ohio," September 17, 1859, and "Speech at New Haven, Connecticut," March 6, 1860, in *Collected Works*, 3:462, 4:24; Eric Foner, "The Ideology of the Republican Party," in *The Birth of the Grand Old Party: The Republicans' First Generation*, ed. Robert Engs and Randall Miller (Philadelphia, 2002), 9–10.

19. Lincoln, "To Horace Greeley," August 22, 1862, "Meditation on the Divine Will," September 2, 1862?, "Emancipation Proclamation," January 1, 1863, "Second Inaugural Address," March 4, 1865, and "To Thurlow Weed," March 15, 1865, in *Collected Works*, 5:388, 403, 6:30, 8:333, 356; Lucius Chittenden, in *Recollected Words of Abraham Lincoln*, comp. and ed. Don Fehrenbacher and Virginia Fehrenbacher (Stanford, CA, 1996), 100.

20. Lincoln, "Speech at New Haven, Connecticut," March 6, 1860, in *Collected Works*, 4:17; "Mr. Lincoln's Reply," in "The Alton Debate," *Lincoln-Douglas Debates*, ed. Sparks, 480; Michael J. Sandel, *Democracy's Discontent: America in Search of a Public Philosophy* (Cambridge, MA, 1996), 22–23; George Anastaplo, *Abraham Lincoln: A Constitutional Biography* (Lanham, MD, 1999), 255.

5

"Fiends . . . Facing Zionwards": Abraham Lincoln's Reluctant Embrace of the Abolitionists

I t has always been one of the ironies of the era of the Civil War and the end of slavery in the United States that the man who played the role of the Great Emancipator of the slaves was so hugely mistrusted and so energetically vilified by the party of abolition. Abraham Lincoln, whatever his larger reputation as the liberator of more than three million black slaves in the Emancipation Proclamation, has never entirely shaken off the reputation of being somewhat halfhearted about it. "There is a counterlegend of Lincoln," acknowledged Stephen B. Oates, "one shared ironically enough by many white Southerners and certain black Americans of our time" who are convinced that Lincoln never intended to abolish slavery, "was a bigot . . . a white racist who championed segregation, opposed civil and political rights for black people," and "wanted them all thrown out of the country."[1]

And a great deal of that reputation is still linked to the denunciations of Lincoln issued by virtually all of those who occupied the abolitionist vanguard, whether they were (as in Frederick Douglass's taxonomy) Garrisonians, Tappanites, Free Soilers, or even old Liberty Party men.[2]

It has been a large part of the task of Lincoln biographers ever since to deplore that image of Lincoln as the sort of extremist rhetoric that abolitionism was pretty generally renowned for; or to insist that Lincoln may have had elements of racism in him but gradually effaced them as he moved on his "journey" to emancipation; or to suggest that Lincoln was all along an abolitionist but dragged his feet over emancipation out of pragmatic political considerations. Josiah Gilbert Holland, whose *Life of Abraham Lincoln* was the first full-dress

Lincoln biography in 1866, ridiculed the way in which "Mr. Lincoln has been assailed . . . for being too slow" to emancipate the slaves. Holland believed that Lincoln certainly "saw the time of emancipation coming," but he "felt himself still withheld from meddling with slavery by any sweeping measure" until 1862 because of his respect for the Constitution and his unwillingness to precipitate the border slave states into secession. Isaac Arnold, a strong antislavery ally of Lincoln's in the Civil War Congress, upped the ante of justification by insisting that "Lincoln in his younger days dreamed of being an emancipator" and "had always wished to emancipate the negroes," but "wished the change to 'come gently as the dews of heaven, not rending or wrecking anything.'" And even much more recently, Michael Burlingame sees Lincoln's "core" value as "a deep hatred of slavery" and believes that "Lincoln was hardly a reluctant emancipator." David Donald reassuringly observes that "Lincoln's views on slavery were not, in fact, so far from those of his critics"; the only reason why he did not join those critics earlier as an abolitionist activist was "because he had so little personal knowledge of slavery." LaWanda Cox, Lincoln's most vigorous academic justifier, writes that there is actually "something breathtaking in his advance from prewar advocacy of restricting slavery's spread to foremost responsibility for slavery's total, immediate, uncompensated destruction by constitutional amendment." It is only because "the constraints under which Lincoln felt he must labor were not always recognized by antislavery men" that Lincoln, then and now, has been charged with "irresolute policy and wavering commitment."[3]

Still, not even the most vigorous apologists for Lincoln can entirely escape the sense of distance, no matter how varying they estimate the distance to be, between the Emancipator and the abolitionists. Indeed, they underestimate it, for the differences the abolitionists saw between themselves and Lincoln were not illusory or mere matters of timing and policy. They involved not only the aggrievement of the righteous but also the irritation of Lincoln himself; and not only quarrels over timetable and voting rights but unbridgeable cultural issues. And only when those differences are allowed their full play can we begin to recognize how deeply Lincoln's place in the story of slavery's end upsets some of the more recent, broad theoretical constructions of the antislavery movement, and how much it questions the moral and political assumptions of American reform, which have drawn strength from the abolitionist example, rather than Lincoln's, ever since.

That the abolitionists disliked Lincoln almost unanimously cannot be in much doubt. They themselves said it too often, beginning as early as the mid-1850s, when Illinois abolitionists looked at Lincoln with a measure of suspicion as a recruit to the antislavery cause. Chicago newspaper editor Charles H. Ray told Elihu Washburne in December 1855 that Lincoln would probably be a highly unreliable ally of the new Republican Party. "I must confess I am afraid of 'Abe'" because "he is Southern by birth, Southern in his associations and Southern, if I mistake not, in his sympathies." Besides, "his wife"—Mary Todd Lincoln—"is a Todd, of a pro-slavery family, and so are all his kin." And the suspicions only became deeper from the moment he stepped into the national spotlight as the Republican candidate for the presidency in 1860. Charles Grandison Finney, the New School revivalist and president of the nation's abolitionist hotbed, Oberlin College, scored Lincoln in the first issue of the *Oberlin Evangelist* to appear after the nominating convention:

> The Republican Convention at Chicago have put in nomination for President Abraham Lincoln of Illinois, a gentleman who became widely known a year and a half ago by his political footrace against S. A. Douglas for the place of United States Senate from their state. In that campaign he won laurels on the score of his intellectual ability and forensic powers; but if our recollection is not at fault, his ground on the score of humanity towards the oppressed race was too low.

As a spectator of the famous Lincoln-Douglas senatorial campaign in 1858, the black Chicago abolitionist Hezekiah Ford Douglass found Lincoln was no significant improvement on Stephen A. Douglas; and Lincoln's stature suffered no improvement for the black Douglass during the 1860 presidential campaign. "We have four parties in this country that have marshalled themselves on the highway of American politics, asking for the votes of the American people," Douglass wrote, but "so far as the principles of freedom and the hopes of the black man are concerned, all these parties are barren and unfruitful; neither of them seeks to lift the negro out of his fetters, and rescue this day from odium and disgrace." And Lincoln was no different from any of them.

> I do not believe in the anti-slavery of Abraham Lincoln, because he is on the side of this Slave Power of which I am speaking, that has possession of the Federal Government. . . . Now, two years ago, I went through the State of Illinois for the purpose of getting signers to a petition, asking the Legislature to repeal the "Testimony Law," so as to permit colored men to testify against white men. I went to prominent Republicans, and among others, to Abraham Lincoln and Lyman Trumbull, and neither of them dared to sign that petition, to give me the right to testify in a court of justice! . . . If we sent our children to school, Abraham Lincoln would kick them out, in the name of Republicanism and anti-slavery![4]

Lincoln's election in November 1860 did little to mollify abolitionist criticism, much less to give them joy at the prospect of a publicly antislavery president in the White House. Lincoln's unwillingness to use the outbreak of the Civil War in the spring of 1861 as a pretext for immediate abolition convinced William Lloyd Garrison that Lincoln was "unwittingly helping to prolong the war, and to render the result more and more doubtful! If he *is* 6 feet 4 inches high, he is only a dwarf in mind!" Garrison had never really believed that Lincoln's Republicans "had an issue with the South," and Lincoln himself did nothing once elected to convince him otherwise. Lincoln's first annual message to Congress, in December 1861, nettled Garrison for its promises to restrain the scope of the war from becoming a "violent and remorseless, revolutionary struggle." Remorseless revolutionary conflict was exactly what Garrison was praying for as a means toward destroying slavery. "What a wishy-washy message from the President!" Garrison exclaimed. "He has evidently not a drop of anti-slavery blood in his veins; and he seems incapable of uttering a humane or generous sentiment respecting the enslaved millions in our land." Frederick Douglass, who had parted fellowship with Garrison over the issue of noninvolvement in politics, hoped for better than Garrison did from Lincoln but only seemed to get more disappointments. Lincoln's presidential inaugural, with its promises not to interfere with Southern slavery if the Southern states attempted no violent withdrawal from the Union, left Douglass with "no very hopeful impression" of Lincoln; if anything Lincoln had only confirmed Douglass's "worst fears." Although Douglass would later go on to cooperate with Lincoln and describe him after his assassination as "emphatically the black man's president," at least until the issuance of the Emancipation Proclamation, Douglass flayed Lincoln as "an itinerant Colonization lecturer, showing all his inconsistencies, his pride of race and blood, his contempt for Negroes and his canting hypocrisy."[5]

Even in Lincoln's Congress, Republican abolitionists—Zachariah Chandler, Henry Wilson, Benjamin Wade, George W. Julian, James Ashley, Thaddeus Stevens—heaped varying amounts of opprobrium on Lincoln's head. Wade, according to Joshua Giddings, "denounced the President as a *failure* from the moment of his election"; it mattered nothing to Wade if the war "continues thirty years and bankrupts the whole nation" unless "we can say there is not a slave in this land." "Lincoln himself seems to have no *nerve* or decision in dealing with great issues," wrote Ohio representative William Parker Cutler in his diary; and Maine senator William Pitt Fessenden erupted, "If the President had his wife's *will* and would use it rightly, our affairs would look much better." Sometimes, Lincoln said to his attorney general, the Missourian Edward Bates, these Radical Republicans were "almost fiendish." "Stevens, [Massachusetts senator Charles] Sumner and Wilson, simply haunt me with the importunities for a Proclamation of Emancipation," Lincoln complained to Missouri senator John B. Henderson. "Wherever I go and whatever way I turn, they are on my trail."[6]

None of the abolitionists, however, was more vituperative in his contempt for Lincoln than the patrician Wendell Phillips. As a self-professed "democrat, a Jeffersonian democrat in the darkest hour," Phillips was already disposed to suspicion of anyone like Lincoln who took Henry Clay, the paladin of the Whigs, as his "beau Ideal of a statesman." While Lincoln eulogized Clay in 1852 as Providence's gift to the nation, Phillips a few months later rejoiced "when we think how the slave trembled at the sound of [Clay's] voice." Phillips thought it was no indiscretion to imagine that "from a multitude of breaking hearts there went up nothing but gratitude to God when it pleased him to call that great sinner from this world." Once Phillips had Lincoln firmly in his sights after the Chicago nominating convention in the spring of 1860, he was no more merciful. "Who is this huckster in politics?" Phillips exclaimed. "Who is this county court advocate?"

> Here is Mr. Lincoln. . . . He says in regard to such a point, for instance as the abolition of slavery in the District of Columbia, that he has never studied the subject; that he has no distinctive ideas about it. . . . But so far as he has considered it, he should be, perhaps, in favor of gradual abolition, when the slave-holders of the district asked for it! Of course he would. I doubt if there is a man throughout the whole South who would not go as far as that. . . . That is the amount of his anti-slavery, if you choose to call it such, which according to the Chicago thermometer, the Northern states are capable of bearing. The ice is so thin that Mr. Lincoln, standing six feet and four inches, cannot afford to carry any principles with him onto it!

Three weeks before Lincoln issued the preliminary Emancipation Proclamation, Phillips was accusing Lincoln of "conducting this war, at present, with the purpose of saving slavery. . . . If he had been a traitor, he could not have worked better to strengthen one side, and hazard the success of the other." Even after the Proclamation took effect, Phillips still raked Lincoln for not doing more. "He is honest," Phillips allowed, "but we must remember the very prejudices and moral callousness which made him in 1860 an available candidate . . . necessarily makes him a poor leader,—rather no leader at all,—in a crisis like this."[7]

It is tempting to write much of this off to the not-inconsiderable egos of many of the abolitionist leaders, to the impatience which three decades of agitation had engendered in the abolitionist faithful, or to the presumably forgivable political naïveté of the abolitionists, who simply did not realize that Lincoln was on their side but had political realities to deal with which they did not understand. For most interpreters, Lincoln and the abolitionists were simply a convergence waiting to happen, and this has become, for the most part, the familiar cadence of the story. Lincoln himself deliberately fed such perceptions from time to time. "Well, Mr. Sumner," Lincoln remarked to the florid Massachusetts Radical in November 1861, "the only difference between you and me on this subject is a difference of a month or six weeks in time." He told the Illinois businessman and politician Wait Talcott that the opinions of "strong abolitionists . . . have produced a much stronger impression on my mind than you may think." And John Roll, a Springfield builder and longtime acquaintance of Lincoln's, heard him reply to a question as to whether he was an abolitionist, "I am mighty near one."[8]

But being "near one" was what the abolitionists thought was Lincoln's fundamental problem. If to be opposed to slavery was to be "near" abolitionism, then almost the entire population of the Northern free states was "near" abolition. But opposition to slavery never entailed outright abolition. Antislavery might just as easily take the form of containment (opposing the legalization of slavery in any new states), colonization (forced repatriation of blacks to Africa), gradual emancipation (freedom keyed to decades-long timetables), or in the minds of most Northerners, nothing at all, so long as slavery got no nearer than it was. "I am a whig," Lincoln wrote to his longtime friend Joshua Speed in 1855, "but others say there are no whigs, and that I am an abolitionist." But this, Lincoln denied: "I now do no more than oppose the *extension* of slavery."[9] Even when he would finally contemplate emancipation, it was not on the abolitionists' terms: His ideal emancipation legislation would "have the three main features—gradual—compensation—and [the] vote of the people," all of which the abolitionists abhorred.[10]

Lincoln's analysis of the abolition radicals as "fiends" has long roots in his own personal history. Lincoln retained only shards of the rigidly predestinarian Separate Baptist religion in which he had been raised, but one which did stick firmly with him was the Separates' suspicion of reformers. Almost as an expression of their Calvinist disbelief in the capacity of human effort to alter the flow of events, the Separates and other radical predestinarian Baptist sects supported no "Secret Societies, Christmas Trees, Cake-Walks, and various other things tolerated and practiced by Arminian churches [and] condemned in plain terms in the New Testament." So, likewise, the mature Lincoln also pulled shy of reform organizations: as a nondrinker, he endorsed the Washington Temperance Society in the 1840s (and delivered one of his earliest surviving full-length speeches to the Springfield, Illinois, chapter of the Washingtonians in 1842), but the success of the Washingtonians was predicated largely on being a secular temperance group which attempted to make no moral judgments on recovering alcoholics. (Nevertheless, Lincoln's Democratic critics accused him of joining the Washingtonians to promote himself politically: "Does any rational man believe for a moment," asked one Democratic newspaper, "that Abraham Lincoln, B. S. Clement and Edward D. Baker have joined the Washingtonian Society from any other than political motives?")[11]

What is vital to see is that, while none of this made him friendly to the abolitionists, none of it made him indifferent to slavery, either. He was not exaggerating when he said, "I have always hated slavery," during his great debates with Stephen A. Douglas in 1858; and in 1854, he explained, "I object to it because it assumes that there CAN be MORAL RIGHT in the enslaving of one man by another."[12] Fundamentally, what set Lincoln apart from the abolitionists was that his definition of slavery was a Whiggish, economic one, rather than an evangelical or moralistic one. When he talked about slavery, what he meant before the 1850s was any relationship of economic restraint, or any systematic effort to box ambitious and enterprising people like himself into a "fixed condition of labor, for his whole life." This "slavery" was what he experienced as a young man under his father, and he came to associate it with agrarianism and the Jeffersonian ideology which protected it. Slavery, in this sense, included anyone, even a "freeman," who is "fatally fixed for life, in the condition of a hired laborer." Abolitionism provided a vastly different framework for opposing slavery, based on a romantic absolutism which repulsed Lincoln. When the Illinois legislature resolved in January 1837 that "property in slaves, is sacred to the slave-holding states by the Federal Constitution," Lincoln and Whig judge Daniel Stone protested that "the institution of slavery is founded on both injustice and bad policy." But the protest bent obligingly in the other direction far enough to add that "the promulgation of abolition doctrines tends rather to increase than to abate its evils." Far from sympathizing with abolitionists in the 1830s and 1840s, Lincoln believed that "the whig abolitionists of New York" had robbed Henry Clay of the 1844 presidential election by wasting crucial votes on the abolitionist Liberty Party. It was one of the things Lincoln pointed out for praise in Henry Clay (in contrast to Wendell Phillips), that although Clay "was, on principle and in feeling, opposed to slavery" and to the idea that "the negroes were to be excepted from the human race," Clay was no abolitionist and had no workable plan "how it could at once be eradicated, without producing a greater evil, even to the cause of liberty itself." Nevertheless, Lincoln insisted that "I can express all my views on the slavery question by quotations from Henry Clay. Doesn't this look like we are akin?"[13] Even after 1854 and the Kansas-Nebraska bill, when it became evident that slavery was not going to accept confinement to the Southern states, but intended to extend itself across the Western territories and perhaps even into the free states, where slave labor could then compete with free wage labor, the only solution Lincoln could imagine was a nonconfrontational program of "gradual emancipation," with financial compensation offered to slave owners, and following that, repatriation back to Africa in American-sponsored colonies.

"My first impulse would be to free all the slaves, and send them to Liberia,—to their own native land," Lincoln remarked in 1854. As late as 1863, as president, Lincoln was still experimenting with colonization schemes; by the testimony (admittedly unreliable) of Benjamin F. Butler, he was still toying with them within a few hours of his death.[14]

Lincoln's fundamental approach to the problem of slavery as a political-economic one stands in dramatic contrast to the most basic instincts of American abolitionism. Dangerous as it is to generalize about a movement as fissiparous as the American abolitionists proved themselves to be over the course of thirty years, there are nevertheless certain common reflexes, and almost all of them run counter to Lincoln's. The most fundamental difference was the location of religion in the abolitionist matrix; for it could be said that, no matter how many abolitionists (including Garrison, Phillips, Abby Kelley, Theodore Dwight Weld, James Birney, and the Grimke sisters) turned their backs on organized Protestantism, nevertheless, evangelical Protestantism *was* the abolitionist matrix. As Robert Abzug has remarked, "Garrison . . . re-created the evangelical drama of American society's sin, declension, and possibility for renewal, and he reset its term." The day that Garrison burnt a copy of the Constitution at the annual Massachusetts Anti-Slavery Society picnic in Framingham was the day Moncure Conway "distinctly recognized that the antislavery cause was a religion" and "that Garrison was a successor of the inspired axe-bearers,—John the Baptist, Luther, Wesley, George Fox."[15]

But this was the position for religion in public life which Lincoln, who was almost pathologically shy about bringing his religious life into public view, deplored. Although as a Whig Lincoln was more receptive to public affirmations of religious postures than previous Democratic presidents, he adamantly refused to allow religion to dictate policy. Religious delegations which came to offer him direction were usually given short shrift, and sometimes a rare display of Lincolnian abruptness; he received the petition of the National Association for the Amendment of the Constitution and their proposal to rewrite the Preamble of the Constitution to recognize "the rulership of Jesus Christ and the supremacy of divine law," but took no action upon it.[16] The religious sentiments which pervade the Second Inaugural are more substantial than those of any other American president, before or since, but they are also remarkable for the message of restraint they contain: that no one possesses sufficient insight to understand the intentions of God.

Lincoln experienced even more distance from the abolitionists once some of the specifics of abolitionist religion came more clearly into view. His disbelief in free will—that "the human mind is impelled to action, or held in rest by some power, over which the mind itself has no control"—had been increasingly rejected by evangelical revivalism in the nineteenth century. Even evangelicals who liked to consider themselves Calvinists redefined their Calvinism in ways that allowed them to preach that conversion to God was a spiritual act one could perform for oneself, at once, instead of waiting mutely for God to do it as *his* choice. And what immediatism was for the revivalists translated into demands for immediate abolition of slavery in the hands of Garrison, Henry Ward Beecher, Elizur Wright, and the Tappan brothers. "Under the government of God, as exhibited in this world, there is but one remedy for sin, and that is available only by a *repentance*, evidenced by reformation," wrote Elizur Wright.

> There is no such thing as holding on to sin with safety. It is not only to be renounced, but the very occasions of it are to be avoided at whatever sacrifice. . . . The entire agency which God has provided to reclaim the world should be adapted to produce *immediate repentance*. . . . The doctrine of the immediate abolition of slavery asks no better authority than is offered by scripture. It is in perfect harmony with the letter and spirit of God's word. . . . It is the duty of the holders of slaves immediately to restore them to their liberty, and to extend to them the full protection of law, as well as its control. . . . Also, it is the duty of all men to proclaim this doctrine—to urge upon slaveholders *immediate emancipation*, so long as there is a slave—to agitate the consciences of tyrants, as long as there is a tyrant on the globe.

But Lincoln was unconvinced that any human action was so completely within the control of the human will that an immediate renunciation of habit and self-interest could be expected from anyone, much less from slaveholders, whose habit was reinforced by racial contempt and whose self-interest was reinforced by the fabulous profits of the cotton trade. And he would have found unrealistic, in both religious and political terms, the kind of immediatist advice Arthur Tappan gave to Theodore Dwight Weld as an agent of the American Anti-Slavery Society in 1834:

> You will inculcate every where, the great fundamental principle of IMMEDI-ATE ABOLITION, as the duty of all masters, on the ground that slavery is both unjust and unprofitable. Insist principally on the SIN of SLAVERY, because our main hope is in the consciences of men. . . . We reprobate the idea of compensation to slave holders, because it implies the right of slavery. . . . We also reprobate all plans of expatriation, by whatever specious pretences covered, as a remedy for slavery, for they all proceed from prejudices against color; and we hold that the duty of whites in regard to this cruel prejudice is not to indulge it, but to repent and overcome it.[17]

Immediatism was not the only religious attitude among the abolitionists that alienated Lincoln. The great obstruction on the road to repentance, according to both the revivalists and the abolitionists, was selfishness. To a certain extent, Lincoln agreed: selfishness described the full extent of human action and even explained his decision to free slaves as an appeal to the self-interest of the slaves which would impel them to take up arms against the South. For the abolitionists, however, selfishness was exactly what they believed they had transcended and expected slaveholders to transcend. "We have no selfish motive to appeal to," Wendell Phillips confidently asserted in 1852. "We appeal to white men, who cannot see any present interest they have in the slave question" and ask them to "ascend to a level of disinterestedness which the masses seldom reach, before we can create any excitement in them on the questions of slavery." But *excitement*, the fuel which Phillips hoped to ignite in order to overcome selfishness, was precisely what Lincoln feared to interject into public discourse. In 1838, he warned that the chief threat to liberty was "the increasing disposition to substitute the wild and furious passions, in lieu of the sober judgments of the Courts." And twenty-three years later, on the eve of the secession of the Southern states from the Union, he was still warning that "though passion may have strained, it must not break our bonds of affection." But Phillips, in outlining the "Philosophy of the Abolition Movement" in 1853 for the Massachusetts Anti-Slavery Society, insisted that passion was the only cure for slavery-inspired moral lethargy. Old School clergy and "Cotton" Whigs, Phillips complained, "are ever parading their wish to draw a line between themselves and us, because *they must be permitted* to wait,—to trust more to reason than feeling,—to indulge a generous charity,—to rely on the sure influence of simple truth, uttered in love, &c., &c." He had no hesitation in accepting the charge that "in dealing with slaveholders and their apologists, we indulge in fierce denunciations, instead of appealing to their reason and common sense by plain statements and fair argument."[18]

On no point, though, did Lincoln feel greater shrinkage from the abolitionists than when he heard them speak in tones of temperamental antirationalism against the Constitution, or worse still, saw them burn it, as Garrison did in 1854. "As to the governments of this world, whatever their titles or forms, we shall endeavor to prove that, in their essential elements, and as at present administered, they are all anti-Christ," Garrison declared, "and that the followers of Jesus should instinctively shun their stations of honor, power, and emolument. . . . Human governments are to be viewed as judicial punishments." Phillips agreed: "The Constitution and government of this country is worth nothing, except it is or can be made capable of grappling with the great question of slavery. . . . The best use of good laws is to teach men to trample bad laws under their feet." Garrison dismissed all talk "about the sacredness of the compact which was formed between the free and slave states, on the adoption of the Constitution" and described it instead as "the infamous bargain." On those terms, the Constitution was actually an obstacle, which trapped well-intentioned abolitionists in its proslavery mire.

> The ballot-box is not an anti-slavery, but a pro-slavery argument, so long as it is surrounded by the United States Constitution, which forbids all approach to it, except on conditions that the voter shall surrender fugitive slaves—suppress negro insurrections—sustain a piratical representation in Congress—and regard man-stealers as equally eligible with the truest friends of human freedom and equality to any or all offices under the United States government.

Illinois abolitionist Ichabod Codding, who tried to nudge Lincoln toward abolitionism, and whom Lincoln politely disliked, warned that the Constitution protected no one from sin: "We are implicated in the *Sin* of Slavery. . . . We stand misrepresented in every case which regards Slavery [and] yet we are taxed to support it." Nor is it easy to imagine Lincoln having any sympathy with Codding's fellow Illinoisan, Owen Lovejoy, in calling for blunt disobedience to the Constitution and the Fugitive Slave Law:

> I will never degrade my manhood, and stifle the sympathies of human nature. . . . Let it echo through all the arches of heaven, and reverberate and bellow along all the deep gorges of hell, where slave catchers will be very likely to hear it; Owen Lovejoy lives at Princeton, Illinois, three-quarters of a mile east of the village, and he aids every fugitive that comes to his door and asks it. Thou invisible demon of Slavery, dost thou think to cross my humble threshold, and forbid me to give bread to the hungry and shelter to the houseless? I BID YOU DEFIANCE IN THE NAME OF MY GOD![19]

And yet Lincoln, in time, paid tribute to the memory of Owen Lovejoy as "my most generous friend" in Congress, and he told Shelby Cullom "that he was one of the best men in Congress." By the same token, Lewis Tappan voted for Lincoln in 1864 ("the first time in his life he had voted for a winning candidate," Bertram Wyatt-Brown reminds us), and William Lloyd Garrison broke ranks with Phillips and other abolitionists and openly supported Lincoln's reelection. "There is no mistake about it in regard to Mr. Lincoln's desire to do all that he can see it right and possible for him to do to uproot slavery," Garrison assured his wife after meeting with Lincoln in the White House in the summer of 1864. And in the end, Lincoln (by a path too well-known to need retelling here) did find his way to the abolition of slavery, first emancipating slaves serving the Confederacy's military interests through the Confiscation Acts of 1861 and 1862, then abolishing slavery in the Confederate states through the Emancipation Proclamation in 1863, and finally eradicating slavery entirely in the United States forever through the Thirteenth Amendment in 1865. Much as he had dreaded the importunities of the radicals in his own party, Lincoln finally had to concede that although they were "bitterly hostile" to him "personally" and "utterly lawless—the unhandiest devils in the world to deal with . . . after all their faces are set Zionwards." As he told John B. Henderson, "Sumner and Wade and Chandler are right about [abolition]. . . . We can't get through this terrible war with slavery existing."[20]

But Lincoln's affection for Lovejoy had its limitations. "If he ever became too radical," Lincoln assured Cullom, "I always knew that I could send for him and talk it over, and he would go back to the floor and do about as I wanted." And the same was true for the abolitionists in general. "Stand with the abolitionist in restoring the Missouri Compromise," Lincoln advised in 1854, "and stand against him when he attempts to repeal the fugitive slave law," because "in the latter case, you stand with the southern disunionist." Lincoln's explanation to Henderson about conceding the need for abolition to the radicals was the preface to an appeal for Henderson and other Missourians to agree to a compensated emancipation plan, "to turn in and take pay for your slaves from the Government." Even after emancipation, Lincoln continued to speak of the abolitionists as though Zion were only occasionally their destination. He told William D. Kelley that he loathed "the self-righteousness of the Abolitionists" and spoke to Eli Thayer of them "in terms of contempt and derision." John Eaton remembered Lincoln exclaiming (of a "well-known abolitionist and orator," probably Phillips), "I don't see why God lets him live!"[21]

Lincoln came to emancipation at last, but came to it by a very different road than the abolitionists. Where they built their argument on the demand of evangelical religion for repentance, Lincoln was reluctant to make religious demands in the public square and instead preferred gradualism and compensation for emancipated slaves. Where they preached from passion and choice, he worked from reason and patience. Where they called for immediatism without regard for consequences, it was precisely the economic consequences of slavery and its extension which kindled Lincoln's opposition in the 1850s. And where they brushed aside the Constitution's implicit sanctions for slavery, and the Constitution with them, Lincoln would proceed against slavery no farther than the Constitution allowed. They were fearless racial egalitarians in an age when racial equality was routinely assumed to be a scientific and physical impossibility; Lincoln was only a Lockean natural-rights equalitarian, who only in the last year of his life began to show glimmerings that the end of slavery would be followed at once by the obligation to guarantee equal civil rights for the freedmen in the postwar future.

And yet, it was the name of Abraham Lincoln—restrained, emotionally chilly, with an unblinking eye for compromise—which ended up at the bottom of the Emancipation Proclamation. This raises, then, the large-scale question, posed by Eric McKitrick, which has so often haunted the literature of the abolitionist movement: "What exactly was the function of William Lloyd Garrison and those who acted similarly, in preparing the way for the ending of slavery and in relation to the other influences converging toward the same end? Where does the extremist—the fanatic, the single-minded zealot—fit in?"[22]

The most recent neo-abolitionist histories from Henry Mayer and Paul Goodman have joined older neo-abolitionists like James McPherson, Howard Zinn, and Martin Duberman in answering this question with a resounding affirmation of the strategic centrality of the abolitionists to the end of slavery. Mayer, for instance, identifies the abolitionists as the *sine qua non* of emancipation. They called up justice from the depths of the American soul; they rolled the stone of law from the door of conscience; they shoved, pushed, and moved the inert center of American politics in the direction of freedom. "William Lloyd Garrison," wrote Mayer in the second sentence of his biography of the abolitionist, "is an authentic American hero who, with a biblical prophet's power and a propagandist's skill, forced the nation to confront the most crucial moral issue in its history."[23] That they were prepared to set aside the Constitution—even the rule of law itself—is only testimony to the inadequacy of law in justifying and redeeming society. By hallowing zealotry, the neo-abolitionists identify direct (even if nonviolent) action as the only morally legitimate stance in American reform. Only by means of incessant agitating of the most radical kind was the nation made ready for abolition; only by means of the dauntless radicalism of *The Liberator* was justice achieved and the way paved for further reform in American society. They never once seemed to feel the degree of self-questioning felt by Lincoln at the deaths of hundreds of thousands of their countrymen and the evaporation of billions of dollars in property in a war that they continued loudly to judge as inadequate until it finally embraced their goal. By extension, we are exhorted to go and do likewise.

This is a comforting, and yet troubling, and even self-congratulatory, way of describing the crooked road which led to emancipation. It forgets how many other strands of thinking besides the unction of moral rectitude went into the making of slavery's end and ignores the potency lent to the antislavery cause by the liberal capitalist argument for free wage labor. Even worse, it sanctions a political ethic built on romantic Kantianism (and hallowed in our times by John Rawls) that stands in stark contrast to the Enlightenment politics of prudence so dear to Lincoln's Lockean and rationalist sense of politics. Lincoln, by contrast, embodied the complexity of American opposition to slavery. He came at the problem only when slavery ceased being content with living under compromises and tried to assert its extension as a solution to the South's dwindling political influence. The end of slavery owed something to a sense of awakened moral responsibility, but that in itself owed far more than we have been willing to admit to the long swing of ideas about political economy and to the public revulsion toward specific public events, such as the effort to "gag" debate over slavery in Congress and the resort to proslavery terrorism in the organizing of the Kansas Territory in the 1850s. Above all, Lincoln was willing to subordinate his own preferences (including his "oft-expressed wish that everyone ought to be free") to the need to build coalitions rather than purify sects. Lincoln had no illusions about his own sanctity or his enemies' depravity, and he was constantly in mind of the price being paid in human lives and treasure for even the noblest of results.

"If I had my way, this war would never have been commenced," Lincoln told the English Quaker activist Eliza P. Gurney a month after issuing the Emancipation Proclamation. "If I had been allowed my way," he continued, "this war would have been ended before this," perhaps before the Proclamation had ever been contemplated. That sentiment has earned him the execration of every abolitionist and neo-abolitionist, from Garrison to (most recently) *Ebony* editor Lerone Bennett, whose book *Forced into Glory: Abraham Lincoln's White Dream* depicts Lincoln as a callous white racist, the kind of fence straddler "we find in almost all situations of oppression." For all of Bennett's rant, Lincoln biographers will ignore him at their peril, because both Garrison and Bennett had a point: Lincoln's best plan for emancipation (without the helping hand of war) *was* a gradualized scheme which might have allowed the grandparents of some of today's adult African Americans to have been born in slavery.[24]

The question Lincoln might have asked the neo-abolitionists was whether the costs of their way of immediate emancipation—costs that included a civil war, 620,000 dead, a national economic body-blow worse than the Great Depression, and the broken glass of Reconstruction to walk over—are also part of their calculation of results. Neither Lincoln's nor the abolitionists' alternative was particularly pretty. (And of the two, I must be candid enough to confess, I cannot see myself in 1861 applauding Lincoln's strategy.) Lincoln never doubted that emancipation was *right* and slavery was *wrong*. But he had an inkling that it was possible to do something right in such a way that it fostered an equally horrifying result and perhaps even an infinitely greater wrong. There is a zeal which is not according to knowledge, and many of the abolitionists had it in spades, and reveled in it. To be pushed into reform merely by the exigencies of war, politics, and the slowly shifting weight of economies was, for them, not to have zeal at all. (British evangelical abolitionists, unlike Garrison and Phillips, had a far greater sense of the need to harness moralism to politics and the long movement of society than their American counterparts.)[25] Still, because their unyielding campaign was followed in 1865 by abolition, it has been easy to conclude that zeal earned its own justification simply through the end of slavery.

But this may be the greatest *post hoc, propter hoc* fallacy in American history. Between the word of abolition and the deed of emancipation falls the ambiguous shadow of Abraham Lincoln. For more than a century, the genius of American reform has steered its course by the constellation of Garrison and Phillips. The realities of reform, however, may have been another matter.

Notes

This essay first appeared as "Lincoln and the Abolitionists," *Wilson Quarterly* 58 (Autumn 2000): 58–71.

1. Stephen Oates, "Lincoln's Journey to Emancipation," in *Our Fiery Trial: Abraham Lincoln, John Brown, and the Civil War Era* (Amherst, MA, 1979), 61.

2. Frederick Douglass, in Ronald Walters, *The Antislavery Appeal: American Abolitionism after 1830* (Baltimore, 1978), 126. See also the varying, and conflicting, taxonomies of abolitionism in Aileen Kraditor, *Means and Ends in American Abolitionism: Garrison and His Critics on Strategy and Tactics, 1834–1850* (New York, 1969); Martin Duberman, ed., *The Antislavery Vanguard: New Essays on the Abolitionists* (Princeton, NJ, 1965); David Brion Davis, *The Problem of Slavery in the Age of Revolution* (Ithaca, NY, 1975); Herbert Aptheker, "Militant Abolitionism," *Journal of Negro History* 26 (October 1941); Eric Foner, "Abolitionism and the Labor Movement in Ante-bellum America," in *Politics and Ideology in the Age of the Civil War* (New York, 1980); and Louis Filler, *The Crusade against Slavery, 1830–1860* (New York, 1960).

3. Josiah Gilbert Holland, *Life of Abraham Lincoln* (Springfield, MA, 1866), 347–48; Isaac Arnold, *The Life of Abraham Lincoln*, ed. James A. Rawley (Lincoln, NE, 1994), 342, 345; Michael Burlingame, "'I Used to Be a Slave': The Origins of Lincoln's Hatred of Slavery," in *The Inner World of Abraham Lincoln* (Urbana, IL, 1994), 20, 357; David Donald, *Lincoln* (New York, 1995), 165, 342; LaWanda Cox, *Lincoln and Black Freedom: A Study in Presidential Leadership* (Urbana, IL, 1985), 6–7. Richard Hart has convincingly shown that, in fact, Springfield had a sizable and active African American community, some of whom lived in Lincoln's own neighborhood, and that Lincoln could not have avoided contact with numerous African Americans, even under Illinois's complicated black codes. See Hart, "Springfield's African Americans as a Part of the Lincoln Community," *Journal of the Abraham Lincoln Association* 20 (Winter 1999), 35–54.

4. Charles H. Ray to Elihu Washburne, December 22, 1855, in Elihu Washburne Papers, Library of Congress; "The Republican Convention at Chicago," *Oberlin Evangelist*, May 23, 1860, 83; "H. F. Douglas, the Negro Orator," *Peoria Daily Transcript*, October 23, 1858; H. F. Douglass, in James M. McPherson, *The Negro's Civil War: How American Negroes Felt and Acted during the War for the Union* (New York, 1965), 5, 7.

5. William Lloyd Garrison, "Annual Meeting of the Massachusetts Anti-Slavery Society," *Liberator*, February 13, 1847; Lincoln, "Annual Message to Congress," December 1861, in *The Collected Works of Abraham Lincoln*, ed. Roy P. Basler (New Brunswick, NJ, 1953–55), 5:49; Garrison to Oliver Johnson, October 7 and December

6, 1861, in *The Letters of William Lloyd Garrison,* vol. 5, *Let the Oppressed Go Free, 1861–1867,* ed. W. M. Merrill (Cambridge, MA, 1979), 37, 47; Frederick Douglass, "The Inaugural Address," April 1861, and "The President and His Speeches," September 1862, in *Life and Writings of Frederick Douglass,* ed. Philip S. Foner (New York, 1950), 3:72–75, 267, 270. Douglass's post-assassination comment on Lincoln is less well known than his later criticism of Lincoln as "pre-eminently the white man's president, entirely devoted to the welfare of white men," but the latter comment was uttered more than ten years later, after Reconstruction had soured Douglass and swung him back to his former opinion of Lincoln. See Michael Burlingame, "'Emphatically the Black Man's President': New Light on Frederick Douglass and Abraham Lincoln," *Lincoln Ledger* 4 (February 1996): 1–5.

6. Joshua Giddings, in J. G. Randall, *Lincoln the President,* vol. 2, *Bull Run to Gettysburg* (New York, 1945), 209; T. Harry Williams, *Lincoln and the Radicals* (Madison, WI, 1941), 10; Allan Bogue, "William Parker Cutler's Congressional Diary of 1862–63," *Civil War History* 33 (December 1987): 320; Francis Fessenden, *Life and Public Services of William Pitt Fessenden* (Boston, 1907), 1:259–60; *The Diary of Edward Bates,* ed. Howard K. Beale (Washington, DC, 1933), 333; Lincoln to John B. Henderson, in Walter B. Stevens, *A Reporter's Lincoln,* ed. Michael Burlingame (Lincoln, NE, 1999), 170–73.

7. Wendell Phillips, "The Labor Question," April 1872, in *Speeches, Lectures, and Letters, Second Series* (Boston, 1905), 171; Phillips, in Ralph Korngold, *Two Friends of Man: The Story of William Lloyd Garrison and Wendell Phillips and Their Relationship with Abraham Lincoln* (Boston, 1950), 269; Phillips, "Philosophy of the Abolition Movement," January 27, 1853, "The Cabinet," August 1, 1862, and "The State of the Country," January 21 and May 11, 1863, in *Speeches, Lectures, and Letters* (Boston, 1863), 113–14, 448, 450, 555.

8. Charles Sumner, Wait Talcott, and John Roll, in *Recollected Words of Abraham Lincoln,* ed. Don Fehrenbacher and Virginia Fehrenbacher (Stanford, CA, 1996), 433, 442, 383.

9. Lincoln, "To Joshua F. Speed," August 24, 1855, in *Collected Works,* 2:323.

10. Lincoln, "To Horace Greeley," March 24, 1862, in *Collected Works,* 5:169.

11. Gilbert Beebe, in Peter J. Wosh, *Spreading the Word: The Bible Business in Nineteenth-Century America* (Ithaca, NY, 1994), 135; Douglas L. Wilson, *Honor's Voice: The Transformation of Abraham Lincoln* (New York, 1998), 262.

12. Lincoln, "Speech at Peoria," October 16, 1854, in *Collected Works,* 2:274.

13. Lincoln, "Protest in Illinois Legislature on Slavery," March 3, 1837, "To Williamson Durley," October 3, 1845, "Eulogy on Henry Clay," July 6, 1852, "Speech at Peoria," October 16, 1854, "Speech at Carlinville, Illinois," August 31, 1858, "Address before the Wisconsin State Agricultural Society, Milwaukee, Wisconsin," September 30, 1859, "Speech at New Haven, Connecticut," March 6, 1860, in *Collected Works,* 1:75, 347, 2:130, 274, 3:79, 478, 4:25.

14. Lincoln, "Speech at Peoria, Illinois," October 16, 1854, in *Collected Works,* 2:255; Benjamin F. Butler, in *Reminiscences of Abraham Lincoln by Distinguished Men of His Time,* ed. Allen Thorndike Rice (New York, 1886), 150–54.

15. Robert H. Abzug, *Cosmos Crumbling: American Reform and the Religious Imagination* (New York, 1994), 144; Moncure Conway, *Autobiography, Memories and Experiences of Moncure Daniel Conway* (Boston, 1904), 1:184.

16. Burlingame, *Inner World*, 177; Morton Borden, "The Christian Amendment," *Civil War History* 25 (June 1979): 160.

17. Lincoln, "Handbill Replying to Charges of Infidelity," in *Collected Works*, 1:382; Elizur Wright, *The Sin of Slavery and Its Remedy; Containing Some Reflections on the Moral Influence of African Colonization* (New York, 1833), 1:42; Arthur Tappan, "Particular Instructions," to Theodore Dwight Weld, in *Letters of Theodore Dwight Weld, Angelina Grimke Weld, and Sarah Grimke, 1822–1844*, ed. G. Barnes and D. L. Dumond (New York, 1934), 1:124–28.

18. Lincoln, "First Inaugural Address—Final Text," March 4, 1861, and "To James C. Conkling," August 26, 1863, in *Collected Works*, 4:271, 6:409; Wendell Phillips, "Sims Anniversary," in *Speeches, Lectures, and Letters* (Boston, 1863), 83, 98, 100.

19. Phillips, "Sims Anniversary," 91; William Lloyd Garrison, "The Great Crisis!" *Liberator*, December 29, 1832, and December 15, 1837; "Twelfth Annual Meeting of the Massachusetts Anti-Slavery Society," *Twelfth Annual Report, presented to the Massachusetts Anti-Slavery Society by its Board of Managers* (Boston, 1844), 3; Owen Lovejoy, "The Fanaticism of the Democratic Party," in *Illinois Literature: The Nineteenth Century*, ed. J. E. Hallwas (Macomb, IL, 1986), 81–82; Ichabod Codding, "Why Discuss This Subject in the North?" in Ichabod Codding Papers, Illinois State Historical Library, Springfield. Lincoln resented Codding's attempt in November 1854 to place Lincoln's name on the newly organized Republican state committee; Lincoln was at that time still firmly committed to the Whig Party, and while he supposed that "my opposition to the principle of slavery is as strong as that of any member of the Republican party . . . I had also supposed that the extent to which I feel authorized to carry that opposition, practically, was not at all satisfactory to that party." "To Ichabod Codding," November 27, 1854, in *Collected Works*, 2:288.

20. Lincoln, "To John H. Bryant," May 30, 1864, in *Collected Works*, 7:366; Bertram Wyatt-Brown, *Lewis Tappan and the Evangelical War against Slavery* (New York, 1971), 337–38; Garrison to Helen E. Garrison, June 11, 1864, in *Letters of William Lloyd Garrison*, 5:212; John Hay, diary entry for October 28, 1863, in *Inside Lincoln's White House: The Complete Civil War Diary of John Hay*, ed. Michael Burlingame and J. R. T. Ettlinger (Carbondale, IL, 1997), 101; John B. Henderson, in Stevens, *Reporter's Lincoln*, 171.

21. Shelby Cullom, in Fehrenbacher and Fehrenbacher, *Recollected Words*, 125; Lincoln, "Speech at Peoria, Illinois," October 16, 1854, in *Collected Works*, 2:273; John B. Henderson, in Stevens, *Reporter's Lincoln*, 172; Eli Thayer and William D. Kelley, in Burlingame and Ettlinger, *Inside Lincoln's White House*, 322 n.233.

22. Eric McKitrick, "The Liberator," *New York Review of Books*, October 21, 1999, 57.

23. Paul Goodman, *Of One Blood: Abolitionism and the Origins of Racial Equality* (Berkeley, CA, 1998), 60; Henry Mayer, *All on Fire: William Lloyd Garrison and the Abolition of Slavery* (New York, 1998), xvii–xxi.

24. Lincoln, "Reply to Eliza P. Gurney," October 26, 1862, in *Collected Works*, 5:478.

25. Christopher L. Brown comments in terms which Lincoln would have appreciated that "if antislavery argument was to have effect, moralists probably would have to do more than simply insist that slavery was wrong. . . . The real burden lay in rethinking the relationship between empire and coerced labor." See "Empire without Slaves: British Concepts of Emancipation in the Age of the American Revolution," *William and Mary Quarterly* 61 (April 1999): 275.

6

APPLES OF GOLD IN A PICTURE OF SILVER:
LINCOLN, THE CONSTITUTION, AND LIBERTY

In the threatening winter of 1860–61, as the United States was being inched ever closer to the outbreak of civil war by the secession of the Southern states over the issue of black slavery, the newly elected president, Abraham Lincoln, opened up a confidential correspondence with a former Southern political colleague, Alexander Stephens of Georgia. Stephens had made headlines in November 1860 in a speech to the Georgia legislature urging Georgia not to follow the South into secession. Lincoln sent him a friendly note, asking for a printed copy of the speech—and perhaps warming Stephens to an invitation to come into Lincoln's cabinet as a gesture of mollification toward the South. Stephens wrote back, apologizing that the speech was not yet in print (apart from the newspaper reports of it that Lincoln had read), but taking the opportunity to urge Lincoln to make some kind of conciliatory promise to the South about staying within the bounds of the Constitution, as president, and not threatening to take federal action against slavery in the South, where slavery had enjoyed a kind of constitutional immunity since the beginnings of the Republic. This, Stephens believed, would deflate the secession fire-eaters better than any cabinet offer, adding (with a phrase borrowed from the Book of Proverbs), "A word fitly spoken by you now would be like 'apples of gold in pictures of silver.'"

Lincoln was disappointed that Stephens seemed to think that he intended some unconstitutional aggression against the South. The president-elect could not believe that conciliatory words from him about the Constitution were really necessary: "Do the people of the South really entertain fears that a Republican administration would, *directly*, or *indirectly*, interfere with their slaves, or with them, about their slaves?" The correspondence died on that point of mutual misunderstanding, and Stephens, rather than entering Lincoln's cabinet, eventually became vice president of the new Southern Confederacy in February 1861. (And nine years later, Stephens would compare Lincoln to Caesar, the destroyer of the Roman republic, and claim that "I do not think he understood" the niceties of constitutional government "or the tendencies of his acts upon them".) But Stephens's anxiety about Lincoln's potential for breaking over the limits of the Constitution stayed in the forefront of Lincoln's thinking, like an irritation he could not rub out. So did the biblical image about apples of gold and pictures of silver, for in January Lincoln wrote out a brief statement on the place of the Constitution in his thinking, perhaps as part of a reply to Stephens, in which Lincoln borrowed precisely Stephens's own image about apples of gold.[1]

"Without the *Constitution* and the *Union*, we could not have attained . . . our great prosperity," Lincoln acknowledged, and therefore he had no intention of treating the Constitution lightly. But "there is something back of these, entwining more closely about the human heart," Lincoln insisted. "That something is the principle of 'Liberty to all'" which is enshrined in the Declaration of Independence, that "all men are created equal." This was a principle which, for Lincoln, slashed straight across the practice of slavery, and if Stephens expected him to pay attention only to the Constitution and ignore the principles which lay "back of these," he would have nothing to expect but disappointment in Lincoln. The Constitution did not exist merely for its own sake, as though it were only a set of procedural rules with no better goal than letting people do what they pleased *with* what they pleased; it was intended to serve the interests of "the principle of 'Liberty to all,'" which meant that the Declaration was "*the* word, *fitly spoken*' which has proved an 'apple of gold' to us." The Constitution, and the federal Union the Constitution created in 1787, "are the picture of silver, subsequently framed around it. The picture was made, not to conceal, or destroy the apple; but to adorn, and preserve it. The picture was made for the apple—not the apple for the picture."[2]

There is no doubt but that the Declaration of Independence was the central statement of Lincoln's political idealism. "I believe that the declaration that 'all men are created equal' is the great fundamental principle upon which our free institutions rest," he wrote in 1858; and two months after his correspondence with Stephens, at Philadelphia's Independence Hall, Lincoln declared that "I have never had a feeling politically that did not spring from the sentiments embodied in the Declaration of Independence." It was "an American Decalogue, which promulgated America's Republican creed." What he hated about the enslavement of blacks was not only its crass disregard of the natural equality of all human beings but the way it forced "so many really good men amongst us into an open war with the . . . Declaration of Independence, and insisting that there is no right principle of action but self-interest." And it was the Declaration's promise of equality which Lincoln made the chapter and verse of his great call for a "new birth of freedom."[3]

But this was precisely what, at bottom, divided Lincoln and Alexander Stephens. For Stephens, the Declaration's proclamation of universal equality was a great mistake; and the Constitution was indeed a set of procedural rules, intended to teach no particular system of political morality, or any other morality for that matter. "The prevailing ideas . . . at the time of the formation of the old Constitution were, that the enslavement of the African was in violation of the laws of nature," Stephens said on March 21, 1861. "Those ideas, however, were fundamentally wrong. They rested upon the assumption of the equality of races. This was an error." Resting the Constitution on the Declaration was the equivalent of building the national house on "a sandy foundation."[4] And there have been some, long after Stephens and even among Lincoln's admirers, who wondered whether Stephens was right, or at least right in apprehending that Lincoln had taken entirely too cavalier an attitude toward the Constitution.

According to the conservative political scientist Willmoore Kendall, Lincoln did not merely set the Declaration and the Constitution into what he imagined was a proper relationship of apples of gold and pictures of silver; he used the Declaration to demolish the Constitution in the name of his own egalitarian ideology. "What Lincoln did . . . was to falsify the facts of history, and to do so in a way that precisely *confuses* our self-understanding as a people," Kendall argued. Gottfried Dietze, a political conservative like Kendall, saw Lincoln's appeal to the Declaration as the "apple of gold" as a democratic pretense which allowed him to demote the Constitution to a mere piece of framework, so that Lincoln would be free to pursue dictatorial glory as president. Lincoln, said Dietze, was "a democratic Machiavellian whose latent desire to achieve immortality broke forth at the first opportunity offered by . . . the Civil War." Or if not glory, Lincoln used the pursuit of equality as an excuse for granting himself "unprecedented and virtually dictatorial powers as president" to tear down the restraints of the Constitution so that he could satisfy a kind of political Oedipus complex. According to Dwight G. Anderson, Lincoln would use the appeal to equality in the Declaration in order to "put himself in Washington's place as the father of his country." For Anderson, Lincoln as president only posed as a defender and maintainer of the Union and the Constitution, while in reality "he actually was transforming it."[5]

And even among Lincoln's admirers, there is a running current of discomfort at Lincoln's apparent willingness to set the Constitution below the Declaration. The great Lincoln biographer James G. Randall, the equally great historian

James Ford Rhodes, and the path-breaking political historian William Dunning all agreed that Lincoln rode roughshod over the Constitution in pursuit of dictatorial powers, although all were quick to add that Lincoln's "wholesome regard for individual liberty" and "the legal-mindedness of the American people" kept him from turning into an outright tyrant. More recently, voices on the political left like Garry Wills, George Fletcher, Charles L. Black, and Mark Tushnet have actually applauded Lincoln for dumping the Constitution in favor the Declaration and creating "in effect, a constitution for a new republic based on nationhood, equality and democracy." According to Wills, the Gettysburg Address, by invoking the Declaration of Independence at the beginning rather than the Constitution, changed "the recalcitrant stuff of that legal compromise, bringing it to its own indictment." At Gettysburg, Lincoln performed "one of the most daring acts of open-air sleight-of-hand ever witnessed by the unsuspecting" and "changed the way people thought about the Constitution." (Willmoore Kendall, in Wills's reading, was actually quite right: Wills merely chose to cheer what Kendall chose to deplore). Howard Jones echoes Wills's judgment by describing the war as "an instrument" Lincoln used "for reshaping the Union of the Constitution into the more perfect Union envisioned by signers of the Declaration of Independence." Even Philip Paludan, who offers the most realistic and persuasive middle path between Kendall and Wills, can only insist that Lincoln was indeed a Declaration of Independence egalitarian, but a *process* egalitarian who believed "that equality would be realized only through the proper operation of existing institutions."[6]

What runs as a common thread through all of these comments, favorable and unfavorable alike, is the peculiar sense that, in varying degrees and for good or ill, Lincoln really does perform a sacrifice of the Constitution to the Declaration. Lincoln's own image of the "apples of gold in the picture of silver" has offered easily quotable support for that, since it suggests all too broadly that the Constitution's importance is largely that of an instrument for implementing the Declaration's ideals. As Lincoln said to a political rally in June 1858: be "ever true to Liberty, the Union, and the Constitution—true to Liberty, not selfishly, but upon principle—not for special classes of men, but for all men, true to the union and the Constitution, as the best means to advance that liberty."[7] Did Lincoln sit at the other extreme from Alexander Stephens and regard the Constitution as a wax nose, to be reshaped according to his own egalitarian idealism? If either Wills or Kendall are even close to being right, the answer would have to be *yes*, to both questions.

The difficulty with resting in this opinion is that we still live under this Constitution; and the Civil War was fought to keep it in place; and very nearly all the advances in civil equality made since the Civil War have been based on appeals to the Constitution. Certainly, no civil rights litigation has achieved success by ignoring the Constitution and directing judges' attention to the Declaration. Casting Lincoln as both Wills and Kendall do—as a subverter of the Constitution—makes Lincoln into a sort of political monster rather than a hero. So what did Lincoln intend when he spoke of the Constitution as a "picture of silver"? And before we confidently conclude that Lincoln had to tear down the Constitution in order to pave the way for equality, what did Lincoln mean by *equality*? For it may turn out that Lincoln was more of a constitutionalist than meets the eye and a very different sort of egalitarian than we think.

It is surprising that Abraham Lincoln, a lawyer's lawyer, would find himself defining the relationship of the Declaration and the Constitution in terms of illustrations and pictures rather than a precise legal equation. But Lincoln was not the only one with that problem. This was because there was no simple consensus in the American Republic about the application of the Constitution, and nowhere was that more dramatically demonstrated than in the ferocious political contests between the Democratic Party of Andrew Jackson and Stephen A. Douglas and the Whig Party of Henry Clay and Abraham Lincoln.

Born in the great political triumph of Thomas Jefferson and his followers in the presidential election of 1800, the Democratic Party saw itself as the party of a virtuous countryside, a party of independent farmers who would keep liberty pure by preventing the fledgling American merchant class from concentrating too much lethal political power in its own hands. For the Democrats, the Constitution was a procedural rulebook, and for the most part, only a procedural rulebook. It prescribed only the minimum of guidelines for government and left the balance to the self-government of American individuals. It bothered the Democrats not at all if those self-governing individuals galloped off in a hundred different cultural and moral directions. Any attempt to prescribe a common cultural standard not only stepped beyond the Constitution, but amounted to a conspiratorial concentration of power. "So long as the individual trespasses upon none of the rights of others, or throws no obstacle in the way of their free and full exercise," wrote Orestes Brownson, "government, law, public opinion even, must leave him free to take his own course."[8]

This heady brand of do-your-own-thing populism (made all the headier by the leadership, first, of Jefferson, and then of Andrew Jackson) had two basic flaws: nations of farmers tend not to do well if they are ever sucked into war with nations of merchants; and, farmers (far from being always virtuous) can just as often be suspicious, provincial, and lecherous. The first of those flaws showed up in the War of 1812, when "War Hawks" led by Henry Clay brought the United States into a war in which the American Republic came within an ace of having its ill-equipped and underweight armies of farmers wiped out by the British. Clay, the sadder but wiser politician, backed away from Jefferson and began insisting that, if the United States wanted its liberty to survive, it had better investigate the acquisition of a little power—eventually Clay created an entirely new party, the Whigs, to promote a national banking system to encourage commercial development (and a national tariff to protect it) and a general combination of business and government in joint effort.

This enraged Democrats. "Our plan may be stated in a phrase of the utmost brevity," erupted Democratic journalist William Leggett, "for it consists merely in the absolute separation of government from the banking and credit system."[9] Clay's so-called American System for the promotion of commerce and industry would only lay open the path to frightening concentrations of power, both inside and outside the government. Once accumulated, that economic power could then be used in political ways—to buy votes for public works projects that benefited the powerful, to finance campaigns for the imposition of evangelical Protestant morality on the working class (like the New York City religious revivals underwritten by the wealthy Whig merchants Arthur and Lewis Tappan), and, even more threatening, to underwrite movements for the abolition of black slavery (which the Tappans were also financing). To Democrats like Leggett, such concentrations of power, and the capacity for social mischief they created, were wildly unconstitutional. The Constitution nowhere gave any sanction to proposals for national banks, national roads, or national meddling with slavery—at least not explicitly.

But *explicitly* was just Clay's point—what the Constitution did not expressly forbid was not *un*constitutional, and so hey-ho for the National Bank. Add to this the guidance given to American jurisprudence by Joseph Story and James Kent in favor of the binding power of contract and the inhibition of state restraints on commerce, and the breakup of state restrictions on banking and interstate business supervised by Chief Justice John Marshall and the Marshall Court, and the way was open to "constitutionalizing" the entire field of domestic economic policy. Instead of the Constitution enjoying a sacred consensus above mere policy disputes, the Constitution in the early Republic became the site of every one of those disputes.[10]

The second flaw in the Democratic reasoning—the unreliability of rural virtue—was something Abraham Lincoln was all too well acquainted with. "I presume I am not expected to employ the time assigned me, in the mere flattery of the farmers, as a class," Lincoln warned the Wisconsin State Agricultural Fair when he was invited to speak there in 1859. "I believe there really are more attempts at flattering them than any other; the reason of which I cannot perceive, unless it be that they can cast more votes than any other." Born in rural Kentucky poverty to the very model of independent Democratic farmers, Lincoln disliked agricultural work and everything attached to it almost from the beginning; and as soon as he came of age in Illinois, he left the farm for the town and the city and never looked back, to become a storekeeper and then a lawyer, two professions which were the midwives for American commercial development. It was this which recruited Lincoln for the Whigs and drove him into politics (even before law), and which made "the name of Henry Clay . . . an inspiration to me."[11] It also determined Lincoln's view of the Constitution, and, as we shall see, gave his understanding of the Declaration an unexpectedly economic twist.

It is only if we suppose that Lincoln thought of nothing *but* the Declaration—only if we ignore his immersion as a highly partisan Whig in the 1830s and 1840s, along with the general propensity of all political partisans then to "constitutionalize" policy debates—that we will be surprised to find Lincoln closely preoccupied with the integrity of the Constitution far earlier than with the Declaration of Independence. For despite the suggestions of some of his critics, Lincoln in the 1840s devoted more attention to the interpretation of the Constitution, and to a far more restrained notion of constitutional interpretation at that, than Wills, Kendall, or Randall claimed. His earliest extended political statement, to the Springfield Young Men's Lyceum, on "The Perpetuation of Our Political Institutions" (January 1838), closes with a ringing denunciation of the role of "passion" in politics (and *passion* was understood to be the Democratic style, as opposed to Whig "reason") and a call for *"general intelligence, [sound] morality* and, in particular, *a reverence for the constitution and laws."* In 1848, as a congressman advocating Clay's programs of tax-supported "internal Improvements," Lincoln attacked proposals to amend the Constitution as a mistake leading to ruin:

> No slight occasion should tempt us to touch it. Better not take the first step, which may lead to a habit of altering it. Better, rather, habituate ourselves to think of it, as unalterable. It can scarcely be made better than it is. New provisions, would introduce new difficulties, and thus create, and increase appetite for still further change. No sir, let it stand as it is. New hands have never touched it. The men who made it, have done their work, and have passed away. Who shall improve, on what *they* did?[12]

Of course, that referred to *changing* the Constitution; as a Whig, he was happy to entertain elasticity in interpreting it, especially when it came to the pet projects of the Whig Party. Participating in his first national political campaign in 1840 as a Whig speechmaker, Lincoln attacked the Democrats' successful dismemberment of the national banking system under Andrew Jackson and Martin Van Buren, a dissolution grounded in Jackson's claim that the Constitution gave no express sanction to a national bank. "As a sweeping objection to a National Bank . . . it often has been urged, and doubtless will be again, that such a bank is unconstitutional," Lincoln told a Springfield audience in

December 1839. "Our opponents say, there is no *express* authority in the Constitution to establish a bank," Lincoln observed, but as a good Whig, he replied,
"The Constitution enumerates expressly several powers which Congress may
exercise, superadded to which is a general authority 'to make all laws necessary
and proper,' for carrying into effect all the powers vested by the Constitution of
the Government of the United States." A national banking system was as good
a means of satisfying that need as any of the simple substitutes the Democrats
were proposing; therefore, on Lincoln's expansive logic, "is it not clearly within
the constitutional power of Congress to do so?"[13]

But this only meant that he read the Constitution as a Whig might read it,
not that he had no regard for it whatsoever. Far from it: his first brief sliver of
national notoriety was his attempt, during his solitary term in Congress, to
force President James K. Polk to reveal his own constitutional high-handed-
ness in triggering the Mexican War, riding roughshod over "the provision of
the Constitution giving the war-making power to Congress." But *as* a Whig,
he was also inclined to read the Constitution as more than merely a procedural document, which secured liberty but refused to do more than express
neutrality on what was done with that liberty. The same spirit in the Whigs
which looked to create a powerful economic republic also looked to sponsor
a powerful spirit of nationalism, which would triumph in the creation of a
single American national identity rather than a diversity of local, regional,
or state identities. "I wish to be no less than National in all the positions I
may take," he said in 1854. What Lincoln found great in Henry Clay was that
"Whatever he did, he did for the whole country. . . . Feeling, as he did, and
as the truth surely is, that the world's best hope depended on the continued
Union of these States, he was ever jealous of, and watchful for, whatever might
have the slightest tendency to separate them." And taken one step further, the
Whigs also encouraged the creation of unified concepts of public morality and
attracted large-scale support from Protestant evangelicals who feared that the
Democrats, in the name of personal liberty, had simply become the party of
moral indifference to right and wrong.[14]

Lincoln never professed very much in the way of religion; but almost as a
way of compensating for his lack of religious profile, he cultivated an unbend-
ing moral uprightness which won him the reputation, which has come down
even to our times, as what his Springfield law partner William Herndon called
"a safe counselor, a good lawyer, and an honest man in all the walks of life."
And it was his moralism which led him into conflict, after 1854, with slavery.
Lincoln's opposition to slavery always had strong moral overtones. "I have
always hated slavery," he declared in his great debates with Douglas in 1858;
and in 1854, he explained, "I object to it because it assumes that there CAN be
MORAL RIGHT in the enslaving of one man by another."[15]

Lincoln did not articulate just what constituted the basis of that moral outrage. (As Southern defenders of slavery delighted to point out, the Bible was singularly silent on condemning slavery, so it would be difficult for him to find a source for antislavery moralism there.) Certainly, one part of this moral loathing for slavery was Lincoln's tendency to associate slaveholding with low-life, nouveau riche forms of loose moral living. He once told a political ally that slavery "was the most glittering ostentatious & displaying property in the world" and was "highly seductive to the thoughtless and giddy headed young men who looked upon work as vulgar and ungentlemanly." And in his 1842 temperance society address in Springfield, Lincoln spoke of the "victory" of reason arriving only "when there shall be neither a slave nor a drunkard on the earth"—implying that slavery and drunkenness were twins.[16]

Another, larger claim for moral indignation was that slavery violated natural law and natural theology. "I think that if anything can be proved by natural theology, it is that slavery is morally wrong." But above all other moral codes, slavery violated the spirit of the Declaration of Independence, and it was in this context—as a contradiction of the secular morality of the Declaration of Independence—that the Declaration first begins to assume, in the 1850s, a significant place in Lincoln's rhetoric. "To us it appears natural to think that slaves are human beings; men, not property," Lincoln said in New Haven in 1860, "that some of the things, at least, stated about men in the declaration of independence apply to them as well as to us." In that case, the enslavement of blacks was a step away from the moral road of the Declaration, and a step away from liberty and toward the enslavement of everyone. "Then we may truly despair of the universality of freedom, or the efficacy of those sacred principles enunciated by our fathers—and give in our adhesion to the perpetuation and unlimited extension of slavery." Slavery was a moral spot on the garment of freedom as laid down in the Declaration. "Our republican robe is soiled, and trailed in the dust," he said in October 1854, in the tones of a parson demanding repentance from his flock: "Let us repurify it. Let us turn and wash it white, in the spirit, if not the blood of the Revolution. . . . Let us readopt the Declaration of Independence, and with it, the practices, and policy, which harmonize with it." Only that will save the Republic from the embarrassment of slavery; and in that case, "we shall have so saved it, that the succeeding millions of free happy people, the world over, shall rise up, and call us blessed, to the latest generation."[17]

The standard Democratic response was to point out that, morality and the Declaration notwithstanding, the Constitution sanctioned slavery, left it untouched in the States where it was legal and maybe even untouchable everywhere else, too. As legal historian Paul Finkelman has remarked, "The word 'slavery' was never mentioned in the Constitution, yet its presence was felt everywhere." The slaveholding states were granted extra representation in Congress based on a census count of three-fifths of their slave populations; recovery of slave runaways—euphemistically described as persons "held to Service or Labour"—was made a matter of interstate comity throughout the Union; the Atlantic slave trade was guaranteed existence for twenty years; and the Constitution's prohibition on export duties granted unearned favors to slave-based agricultural products.[18]

Some of the most extreme Southern Democrats argued that the Declaration not only had nothing to do with the Constitution, but it had actually been a philosophical mistake for the United States to adopt such ideas in its founding documents. Northern Democrats, like Lincoln's great Illinois rival, Stephen A. Douglas, would not go so far as to reject the Declaration out of hand, but they would argue that the Declaration's ideas about freedom and equality applied only to white people. "In my opinion the signers of the Declaration [of Independence] had no reference to the negro whatever when they declared all men to be created equal," Douglas remarked in the great debates of 1858. And this left him free to deal with the Constitution purely as a procedural document which made no claims to any moral judgments whatsoever. It was not that Douglas actually favored slavery; it was that he believed that the rights of black people were "a question which each State of this Union must decide for itself." This was because "our Government was formed on the principle of diversity in the local institutions and laws, and not on that of uniformity."[19]

The response of many antislavery Whigs in the 1840s and Republicans in the 1850s was to concede this point and flee from the Constitution to the Declaration as some sort of alternative standard of government.[20] And for Lincoln, too, the Declaration surfaces in the 1850s as a vital authority to appeal to when Democrats reached out to white racial prejudice as a way of silencing Northern unease with slavery. But Lincoln showed no sign that he believed the Constitution now had to be reshelved to a lower point, or that he had ever believed other than that the Constitution was a moral document, with moral implications about liberty and equality which coincided perfectly with the Declaration.

As the image of the apple of gold and the picture of silver indicates, Lincoln believed that the Declaration and the Constitution needed each other. The Declaration was a statement of foundational natural rights and natural rights which were shared everywhere by every human being. But it was not, and could not be, a statement about civil or political rights, which were a different thing altogether. "I have said that I do not understand the Declaration to mean that all men were created equal in all respects"—the details of specific *civil* and political rights were up to each community to grant. And the granting of such rights was very much a power left to the states in the early nineteenth century, within the very general framework of the federal Constitution. Even up through the last weeks of his life, Lincoln was reluctant to commit the federal government to a national statement about black civil rights, because the Constitution gave the federal government no power to delimit those rights. (Not that Lincoln had *no* concern for black civil rights: this is why he delicately pestered Reconstruction governors like Michael Hahn to enfranchise the freedmen, because civil rights like the franchise were understood, before the Reconstruction Amendments, to be the proper constitutional bailiwick of the states.)

But in the basic natural rights that belonged to everyone, Lincoln believed that blacks and whites alike shared a common, equal ground which forever forbade one race from enslaving the other. "Though it does not declare that all men are equal in their attainments or social position, yet no sane man will attempt to deny that the African upon his own soil has all the natural rights that instrument vouchsafes to all mankind." And in no case was that natural equality more evident than in the case of economic rights. Every man, "in the right to put into his mouth the bread that his own hands have earned . . . is the equal of every other man, white or black."[21]

This did not mean, however, that the Declaration and the Constitution were two entirely different sorts of document, the one strictly about ideas and the other strictly about technical process. A close reading of the historical context of the Constitution would demonstrate that the Constitution was animated by the same moral commitment to liberty as the Declaration. True, the Constitution gave some measure of legal sanction to slavery, but this was only because the choice in 1787 was between making those concessions and getting a national Constitution, or a descent into national anarchy and misrule; and only because the authors who made those concessions made them in the expectation that slavery would gradually die out anyway on its own. "You may examine the debates under the Constitution and in the first session of Congress and you will not find a single man saying that Slavery is a good thing," Lincoln wrote in 1859. "They all believed it was an evil."[22]

Whatever indirect immunities the Constitution originally conferred upon slavery, "I believe that the right of property in a slave is *not* distinctively and expressly affirmed in the Constitution." For instance: "there was nothing said in the Constitution relative to the spread of slavery in the Territories, but the same generation of men said something about it in [the] ordinance of [17]87," the Northwest Ordinance which restricted the spread of slavery into the old Northwest Territory. What was more, "they placed a provision in the Constitution which they supposed would gradually remove the disease by cutting off its source. This was the abolition of the slave trade," once the initial twenty-year sanction for it had expired.

A European, be he ever so intelligent, if not familiar with our institutions, might read the Constitution over and over again and never learn that Slavery existed in the United States. The reason is this. The Framers of the Organic Law believed that the Constitution would *outlast* Slavery and they did not want a word there to tell future generations that Slavery had ever been legalized in America.[23]

Lincoln did not feel any necessity for setting the Constitution and the Declaration in tension with each other because he supposed that the common intentions of their common authors on the point of equality and liberty spoke sufficiently well for themselves. And this, he explained, was why he had not stepped forward as an antislavery partisan before 1854 and the adopting of the Kansas-Nebraska bill, permitting the extension of slavery into the Western territories. "I have always hated it, but I have always been quiet about it until this new era of the introduction of the Nebraska bill began. I always believed that everybody was against it, and that it was in the course of ultimate extinction. . . . The adoption of the Constitution and its attendant history led the people to believe so." The "theory of our government is Universal Freedom," Lincoln said in 1854. "'All men are created free and equal,' says the Declaration of Independence. The word 'Slavery' is not found in the Constitution."[24]

And so he continued to believe. Unlike many fellow Republicans, Lincoln would not demand an end to the obnoxious provisions of the Fugitive Slave Law of 1850, because however much he disliked the operation of it, it was guaranteed to the South under the Constitution. As Lincoln wrote Joshua Speed in 1855, "I confess I hate to see the poor creatures hunted down, and caught, and carried back to their stripes, and unrewarded toils." But "I also acknowledge *your* rights and *my* obligations, under the constitution, in regard to your slaves," and he wanted Speed to appreciate "how much the great body of the Northern people do crucify their feelings, in order to maintain their loyalty to the constitution and the Union." Lincoln declared at the end of the Lincoln-Douglas debates, "I have neither assailed, nor wrestled with any part of the constitution. The legal right of the Southern people to reclaim their fugitives I have constantly admitted. The legal right of Congress to interfere with the institution in these states, I have constantly denied." In 1859, he actually advised Salmon Chase to restrain the Ohio state Republican committee from asking for a repeal of the Fugitive Slave Law to be included in the 1860 Republican national campaign platform. "The U.S. Constitution declares that a fugitive slave *shall be delivered up.*"[25]

But to argue from that premise that the Constitution somehow gave slavery the broad right to plant itself in new areas and sprout new dominions for itself, under the shelter of Douglas's argument that the Constitution made no moral judgments about what people did in those new dominions, was actually a denial of the Constitution's true purpose of implementing the Declaration's natural-rights philosophy. Even when the infamous *Dred Scott* decision in 1857 seemed to suggest that the Constitution actually did protect the extension of slavery into the territories, Lincoln refused to see it as any reason to surrender confidence in the ultimate justice of the Constitution. In his mind, *Dred Scott* was not an interpretation of the Constitution but a perversion of it.

> If this important decision had been made by the unanimous concurrence of the judges, and without any apparent partisan bias . . . it then might be, perhaps would be, factious, even revolutionary, to not acquiesce in it as a precedent. But when, as it is true we find it wanting in all these claims to the public confidence, it is not resistance, it is not factious, it is not even disrespectful, to treat it as not having yet quite established a settled doctrine for the country.

And yet, even at that moment, Lincoln would not call for defiance of the Court, but rather for patience in awaiting a new decision. "We do not propose that when Dred Scott is decided to be a slave, that we will raise a mob to make him free," Lincoln warned during the Lincoln-Douglas debates. "If there be any man in the Republican party who is impatient . . . of the constitutional guarantees thrown around it, and would act in disregard of these . . . that man is misplaced, and ought to leave us."[26] This is not what we expect to hear from a man who sits lightly by the Constitution. But it is what we expect to hear from one who believes that the Constitution was written to pursue, more than just procedural goals, a set of moral goals.

For Lincoln, the place of the Declaration of Independence as an "apple of gold" was not intended to diminish the importance of the Constitution as a "picture of silver"; nor was a description of the Constitution as a means to realizing the goals set out in the Declaration a way of writing off the Constitution. Much as he appealed to Douglas's followers in 1856 to "Throw off these things, and come to the rescue of this great principle of equality," he also added, "Don't interfere with anything in the Constitution. That must be maintained, for it is the only safeguard of our liberties." Nor was he exaggerating for political effect when, en route to his inauguration in 1861, he remarked, "When I shall speak authoritatively, I hope to say nothing inconsistent with the Constitution, the union, the rights of all the States, of each State, and of each section of the country." Moreover, as an "old Henry Clay Whig," he persisted in taking a minimalist view of his own powers as president under the Constitution. "My political education strongly inclines me against a very free use of any of these means, by the Executive, to control the legislation of the country. As a rule, I think it better that congress should originate, as well as perfect its measures, without external bias."[27]

The tragedy of what happened with the secession of the Southern states and the beginning of the Civil War was that, with such views of the Constitution, Lincoln as president was actually a better safeguard for the continued existence of slavery in the South than secession. If it were a case, Lincoln explained in his First Inaugural, where a majority was forcibly depriving a minority of their constitutional rights, secession—or rather, revolution—might well be justified. "But such is not our case. All the vital rights of minorities, and of individuals, are so plainly assured to them . . . in the Constitution, that controversies never arise concerning them." Nor should they be worried that his private intentions might somehow subvert these rights. "By the frame of the government under which we live, this same people have wisely given their public servants but little power for mischief; and have, with equal wisdom, provided for the return of that little to their own hands at very short intervals."[28] Just as only Nixon could have gone to China, only Lincoln, with the moral weight of the Republican Party, could have enforced national respect for the constitutional safeguards that prevented interference with Southern slavery.

But this did not happen, and secession plunged the nation into a situation for which the Constitution granted little guidance. Just as the Constitution granted no right to secede, it granted the president no direction about how to proceed with the seceders. His guiding star in that case, however, was the fact of the Constitution itself and his insistence that the Constitution was permanent and unbreakable. "My opinion is that no state can, in any way lawfully, get out of the Union, without the consent of the others," he told Thurlow Weed in 1860, "and that it is the duty of the President, and other government functionaries to run the machine as it is." Just as slavery was a violation of the spirit of the Declaration, secession was a violation of the whole idea of constitutional government. "A majority, held in restraint by constitutional checks, and limitations, and always changing, with deliberate changes of popular opinions and sentiments, is the only true sovereign of a free people." But secession was an insult to the notion of majority rule and constitutional government, a flight "to anarchy or despotism."[29]

The constitutional uncertainties of dealing with secession led Lincoln into a series of actions in the spring of 1861 which were, by his own public admission, of debatable constitutionality in peacetime: suspending the writ of habeas corpus, authorizing the raising of a national army, spending public money to buy supplies, imposing a blockade. What Lincoln reminded his critics was that this was not peacetime, but war, and war of such a nature that no one who wrote the Constitution had ever anticipated, and war that had broken out while Congress was not only between sessions but in the midst of completing congressional elections. (Lincoln's decision in April not to call a special session of Congress before July 4, 1861, was dictated in large measure by the fact that, under the old staggered system of congressional elections, a number of key border-state congressional districts had not yet finished balloting for new representatives.) Similarly, the exigencies of the war meant that the executive branch of the government swelled to unprecedented size under Lincoln's administration, leading Lincoln's critics to claim that Lincoln was the original author of "big government." But these charges generally miss how dramatically the federal government shrank back to its prewar proportions after 1865 and stayed that way for another half century. Congress, fully as much as the executive branch, filled the role of "big government" during the war: each wartime Congress, the 37th and 38th, doubled the number of bills passed by the record 27th Congress of 1841–43. But once the war was over, an equally massive retrenchment became the order of the day.[30]

It also needs remembering how comparatively limited Lincoln's early extraconstitutional wartime gestures were. The original unilateral suspensions of the writ of habeas corpus were only operative in areas of military confrontation; the recruiting and supplying of the armies were submitted to Congress for *post facto* approval, and, despite the clamor of offended Democrats during the war, wartime arrests and limitations of civil liberties were extraordinarily few, especially by comparison with the Red Scares and wholesale confinement of Japanese Americans in the twentieth century's American wars. And one good measure of Lincoln's cautious constitutionalism is the care with which he strove to justify even these measures. He was meticulous in seeking out legal opinions to support actions as commander in chief as minor as the appointment of a temperance representative as an officer or the remission of a fine imposed on a restaurant owner for selling brandy to a wounded soldier; he rigidly segregated those decisions which he believed as commander in chief he needed to take to "best subdue the enemy" from those meddling in "the permanent legislative functions of the government."[31]

Like his Whig predecessors, Lincoln was troubled by any expansion of government built on nothing more than raw executive power. The adoption of measures on the sole ground that "I think the measure politically expedient, and morally right" bothered Lincoln. "Would I not thus give up all footing upon constitution or law? Would I not thus be in the boundless field of absolutism? Would it not lose us . . . the very cause we seek to advance?" And he submitted himself to the most obvious of all tests of constitutionality, the reelection campaign of 1864, which he could easily have suspended by bayonet, although it never seems even to have crossed his mind as a possibility. In fact, his only recorded discussion about a response to an unfavorable electoral verdict was the extraction of a promise from all his cabinet that they would abide by the legal results. As Don Fehrenbacher remarked, "he placed the principle of self-govern-ment above even his passion for the Union" and "affirmed his adherence to the most critical and most fragile principle in the democratic process—namely, the requirement of minority submission to majority will."[32]

It was, in fact, a matter of frustration to the most radical members of Lincoln's own party that he seemed so unwilling to step out from behind the Constitution and deal with the Confederate states as they thought he ought to do. Despite the clamor of Charles Sumner, Ben Wade, and Zachariah Chandler in Congress, Lincoln never seriously entertained any notion of destroying the identity of the rebel states, and he aimed at a speedy reconstruction with those states' identities intact. He issued the Emancipation Proclamation only after he had satisfied his own mind that it could be applied strictly as a military measure, under his own authority as commander in chief in time of war, and only with strict application to those parts of the Confederacy still in actual rebellion.

Even then, his preface to the proclamation identified its "object" as "prac-tically restoring the constitutional relation between the United States, and each of the states . . . in which states that relation is, or may be suspended, or disturbed." (He refused, for instance, Salmon Chase's urging to extend the proclamation to federally occupied parts of Virginia and Louisiana on the grounds that these areas were no longer under his purview as military zones, and that the proclamation "has no constitutional or legal justification, except as a military measure.") He admitted to Alexander Stephens at the Hampton Roads Conference in February 1865, "that as the proclamation was a war measure and would have effect only from its being an exercise of the war power, as soon as the war ceased, it would be inoperative for the future. It would be held to apply only to such slaves as had come under its operation while it was in active exercise. . . . So far as he was concerned, he should leave it to the courts to decide." He appeared, as Mark Neely has remarked, "to some antislavery advocates at the time and to many historians since to have been strangely stricken with a paralyzing constitutional scrupulousness."[33] Conscious of his constitutional limitations as president, rather than simply attempt to enforce it by bayonet, Lincoln turned in 1864 to having emancipa-tion, in more sweeping form, written into the Constitution as the Thirteenth Amendment. It is hardly likely that a "dictator," or an egalitarian ideologue who believed that the Declaration of Independence trumped all questions, would even have bothered.

There is no easy formula for describing the living connection between Lin-coln's well-known awe for the Declaration and his restrained constitutionalism. It is doubtful whether he himself had one, at least explicitly, and his best effort at describing it was only a biblical metaphor. He had no constitutional theory as such, if only because he believed that the original intent of the Founders was actually quite easy to discover in the text of the Constitution and in the writings of the Founders—which, preeminently, included the Declaration of Independence. But he was convinced that such a connection existed, that as the Declaration set out a political ideal for all Americans, the Constitution remained the single greatest vehicle for realizing, implementing, and occasionally restraining that ideal.

This does not make Lincoln, by any stretch of the imagination, into either Kendall's or Wills's closet revolutionary, undermining a Constitution that he resented as an obstacle to either ambition or liberty. Gideon Welles, Lincoln's secretary of the navy and a former Democrat who was keen to scent Republican improprieties, remarked that

> Mr. Lincoln . . . though nominally a Whig in the past, had respect for the Constitution, loved the federal Union, and had a sacred regard for the rights of the States. . . . War two years after secession brought emancipation, but emancipation did not dissolve the Union, consolidate the Government, or clothe it with absolute power; nor did it impair the authority and rights which the States had reserved. Emancipation was a necessary, not a revolutionary measure, forced upon the Administration by the secessionists themselves, who insisted that slavery which was local and sectional should be made national.

It is one of the great oddities of modern American life that (as Michael Sandel has written) our political discourse has tended to follow, not the path of Lincoln, but the path of Stephen A. Douglas, toward insisting that the Constitution provides only a procedural framework in which morally unencumbered individuals scream in protest at any attempt to "legislate morality."[34] To the extent that Sandel is right, perhaps Abraham Lincoln is a revolutionary after all, for our times, if not for his own.

Notes

This essay first appeared in *The Lincoln Enigma: The Changing Faces of an American Icon*, edited by Gabor Boritt (Oxford University Press, 2001).

1. Lincoln, "To Alexander H. Stephens," December 22, 1860, in *The Collected Works of Abraham Lincoln*, ed. Roy P. Basler (New Brunswick, NJ, 1953–55, 4:160–61; A. H. Stephens, *A Constitutional View of the Late War between the States* (Philadelphia, 1870, 2:266–70, 447; Thomas E. Schott, *Alexander H. Stephens of Georgia: A Biography* (Baton Rouge, 1988), 309–10.

2. Lincoln, "Fragment on the Constitution and the Union," in *Collected Works*, 4:168–69.

3. Lincoln, "Speech at Peoria, Illinois," October 16, 1854, "To James M. Brown," October 18, 1858, and "Speech in Independence Hall," February 22, 1861, in *Collected Works* 2:255, 3:327, 4:240; Joseph R. Fornieri, "Lincoln's Political Faith in the Peoria

Address," in *Lincoln Revisited: New Insights from the Lincoln Forum*, ed. John Y. Simon et al. (New York, 2007), 6; Douglas L. Wilson, *Lincoln's Sword: The Presidency and the Power of Words* (New York, 2006), 203–8; William Lee Miller, *Lincoln's Virtues: An Ethical Biography* (New York, 2002), 374.

4. Alexander H. Stephens, "Cornerstone Address," in *Southern Pamphlets on Secession, November 1860–April 1861*, ed. Jon L. Wakelyn (Chapel Hill, NC, 1996), 405–6; Daniel Farber, *Lincoln's Constitution* (Chicago, 2003), 103.

5. Leo de Alvarez, preface to *Abraham Lincoln, the Gettysburg Address and American Constitutionalism*, ed. Laurence Berns et al. (Irving, TX, 1976), 1; Willmoore Kendall, "Equality: Commitment or Ideal?" *Intercollegiate Review* 24 (Spring 1989): 27–28; Gottfried Dietze, in Merrill Peterson, *Lincoln in American Memory* (New York, 1994), 333–34; Dwight G. Anderson, "Quest for Immortality: A Theory of Abraham Lincoln's Political Psychology," in *The Historian's Lincoln: Pseudohistory, Psychohistory, and History*, ed. Gabor Boritt (Urbana, IL, 1988), 265, 267, 268, 269.

6. Peterson, *Lincoln in American Memory*, 299–300; Mark E. Neely, *The Fate of Liberty: Abraham Lincoln and Civil Liberties* (New York, 1991), 226–31; Garry Wills, *Lincoln at Gettysburg: The Words That Remade America* (New York, 1992), 38–39, 145–46. See Mark Tushnet, *Taking the Constitution away from the Courts* (Princeton, NJ, 1999); Charles L. Black, *A New Birth of Freedom: Human Rights, Names and Unnamed* (New York, 1998); George Fletcher, *Our Secret Constitution: How Lincoln Redefined American Democracy* (New York, 2001), 68, 80; Andrew McLaughlin, "Lincoln, the Constitution and Democracy," in *Abraham Lincoln Association Papers* (Springfield, IL, 1937), 29–30; Howard Jones, *Abraham Lincoln and a New Birth of Freedom: The Union and Slavery in the Diplomacy of the Civil War* (Lincoln, NE, 1999), 15; Philip Paludan, *The Presidency of Abraham Lincoln* (Lawrence, KS, 1994), 18–19, and "Lincoln and the Rhetoric of Politics," in *A Crisis of Republicanism: American Politics in the Civil War Era*, ed. Lloyd Ambrosius (Lincoln, NE, 1990), 77; Harry V. Jaffa, *A New Birth of Freedom: Abraham Lincoln and the Coming of the Civil War* (Lanham, MD, 2000), 502.

7. Lincoln, "To Anton C. Hesing, Henry Wendt, Alexander Fisher, Committee," June 30, 1858, in *Collected Works*, 2:475.

8. Orestes Brownson, in Lawrence Kohl, *The Politics of Individualism: Parties and the American Character in the Jacksonian Era* (New York, 1989), 109; Patrick W. Carey, *Orestes A. Brownson: American Religious Weathervane* (Grand Rapids, MI, 2004), 53.

9. William Leggett, "Separation of Bank and State," May 27, 1837, in *Democratick Editorials: Essays in Jacksonian Political Economy by William Leggett*, ed. L. W. White (Indianapolis, IN, 1984), 142.

10. Daniel Feller, *The Jacksonian Promise: America, 1815–1840* (Baltimore, 1995), 33–52; Daniel Walker Howe, *The Political Culture of the American Whigs* (Chicago, 1979), 23.

11. Lincoln, "Address before the Wisconsin State Agricultural Society, Milwaukee, Wisconsin,," September 30, 1859, in *Collected Works*, 3:472–73; Gabor S.

Boritt, *Lincoln and the Economics of the American Dream* (Memphis, TN, 1978), 79–91; Lucius E. Chittenden, in *Recollected Words of Abraham Lincoln*, ed. Don and Virginia Fehrenbacher (Stanford, CA, 1996), 99; Olivier Fraysse, *Lincoln, Land and Labor, 1809–60*, trans. Sylvia Neely (Chicago, 1994), 30–32.

12. Lincoln, "On the Perpetuation of Our Political Institutions," January 27, 1838, and "Speech in United States House of Representatives on Internal Improvements," June 20, 1848, in *Collected Works,* 1:115, 488.

13. Lincoln, "Speech on the Sub-Treasury," in *Collected Works,* 1:171–72; Paul Angle, *"Here I Have Lived": A History of Lincoln's Springfield* (Chicago, 1971), 110–11; Boritt, *Lincoln and the Economics of the American Dream,* 65–71; Douglas L. Wilson, *Honor's Voice: The Transformation of Abraham Lincoln* (New York, 1998), 200–201.

14. Lincoln, "To William Herndon," February 15, 1848, "Speech at Peoria, Illinois," October 16, 1854, and "Eulogy on Henry Clay," July 6, 1852," in *Collected Works,* 1:451, 2:126, 130, 248; Michael Lind, *What Lincoln Believed: The Values and Convictions of America's Greatest President* (New York, 2004), 88–100; John Channing Briggs, *Lincoln's Speeches Reconsidered* (Baltimore, 2005), 122–23; Stewart Winger, *Lincoln, Religion, and Romantic Cultural Politics* (DeKalb, IL, 2003), 81–85.

15. William H. Herndon, "Lincoln in Springfield," in *The Hidden Lincoln: From the Letters and Papers of William H. Herndon,* ed. Emmanuel Hertz (New York, 1938), 424; Lincoln, "Speech at Peoria," October 16, 1854, in *Collected Works,* 2:274.

16. Gillespie to William H. Herndon, in *Herndon's Informants: Letters, Interviews, and Statements about Abraham Lincoln,* ed. Douglas L. Wilson and Rodney O. Davis (Urbana, IL, 1998), 183; Lincoln, "Temperance Address," February 22, 1842, in *Collected Works,* 1:279.

17. Pauline Maier, *American Scripture: Making the Declaration of Independence* (New York, 1997), 202; Lincoln, "Speech in Hartford, Connecticut," March 5, 1860, "Speech in New Haven, Connecticut," March 6, 1860, "Speech in Peoria, Illinois," and "Speech at Carlinville," August 31, 1858, in *Collected Works,* 2:222, 276, 3:81, 4:3, 16; Farber, *Lincoln's Constitution,* 11; Joseph R. Fornieri, *Abraham Lincoln's Political Faith* (DeKalb, IL, 2003), 37.

18. Rush Welter, *The Mind of America, 1820–1860* (New York, 1975), 419; Jean Baker, *Affairs of Party: The Political Culture of Northern Democrats in the Mid-Nineteenth Century* (Ithaca, NY, 1983), 153; Paul Finkelman, *Slavery and the Founders: Race and Liberty in the Age of Jefferson* (Armonk, NY, 1996), 31–32; Don E. Fehrenbacher, *The Slaveholding Republic: An Account of the United States Government's Relations to Slavery* (New York, 2001), 12–13.

19. "Mr. Douglas's Speech," in "The Jonesboro Debate," in *The Lincoln-Douglas Debates of 1858,* ed. E. E. Sparks (Springfield, IL, 1908), 224–26; David Zarefsky, *Lincoln, Douglas and Slavery: In the Crucible of Public Debate* (Chicago, 1990), 173.

20. J. David Greenstone, *The Lincoln Persuasion: Remaking American Liberalism* (Princeton, NJ, 1993), 241; Harold Hyman, *A More Perfect Union: The Impact of the Civil War and Reconstruction on the Constitution* (New York, 1973), 59.

21. Lincoln, "Speech at Carlinville, Illinois," August 31, 1858, and "Speech in Springfield, Illinois," July 17, 1858, in *Collected Works,* 2:520, 3:79.

22. George Anastaplo, "Slavery and the Federal Convention of 1787," in *Abraham Lincoln: A Constitutional Biography* (Lanham, MD, 1999), 61, 66; Lincoln, "Speech at Elwood, Kansas," November 30, 1859, in *Collected Works,* 3:496.

23. "Mr. Lincoln's Reply," in "The Galesburg Debate," in Sparks, *Lincoln-Douglas Debates,* 359; Lincoln, "Speech in Indianapolis," September 19, 1859, "Speech at Springfield, Illinois," October 4, 1854, and "Speech at Elwood, Kansas," November 30, 1859, in *Collected Works,* 2:245, 3:456, 496.

24. Lincoln, "Speech in Chicago," July 10, 1858, and "Speech at Springfield," October 4, 1854, in *Collected Works,* 2:245, 492.

25. Lincoln, "To Joshua F. Speed," August 24, 1855, "Speech in Springfield," October 30, 1858, and "To Salmon P. Chase," June 9, 1859, in *Collected Works,* 3:320, 334, 384.

26. Lincoln, "Speech at Springfield, Illinois," June 26, 1857, in *Collected Works,* 2:401; "Mr. Lincoln's Speech," in "The Quincy Debate," in Sparks, *Lincoln-Douglas Debates,* 405.

27. Lincoln, "Speech at Kalamazoo, Michigan," August 27, 1856, "Speech in Buffalo, New York," February 18, 1861, and "Speech at Pittsburgh, Pennsylvania," February 15, 1861, in *Collected Works,* 2:366, 4:214, 221.

28. Lincoln, "First Inaugural Address—Final Text," March 4, 1861, in *Collected Works,* 4:267, 270.

29. Lincoln, "To Thurlow Weed," December 17, 1860, "Message to Congress in Special Session," July 4, 1861, and "First Inaugural Address—Final Text," March 4, 1861, in *Collected Works,* 4:153, 430, 268.

30. Paludan, *Presidency of Abraham Lincoln,* 109; Mark R. Wilson, *The Business of Civil War: Military Mobilization and the State, 1860–1865* (Baltimore, 2006), 202–3.

31. Lincoln, "To Simon Cameron," July 17, 1861, "To Edward Bates," June 15, 1862, "Reply to Emancipation Memorial Presented by Chicago Christians of All Denominations," September 13, 1862, and "To Orville H. Browning," September 22, 1861, in *Collected Works,* 4:451, 532 and 5:271, 421.

32. Lincoln, "To Salmon P. Chase," September 2, 1863, in *Collected Works,* 6:429; Don E. Fehrenbacher, "Lincoln and the Constitution," in *Lincoln in Text and Context: Collected Essays* (Stanford, CA, 1987), 127.

33. Lincoln, "Preliminary Emancipation Proclamation," September 22, 1862, and "To Salmon P. Chase," September 2, 1863, in *Collected Works,* 5:433–34, 6:428; Stephens, *Constitutional View,* 2:610; Neely, *Fate of Liberty,* 218.

34. Gideon Welles, "Administration of Abraham Lincoln, I," in *Selected Essays by Gideon Welles: Lincoln's Administration,* ed. Albert Mordell (New York, 1960), 72–73; Michael Sandel, *Democracy's Discontent: America in Search of a Public Philosophy* (Cambridge, MA, 1994), 24–25.

7

UNDERSTANDING EMANCIPATION: LINCOLN'S PROCLAMATION AND THE END OF SLAVERY

The most common trope which governs understanding of Abraham Lincoln and emancipation is that of *progress*. The variations on this trope are legion, and they include notions of Lincoln's *journey* toward emancipation, his *growth* in understanding the justice of emancipation, or his *path* to the Emancipation Proclamation. "Lincoln was," as Horace Greeley put it, "a growing man," growing in this case from a stance of moral indifference and ignorance at the time of his election in 1860, toward deep conviction about African American freedom by the time of the Emancipation Proclamation, less than two years later. This was a generous sentiment, since it credited Lincoln with being "breathtaking in his advance from prewar advocacy of restricting slavery's spread to foremost responsibility for slavery's total, immediate, uncompensated destruction by constitutional amendment."[1]

But it was also an unconvincing one, since a *journey* may not be about *growth* at all if it is an unwilling one, or one guided purely by opportunism. Neo-Beardian historians like Richard Hofstadter read Lincoln as a political poseur for whom *growth* was synonymous with a keen eye for the main chance.[2] In the backwash of the civil rights movement, embittered dissenters within the African American world brooded over the casual racism which accompanied Lincoln's prewar utterances on slavery and wondered why they should offer homage to a white man whose principal act of emancipation was limited to slaves he could not free, while ignoring the plight of the slaves he could. "Lincoln grew during the war," conceded *Ebony* editor Lerone Bennett in a sensational article on Lincoln in 1968, "but he didn't grow much. On every issue relating to the black man . . . he was the very essence of the white supremacist with good intentions."[3]

In the face of such skepticism, a second—and even more generous—trope has been applied to Lincoln which finds him not *growing*, but *waiting*. In this scenario, Lincoln already possesses in 1861 all the racial goodwill necessary for emancipation but *waits* until the right moment in the war, or the right moment in the growth of Northern acceptance of the idea of emancipation. Lincoln "saw the time of emancipation coming" and was "quick to see the tendency of the public mind," said Lincoln's earliest serious biographer, Josiah G. Holland, in 1866. "He was clearing away obstacles, and preparing his ground" for emancipation. He was (in a more recent version by LaWanda Cox) "cautious, advancing one step at a time, and indirect, exerting influence behind the scenes." This has had the advantage of casting Lincoln as a sort of political seer, biding his time until the nation can see the future as clearly as he sees it, and it turns his yearlong delay in issuing the proclamation into a compliment to his political wisdom. But it also has generated its share of disappointment, since unappeased critics wanted to know how long one should *wait* to do right. "After all, he came into office in 1861. How come it took him two whole years to free the slaves?" asked a suspicious Julius Lester in 1968. "His pen was sitting on his desk the whole time."[4]

But a better reason for skepticism about these tropes is that there is so little evidence behind them. The Radicals of Lincoln's own party found his refusal to embrace immediate abolition infuriating; they never spoke of Lincoln in terms of *progress* or *waiting*, but instead in terms of "imbecility," "perverseness," or "vacillation." Those who had been closest to Lincoln both before and during the war believed that, far from needing *growth*, Lincoln arrived in the presidency fully committed to implementing an emancipation program, and without *waiting*. Lincoln, wrote Isaac Arnold in 1866, "had it in his mind for a long time to war upon slavery until its destruction was effected." But the most important testimony comes from Lincoln himself. "I have always thought that all men should be free," he insisted in 1865. "I am naturally anti-slavery," he told Albert Hodges and Thomas Bramlette in 1864. "If slavery is not wrong, nothing is wrong. I can not remember when I did not so think, and feel." Far from having waited for the right moment to issue the proclamation, Lincoln was sure that the moment could not have been more politically inapt. "When I issued that proclamation," Lincoln frankly told Methodist educator John McClintock, "I was in great doubt about it myself. I did not think that the people had been quite educated up to it, and I feared its effects upon the border states."[5]

Nevertheless, the prevailing view of Lincoln and emancipation has been almost entirely governed by these tropes, as almost any biography of Lincoln written in the last hundred years will attest. They are intended as a shield to Lincoln's iconic place in American historical consciousness. But they also serve to diminish that place by substituting a shorthand character analysis for political perception. Understanding the Emancipation Proclamation rests, not with Lincoln's "vacillation" or his "patience" or even with Lincoln himself, but with the varieties of emancipation on offer at the onset of the Civil War, the legal mechanisms necessary to give emancipation permanence, the necessity of keeping the question out of the hands of the federal court system once the war was over, and the vastly underestimated political instability threatened by General George B. McClellan and the Army of the Potomac from July to November 1862.

From those complexities, however, two things become apparent: First, that Lincoln had determined that his presidency would be the one which finally drew the line which would permanently contain slavery. The Kansas-Nebraska Act would be overturned and the territories of the old Louisiana Purchase would be reserved solely for free settlement. In theory, once those territories achieved statehood, they had the sovereign right then to legalize slavery, but Lincoln could not believe that any territory, once free, would "do such an extraordinary thing as to adopt a Slave Constitution." And none did.[6]

Second, that once slavery's growth was contained, federally funded programs of gradual, compensated emancipation would be dangled in front of the border states, where slavery had the weakest hold, setting up a process which would, with increasing speed, peacefully eliminate slavery by the end of the century. Under this system, the slave states would do the work of emancipation themselves, without the legal risks which would result from federal emancipation, and the federal government would only have to provide the self-interested motive of money. But once again, none did—which is why there had to be an Emancipation Proclamation.

Although the Emancipation Proclamation is routinely spoken of as though it were a single document, there are in fact four Emancipation Proclamations—the so-called "First Draft" of July 22, 1862; the "Preliminary" Emancipation Proclamation of September 22, 1862; the final draft, submitted and discussed at the cabinet meetings of December 29 and 31, 1862; and the formal proclamation of January 1, 1863—all of which differ markedly from each other, and some parts of which were not even of Lincoln's composing. But there are also three other Lincoln documents which qualify as emancipation proclamations which are far less well known—the November 1861 plan for compensated emancipation, which Lincoln drew up for George P. Fisher to introduce into the Delaware legislature; the March 6, 1862, joint resolution he drafted for, and presented to, Congress to endorse national compensated emancipation; and the July 14, 1862, bill he drafted for Congress to implement the national compensated emancipation plan. And then there are five other emancipation proclamations, not of Lincoln's authorship and, in some cases, rivals to Lincoln's own plans. These are the local emancipations announced by John Charles Frémont in Missouri and Major General David Hunter in the occupied Carolina coastal districts (and subsequently cancelled by Lincoln), and Congress's own emancipation decrees—the First Confiscation Act of August 1861; the emancipation bill for the District of Columbia in April 1862; and the Second Confiscation Act of July 17, 1862—all of which were described as "emancipation proclamations" in the national press.

Surveying them together, the broad picture which emerges from these documents over the course of thirteen months in 1861 and 1862 is the clarity with which Lincoln's face was set toward emancipation from the first. The time that elapsed between Lincoln's inauguration and the issue of the proclamation was not a question of emancipation itself, nor was it a question of whether emancipation was secondary to the preservation of the Union, nor even the supposed practicability of emancipating slaves lest it jeopardize the Union. It was a question about the *means* of emancipating, and that was complicated in Lincoln's understanding, first by the political and legal entanglements of slavery, and then by the war. No single factor in this was more important in Lincoln's mind than the limited reach of the federal government; slavery was a matter of individual state enactments, and even the slave code which governed the District of Columbia was only an enforcement of the existing Maryland and Virginia codes, not a product of federal statute. "As an anti-slavery man I have a motive to desire emancipation, which pro-slavery men do not have," Lincoln wrote, but "the general government, sets up no claim of a right, by federal authority, to interfere with slavery within state limits, referring, as it does, the absolute control of the subject, in each case, to the state and it's people, immediately interested."[7]

But this did not mean that the federal government could not put motives to emancipate in their minds that would hasten the decision, something which both Lincoln and the Southern secessionists keenly appreciated. Principally, the federal government could offer financial incentives, by providing emancipation subsidies to the slave states, and social incentives, by allowing the state legislatures to set their own emancipation timetables, "making the emancipation gradual and compensating the unwilling owners." Compensation would be costly, but it would not be nearly so costly as civil war. "Mr. Lincoln always contended that the cheapest way of getting rid of slavery," recalled Joseph Gillespie, "was for the nation to buy the slaves & set them free." Similarly, gradualism delayed the promise of full freedom for at least a generation. But in Lincoln's mind, it had the virtue of allowing former slaves and slave owners to find "some practical system by which the two races could gradually live themselves out of their old relation to each other, and both come out better prepared for the new." It also avoided the virtually automatic associations immediate emancipation had with slave insurrection, a racial fantasy which had enormous currency based on the San Domingo slave revolt, Nat Turner's insurrection in 1831, and, ultimately, John Brown's raid on Harper's Ferry. Above all, using compensation and gradualism to solicit the cooperation of the state legislatures would keep emancipation out of the federal courts. In a federal judicial system headed by Chief Justice Roger B. Taney, who only four years before had written the majority opinion in *Dred Scott* and further tried to cripple the Union war effort in *ex parte Merryman* and *Prize Cases*, any unilateral move by Lincoln on the federal level would inevitably generate constitutional challenges that gave presidential emancipation little likelihood of survival. Emancipation must, as Lincoln wrote to Horace Greeley in 1862, have "three main features—gradual—compensation—and [the] vote of the people." With that, Lincoln told Gilbert Greene that "he was quite sure [slavery] would not outlive the century. It seemed to him that gradual emancipation and governmental compensation, would bring it to an end."[8]

Although in his First Inaugural, Lincoln promised to abide by the Fugitive Slave Law of 1850, refrain from thrusting obnoxious appointees into federal positions in the South, and even pose "no objection" to a constitutional amendment "to the effect that the federal government, shall never interfere with the domestic institutions of the States, including that of persons held to service," the fact was that everything he had said about gradual emancipation was perfectly consistent with these apparently conciliatory offers. It was what he did *not* promise—to permit the extension of slavery into the territories, to broaden the fugitive slave statutes, or to back the Crittenden Compromise—which was held decisive by the people for whom it mattered the most, the Southern slaveholders, since they understood that, without such promises, Lincoln was leaving himself all the opportunity he needed to set the national political clock ticking toward emancipation. (This was a tactic Lincoln had often practiced in the Illinois courts: Leonard Swett once remarked that Lincoln was notorious for graciously giving away point after point to opposing counsel until, "when the whole thing is unravelled, the adversary begins to see that what he was so blandly giving away was simply what he couldnt get & Keep. By giving away 6 points and carrying the 7th he carried his case and the whole case hanging on the 7th he traded away every thing which would give him the least [aid] in carrying that").[9]

The most likely place to begin a campaign for gradual, compensated emancipation would be the border states—the slave states of Missouri, Kentucky, Maryland, and Delaware—where slavery was at its weakest; and among the border states, none was weaker in its hold on slavery than Delaware. Once persuade a state like Delaware to adopt emancipation with the carrot of compensation, and the other border states would follow; let slavery disappear from the border states, and slave owners would either have to agree to accept compensation and emancipate their slaves, or else move further south. The more the territory open to slavery shrank, the more slaves would be crowded into it by panicky slaveholders; the more the number of slaves crowded into those states grew, the more their price would decline, until they either became worthless, or until the next round of slave states decided to cut their losses, embrace emancipation, and accept federal compensation.

Nor was this scenario merely speculation. Each of Lincoln's "three main features" was patterned after the gradual emancipation plans adopted by the Northern states between 1780 and 1827 and upon the most successful large-scale emancipation scheme of the day, Britain's emancipation in 1833 of the slaves it held in the West Indies. The West Indian emancipation was both gradual and compensated and enjoyed the support, even if reluctant, of the West Indian assemblies. Its gradualism was embodied in limitations which provided for long-term apprenticeships, and a compensation fund for the West Indian planters cushioned the economic blow of lost capital investment. Compensation was not, as it might seem, a payoff to the planters, so much as it was a cash-flow subsidy which would allow the planters immediately to begin paying wages to black apprentices. Even more significant, the restless-ness of the ex-slaves under apprenticeship forced the telescoping of the terms of apprenticeship from twenty years to four. Emancipation, in every instance in the Western hemisphere, was a process which inevitably acquired its own speed, and every observer of the West Indian scene could understand that even the most halting first step away from slavery always accelerated beyond the timetables and scope of its authors.[10]

The solution to the problem posed by Southern secession from the Union was, on those terms, quite simple: reunite the nation first, either by the North's numerical and military superiority, or by politically undermining the Confed-erate elite. This meant that saving the Union was actually the indispensable means to emancipation (rather than the other way round), since only within the constraints imposed by being part of the Union did Lincoln have any le-verage over the slave states. It also meant that he could not tolerate any effort to stampede him toward more immediate federal solutions, and that included especially the voices that demanded that he use the war as a platform from which to declare military emancipation. That might stampede the loyal border slave states into joining the Confederacy and put both military victory and the South's slaves permanently beyond his reach. "I think to lose Kentucky is nearly the same as to lose the whole game. Kentucky gone, we can not hold

Missouri, nor, as I think, Maryland," Lincoln wrote. "These all against us, and the job on our hands is too large for us. We would as well consent to separation at once, including the surrender of this capitol." So, when Lincoln's headstrong commander in Missouri, John Charles Frémont, issued a martial-law emancipation edict on August 31, 1861, Lincoln ordered him to "modify" it and then relieved him of command two months later. When Major General David Hunter did the same in the occupied coastal district of South Carolina in May 1862, Lincoln declared Hunter's proclamation "altogether void," and Hunter was soon recalled as well.[11]

These revocations, as much as any battle, saved the border for the Union, and with it, severely diminished the certainty of Confederate survival. They also underscored how unconvinced Lincoln was that anything *except* gradualism and compensation would be able to guarantee emancipation legal permanence. Nevertheless, the comfortable majorities given Republicans by the 1860 congressional elections encouraged the antislavery Radicals in the Republican ranks to press for political counterparts to martial-law emancipation. At the end of the special session called by Lincoln in midsummer 1861, Congress adopted the First Confiscation Act, which permitted the seizure of rebel property—including slaves, if found working for the Confederate forces. (This had a nice irony to it, since Southern defenders of slavery in Congress had always defended it from federal interference on the grounds that slaves were property, and property rights were inviolable.) This was followed by a Second Confiscation Act in July 1862, which upped the ante by declaring free the slaves of any slave owner in active rebellion against the United States, whether or not those slaves were actually employed in war-related service. From there, presumably, one could justify further confiscation legislation which would seize any slave remaining in bondage.[12]

But confiscation, while it satisfied the political urge to strike at slavery directly, also held serious legal perils. Property confiscation in time of war is as old as war itself, but from the time of Hugo Grotius, the seventeenth-century Dutch "father" of the "law of nations," lawyers and judges had struggled to construct a code of rules and laws that would restrain the most vicious examples of it.[13] In the United States, the authors of the federal Constitution, remembering that they had once themselves come close to having everything they owned confiscated for rebelling against the king, authorized Congress "to define and punish" breaches of "the law of nations" (Article 1, section 8) and put explicit limits on property seizures and the use of martial law on their own fellow-citizens. Article 1, section 9, of the Constitution outlawed bills of attainder (which allowed legislatures to inflict the death penalty for treason without jury trials), while the punishment of treason itself was hedged in by

Article 3, section 3, which forbade Congress to "work Corruption of Blood"—in other words, to pass bills of "pains and penalties" that went beyond punishing traitors themselves and reached down to impoverish their families by permanently confiscating a convicted traitor's property.

For those reasons, trying to achieve emancipation through confiscation was less easy than it looked. During the War of 1812, the U.S. Supreme Court had held that the property of British subjects in the United States could not be taken without "some legislative act expressly authorizing its confiscation," and so when the First Confiscation Act was proposed during the special summer session of 1861, the matter was referred to the Senate Judiciary Committee—where, as it turned out, Illinois senator Lyman Trumbull was one of the rare Radical Republicans sitting as chair of a congressional committee. What Trumbull's committee came back with on July 15, 1861, was a confiscation bill that tried to evade the constitutional restriction on "pains and penalties" by declaring the property of anyone "aiding, abetting or promoting insurrection" open to seizure as "prize and capture," as though all such property resembled the capture of "prizes" at sea. This would, in particular, render slaves used by the Confederate military liable to federal confiscation, since by invoking the law of prize, the constitutional ban on attainder would have no application.[14] But confiscating slaves, and doing it during a civil war, meant stretching the law of nations, prize law, and admiralty law to cover categories they had never included before. Moreover, any confiscations of property were regarded by the textbook authors as justified actions in time of war only between belligerent nations. The law of prize might work very well when the captured cargoes of ships belonged to the citizens of enemy nations; but Lincoln's contention from the start of the war was that the Confederacy was *not* a nation. It was merely an insurrection because secession from the Union was a constitutional impossibility. This made the Confiscation Act, even as prize law, an action directed against the property of one's own citizens, and even in cases of treason, that ran afoul of the Constitution's ban on bills of attainder.[15]

Nevertheless, in the turbulent atmosphere following the humiliating defeat at First Bull Run, Congress passed Trumbull's Confiscation Act, and Lincoln signed it, albeit grudgingly. "The President had some difficulty in consenting to approve the act of Congress," wrote Treasury Secretary Salmon P. Chase, and according to the *New York Times*, Lincoln "finally consented only upon the most urgent entreaties of prominent members of the Senate." When the Second Confiscation Act was placed before him by Congress in July 1862, Lincoln threatened to balk again and on the same grounds. Much as he saw "no formal attainder" in the Second Confiscation Act, "I am constrained to say I think this feature of the act is unconstitutional," and he was ready to veto it until Congress hurriedly passed a joint resolution which denied that "proceedings under said act" should "be so construed as to work a forfeiture of the real estate of the offender beyond his natural life." But even then, Lincoln showed little energy in enforcing the bill. He gave no directions on enforcement to Attorney General Edward Bates, and Bates, a geriatric Missouri Whig who had no use for any emancipation that did not immediately deport the blacks it emancipated, declined to issue a circular of directions to federal attorneys unless they asked for it point-blank. "It cannot be said," recalled the Maine congressman James G. Blaine, "that the results flowing from the measure, either in restraining the action of Southern men or in securing to the National Treasury money derived from confiscated property, were at all in proportion to the importance ascribed to it in the discussions of both branches of Congress."[16]

The Frémont and Hunter proclamations suffered from the opposite problem. As commander of the Department of Missouri in the summer of 1861, Frémont tried to deal with the annoyance of guerilla warfare by proclaiming martial law on August 30, and in the spirit of the First Confiscation Act of two weeks before, he proposed punishing rebel sympathizers who sponsored the guerillas with his own version of confiscation: "The property, real and personal, of all persons . . . who shall take up arms . . . or who shall be directly proven to have taken an active part with their enemies in the field, is declared to be confiscated to the public use, and"—here was the red flag—"their slaves, if any they have, are hereby declared free men." The political consequences of Frémont's decree in the border states were, just by themselves, enough to move Lincoln to "modify" it. "No doubt the thing was popular in some quarters, and would have been more so if it had been a general declaration of emancipation," Lincoln explained to Orville Hickman Browning. But in the border states it could backfire: "the very arms we had furnished Kentucky would be turned against us." Still, the principal reason why Lincoln believed that Frémont had "no authority" to issue martial-law decrees about emancipation was because no one in American law really knew what standing martial-law emancipations might have if, after the period of martial law expired, they were appealed to the civil courts. In *Fleming v. Page*, Chief Justice Taney had so circumscribed the effect of martial law by United States forces that he denied the appeal of several Philadelphia merchants against the levy of customs on goods shipped from the American-occupied Mexican port of Tampico during the Mexican War, on the grounds that American military occupation of Tampico had done nothing to change its civil status as a foreign port. "Martial law is a thing not mentioned by name, and scarcely as much as hinted at, in the Constitution and statutes of the United States," admitted Caleb Cushing, onetime attorney general, in 1856. "I say, we are without law on the subject." At best, Lincoln explained, a commander might be able to *seize* property for use, but only "as long as the necessity lasts." He could not *emancipate* it from its owner. "That must be settled according to laws made by law-makers," and not by military proclamations. Anything other than that was simply "dictatorship," and even the best-intentioned dictatorship would mean the death of "any government of Constitution and laws."[17]

The common defect in both of these devices for emancipating slaves—confiscation and martial law—was their lack of legal permanence once the war emergency was over. Moreover, neither of them did anything to the institution of slavery itself, which would remain perfectly legal in both scenarios, no matter how many individual slaves were emancipated. Worst of all, if either of them failed to survive a court challenge, and a federal decision made the federal judiciary the guarantor of slavery, the prospect for all future emancipation would be set back in just the same way as *Dred Scott* had set back the struggle to keep slavery out of the territories. And this was before any consideration of the possible political debris these schemes would shake out in the border states or in Congress. In the wake of Bull Run, recalled James Blaine, "the military situation was so discouraging that in the president's view it would have been wiser for Congress to refrain from enacting laws which, without success in the field, would be rendered unnecessary."[18]

Yet, in the end, it was not Lincoln's favored path of gradual, legislated emancipation which he finally adopted, and Delaware shows us why. As early as November 1861, Lincoln began preparatory work for compensated emancipation by drawing up a plan for emancipation in Delaware and met with antislavery Delawareans with a view toward getting the assent of the minuscule Delaware legislature to compensation. This would then allow Lincoln to approach Congress with a request for funding, and by the time the Delaware legislature met in the spring of 1862, both federal funding and the goodwill of the legislature would allow the first compensated emancipation to be put in motion. The plan, presented by Lincoln to Delaware's lone member of the House of Representatives, George P. Fisher, would free all children born to Delaware slaves after the adoption of the bill and all Delaware slaves over the age of thirty-five; all others would become free at age thirty-five, although free children with slave mothers might still be subject to compulsory apprenticeship until age twenty-one for males and age eighteen for females. For this, Congress would pay the State of Delaware $719,200 in 6 percent United States bonds, doled out in thirty-one annual installments. Given the likelihood that the emancipation timetable would generate its own increased momentum, Lincoln additionally offered to compress the compensation into ten payments of $71,920, which would completely eliminate slavery in Delaware by 1872.[19]

By the time Congress was ready to convene for its new session in December, Lincoln was confident that Delaware would accede. Orville Hickman Browning, who arrived in Washington the day before the session opened, stopped by the White House and found Lincoln "very hopeful of ultimate success." The Delaware "proposition" could then "be made use of as the initiative to hitch the whole thing to." Slavery would be on the short road to extinction, and as an added benefit, the Confederates would be disheartened and sue for peace. "If Congress will pass a law authorizing the issuance of bonds for the payment of the emancipated Negroes in the border states, Delaware, Maryland, Kentucky, and Missouri will accept the terms." Once the impetus of legislative emancipation began, the Confederates, staking their hopes for success on wooing the border states into rebellion, would collapse in dismay. By these means, "it seemed to him that gradual emancipation and governmental compensation" would bring slavery "to an end."[20]

But Lincoln was surprised to find that even Delawareans "who look upon slavery as a curse" were so deeply dyed by racial hatred that "we also look upon freedom possessed by a negro, except in a very few cases, as a greater curse." Fisher published the text of Lincoln's "Act for the Gradual Emancipation of slaves in the State of Delaware" in the newspapers at the beginning of February 1862 and squeaked it through the Delaware Senate by a five-to-four vote, despite the senate's Democratic majority. But in the Delaware House, a straw poll showed Fisher that the bill would fail by a single vote. Hoping to fight another day, Fisher had the bill withdrawn. "No man in his senses," the Democratic newssheets in Delaware crowed, "supposes that the Government intends to give Delaware $900,000" to buy out slavery. "If it ever buys the slaves Delawareans will be saddled with the cost."[21]

The vigor with which Delaware threw compensated emancipation back in Fisher's—and Lincoln's—face should have said something to Lincoln about misjudging how fanatically resistant the border states might be to translating Unionism into emancipation. Instead, Lincoln preferred to treat the Delaware refusal as a temporary setback which could be remedied by the next session of the legislature. Three weeks after Fisher's bill died for want of support in the Delaware House, Lincoln sent to Congress a proposed joint resolution which not only restated most of the terms of the Delaware plan but extended its offer of compensated emancipation to all of the border states. "I recommend," Lincoln wrote to Congress on March 6, 1862, "*Resolved* that the United States ought to co-operate with any state which may adopt gradual abolishment of slavery, giving to such state pecuniary aid, to be used by such state in its discretion, to compensate for the inconveniences public and private, produced by such change of system." He could not believe, even after the failure of the Delaware proposal, "that it would not soon lead to important practical results." The resolution passed the House on March 11 by a vote of 89 to 31; after little more than a week of debate, the Senate approved it on April 2 by a vote of 32 to 10. A week later, Lincoln signed the joint resolution and sent it out to the border states for their action. "The Proposition of the Presidt. is an epoch," exulted Charles Sumner, "& I hope it will commence the end." Lincoln told Horace Greeley at the end of March that "if some one or other of the border-states would move fast, I should greatly prefer it," but his main concern was that emancipation be presented with as little apparent arm-twisting as possible. "We should urge it *persuasively*, not *menacingly*, upon the South." It was less important to him to get emancipation put on a timetable than that it be framed in a way that would avoid a challenge in the federal courts, and he assured Carl Schurz that "he was not altogether without hope that the proposition he had presented to the southern states in his message of March 6th would find favorable consideration."[22]

And perhaps it might have, had Lincoln been given time. But time was what he had less of than he thought, and that reality was brought home to him by the general in chief of the Union armies, George Brinton McClellan. When McClellan failed to capture Richmond and sullenly pulled his numerically superior Army of the Potomac back to its base around Harrison's Landing in June 1862, Lincoln decided to send himself to the Peninsula to gain his own perspective on McClellan's predicament.[23] "The object of the presidential visit was to see the condition of the army, and learn what change of plans, if any, were deemed necessary by Gen. McClellan," reported the *Washington Sunday Morning Chronicle*, but the changes of plans McClellan had in mind were political rather than military in nature, all of which were included in a letter McClellan had prepared for Lincoln upon his arrival. The Harrison's Landing Letter may have been the most insubordinate communication ever made by an American officer to his civilian commander in chief. It declared that "Military power should not be allowed to interfere with the relations of servitude, either by supporting or impairing the authority of the master"; otherwise, "a declaration of radical views, especially upon slavery, will rapidly disintegrate our armies."[24]

Given the general's temperamental reluctance to act, few of McClellan's biographers have been sure whether he was simply politically clumsy, or whether he was actually flirting with the idea of a *coup d'etat*.[25] Nevertheless, for months there had been whispers about McClellan's "putting his sword across the government's policy," about "his sympathies with the South," and his "incapacity and want of loyalty." Quartermaster General Montgomery Meigs was appalled to hear "officers of rank" in the camp at Harrison's Landing speak easily about "a march on Washington to 'clear out those fellows.'" One of McClellan's generals, William F. "Baldy" Smith, protested that tolerating even the cheapest camp-talk on that subject "looks like treason: & that it will ruin you and all of us." But if McClellan paid no attention, Lincoln did. Navy Secretary Welles remembered that McClellan's "singular letter . . . struck the President painfully," and McClellan made matters worse by scattering around careless hints about "taking my rather large military family to Washn to seek an explanation of their course." He wrote his wife on July 11 that "I have commenced receiving letters from the North urging me to march on Washington & assume the Govt!!" And a month later he hinted at the possibility of a "coup," "after which "everything will be changed in this country so far as we are concerned & my enemies will be at my feet."[26]

Lincoln returned to Washington on July 10, "grieved with what he had witnessed." McClellan's ultimatum destroyed the illusion that time was on Lincoln's side, that gradual emancipation could be tended slowly and calmly while the war went doggedly on to its conclusion. He now feared that if he acted at once to cashier McClellan, "his dismissal would provoke popular indignation"—not to mention the indignation of the Army of the Potomac—"and shake the faith of the people in the final success of the war." If he were to begin the emancipation of slaves, it would have to be preemptive, no matter what McClellan's ultimate plans were, and that meant that it would need to happen at once. "Oh," Lincoln groaned to Isaac Arnold and Owen Lovejoy, "if the border States would accept my proposition! Then . . . you, Lovejoy, and Arnold, and all of us, would not have lived in vain! The labor of your life, Lovejoy, would be crowned with success—you would live to see the end of slavery." But the border staters would do nothing to help him put compensated emancipation into action now. It was time, Lincoln concluded after returning from Harrison's Landing, to stop waging war "with elder-stalk squirts, charged with rose water." From that point, he would not leave "any available means unapplied."[27]

The "means" Lincoln had in view were anything but humdrum, for he was now determined to resort to the kind of military emancipation he had forbade Frémont from decreeing a year before. On July 22, 1862, Lincoln laid before his cabinet what has been designated as the "First Draft" of an emancipation proclamation, and it was clearly a military proclamation. How long Lincoln had been composing this document is unclear: Vice President Hannibal Hamlin insisted on at least three occasions in later years that Lincoln had read a version of this to him in mid-June; Francis Carpenter and Joseph Barrett thought it was "undoubtedly true" that Lincoln had begun composing the "First Draft" on July 9, while still en route back to Washington from Harrison's Landing; Navy Secretary Gideon Welles was convinced that Lincoln had not begun work on the proclamation until July 14, after a final meeting with the border-state congressional delegations, which met with a blank refusal of cooperation. What is certainly true is that, as soon as it finally became clear that the border states would not accept even the most generous compensation plan, Lincoln began dropping portentous hints that he had given emancipation "much thought and had about come to the conclusion that it was a military necessity absolutely essential for the salvation of the Union, that we must free the slaves or be ourselves subdued."[28]

The "military" means Lincoln had in view was a particular form of martial law known as the "war powers." The Constitution designates the president as the commander in chief of the armed services in time of war, and in war, the president was presumed to possess a set of war powers which occupied a vague and untested middle ground between martial law and civil law. This presumption had a shaky history: the only body of opinion which described the war powers was a series of comments made by John Quincy Adams on the floor of the House of Representatives in 1836 and again in 1841 and 1842, in which he goaded Southern congressmen with the premise that Congress had the "authority to interfere with the institution of slavery" in time of national emergency, including the power "to abolish it by treaties of peace." Under these war powers, the president might exercise certain martial-law prerogatives, but without invoking widespread military policing or the closure of the civil courts.[29]

As we will see in the final essay, many legal commentators hotly denied that any such war powers existed in the Constitution. But the notion refused to die, and it was with the war powers in mind that Lincoln composed the "First Draft" of the Emancipation Proclamation. The "First Draft" does not, at first glance, appear to be a proclamation at all, since it seems to begin as the enabling announcement required by the Second Confiscation Act, which he had just signed the week before.

> In pursuance of the sixth section of the act of congress entitled "An act to suppress insurrection and to punish treason and rebellion, to seize and confiscate property of rebels, and for other purposes" Approved July 17, 1862, and which act, and the Joint Resolution explanatory thereof, are herewith published, I, ABRAHAM LINCOLN, President of the United States, do hereby proclaim to, and warn all persons within the contemplation of said sixth section to cease participating in, aiding, countenancing, or abetting the existing rebellion, or any rebellion against the government of the United States, and to return to their proper allegiance to the United States, on pain of the forfeitures and seizures, as within and by said sixth section provided.

But that much said, Lincoln proceeded to transform confiscation from Lyman Trumbull's bizarre application of the law of prize to an executive decree based on the "war powers."

And, as a fit and necessary military measure for effecting this object, I, as Commander-in-Chief of the Army and Navy of the United States, do order and declare that on the first day of January in the year of Our Lord one thousand, eight hundred and sixtythree, all persons held as slaves within any state or states, wherein the constitutional authority of the United States shall not then be practically recognized, submitted to, and maintained, shall then, thenceforward, and forever, be free.[30]

By confining confiscation to the *states, wherein the constitutional authority of the United States shall not then be practically recognized*—in other words, the Confederacy—the border states, with their civil courts open and laws (including laws on slavery) untainted by rebellion, were now exempt. Those states not being in rebellion, Lincoln had no grounds for extending his "war powers" to them. The states of the Confederacy were another matter, and here Lincoln opened the scope of the act dramatically. Under the rubric of those powers, Lincoln was prepared to do what no president under any other rubric could have done, and that was declare general emancipation—not just of slaves used in Confederate war service, or the slaves of disloyal masters—but of all the slaves, without exception, in all rebellious areas. And not merely seized as "contraband," or vaguely "free," but permanently free, *thenceforward, and forever*.

This was taking a long chance, especially with the Federal armies stumbling from one defeat to another. Secretary of State William H. Seward "thought it would be well to postpone the whole subject to a more auspicious period." Lincoln eventually agreed and "put the draft of the proclamation aside" in order to wait for a Union victory, so that it would appear "supported by military success." But in this instance, *waiting* was the strategy of Seward, not Lincoln.[31]

If Lincoln regarded the proclamation as a grudging necessity, he showed no sign of it by the way he freely leaked rumors of it. New York politico James A. Hamilton gave New York governor Edwin Morgan a garbled version of the proclamation, with the proclamation being presented to Lincoln "by several members of Congress and other gentlemen." Lincoln, as Hamilton heard, "approved of the policy thereby indicated, and declared that, with slight modifications, he would issue it," but "this purpose was frustrated by two members of his cabinet." Lincoln certainly read it to James Speed, the brother of Joshua Speed, only to have Speed conclude that "it will do no good; probably much harm." Southern Unionist Robert J. Walker brought the novelist and journalist James R. Gilmore to meet Lincoln on August 18, whispering to Gilmore that "I have good news for you, but it must be strictly confidential,—the Emancipation Proclamation is decided upon," news which Lincoln then authorized Gilmore to leak privately to Gilmore's boss at the *New York Tribune*, Horace Greeley. Leonard Swett related to John Nicolay that Lincoln had read the proclamation to him at the White House on the evening of August 20. Hiram Barney, the Collector of the Port of New York and a key figure in New York Republican politics, also claimed fifteen years later that Lincoln had read him a draft of the proclamation "in his own hand writing and in his pocket when we were together" in Washington on September 5.[32]

The rumors, in turn, gave way to demands. Lydia Maria Child and Horace Greeley both published calls to Lincoln as editorials, Greeley's "The Prayer of Twenty Millions" in the *Tribune* on August 19, and Child's "To the President of the United States" in the *Washington National Republican* on August 22; and in September, the New York City Central Republican Committee adopted resolutions calling on Lincoln "to issue a proclamation of emancipation, and declare that all slaves of rebels in this Union are forever free"—language which approximated the "First Draft" a little too closely to have been an accident. On September 17, the veteran abolitionist Robert Dale Owen wrote Lincoln a lengthy letter, enclosing an emancipation proclamation he had drafted himself for Lincoln's use. But Lincoln stuck grimly to Seward's advice, letting public demand and the military situation seem to draw the proclamation out of him. On August 30, the rebel Army of Northern Virginia soundly beat a federal army at Manassas, Virginia, and the following week, Lee's army crossed the Potomac River into Maryland, invading Union territory for the first time in the war. On September 17, Lee was attacked by the Army of the Potomac under McClellan along the Antietam Creek at Sharpsburg, Maryland. In an all-day battle of unprecedented ferocity, Lee was almost hammered to destruction and withdrew across the Potomac the following evening. Lincoln would have preferred that Lee had been cornered and crushed, but he was willing to accept the results of the Antietam battle as a victory. And a victory was what he needed to undergird the proclamation. "When Lee came over the river," Lincoln told Massachusetts congressman George Boutwell,

> I made a resolve that when McClellan drove him back—and I expected he would do it sometime or other—I would send the Proclamation after him. I worked upon it and got it pretty much prepared. The battle of Antietam was fought on Wednesday [September 17], but I could not find out till Saturday [September 20] whether we had really won a victory or not. It was then too late to issue the Proclamation that week, and I dressed it over a little on Sunday, and on Monday [September 22] I gave it to them [the cabinet].[33]

This time, no one in the cabinet was surprised. When a visitor to the White House told Secretary Chase on Sunday that the president, "being very busy writing, could not see him," Chase immediately concluded, "Possibly engaged on Proclamation." A special cabinet meeting was called for noon on Monday, and Lincoln began business by briefly reminding everyone that "for several weeks the subject [of emancipation] has been suspended, but . . . never lost sight of." He had waited for the victory Seward had cautioned him to await, and perhaps more remarkable for a man of so little religious visibility, "he had made a vow, a covenant, that if God gave us the victory in the approaching battle, he would consider it an indication of Divine will, and that it was his duty to move forward in the cause of emancipation." This version of the proclamation document was entirely a military pronouncement, not a civil proclamation wrapped in a protective military justification. What was more, emancipation was not only a military decree, it would be a military *act*, backed explicitly by Federal bayonets: "The executive government of the United States, including the military and naval authority thereof, will recognize and maintain the freedom of such persons, and will do no act or acts to repress such persons, or any of them, in any efforts they may make for their actual freedom."[34]

The announcement that he would "recognize and maintain" any freedom the slaves might wrest for themselves may have been the most shocking statement in any of the four versions of the proclamation, since it pledged that the Federal armies would do nothing to repress "any efforts they may make for their actual freedom." Those "efforts," quite conceivably, could include slave insurrection. (Assistant Secretary of War Charles Dana told William Seward that this was the "bad egg in the pudding—& I fear may go far to make it less palatable than it deserves to be.") But Lincoln was undeterred. Once the proclamation took effect, Lincoln remarked to Indiana judge T. J. Barnett, "the character of the war will be changed. It will be one of subjugation and extermination."[35]

The "Preliminary" Emancipation Proclamation was countersigned by Secretary of State Seward and issued the next day, with every major Northern newspaper printing and commenting on it. "How utterly insignificant seemed my personal fortunes, disappearing from my own mind in the radiance and glow of this, to me, the greatest human utterance," wrote Ohio congressman Albert G. Riddle. "It was like speaking a new world into being by Omnipotence."[36]

The Confederates were given one hundred days, until January 1, 1863, to submit or face the legal reality of emancipation. They, of course, showed no signs of repentance, and at the end of December, Lincoln put copies of the proclamation into the hands of each cabinet member for final comments. The comments do not make particularly instructive reading, since they touched mainly on two issues—the precise identification of which states and parts of states were exempt from the proclamation since they were now under Union occupation, and the promise that the "Executive . . . will recognize and maintain the freedom of said persons and will do no act, or acts to repress said persons, or any of them, in any suitable efforts they may make for their actual freedom." Lincoln thought he had softened objections to his recognize-and-maintain threat by adding, in this "Final Draft," an additional "appeal to the people so declared to be free, to abstain from all disorder, tumult, and violence, unless in necessary self defence." But Bates, Seward, Blair, and even Chase all urged him to strike it out entirely, and two days later, when the cabinet met to review the "Final Draft," both Chase and Seward proposed a rewriting "enjoining upon, instead of appealing to, those emancipated, to forbear from tumult." In the end, Lincoln would concede and "enjoin upon the people so declared to be free to abstain from all violence, unless in necessary self-defence; and I recommend to them that, in all cases when allowed, they labor faithfully for reasonable wages."[37]

The origins of the trope of *progress* lie largely in the Radical Republicans' perceptions that Lincoln did not appreciate the urgency of the opportunity the elections of 1860 had put into antislavery hands, just as the trope of *waiting* was cultivated as a rejoinder (and a rebuke) to the notorious "impatience" of the Radicals. In defense of the Radicals, it has to be said that they had little reason to be patient. The Republicans held political power in Congress for the first time in 1861, and it was imperative for them to move as rapidly and comprehensively as possible lest the Radical moment pass in the next election. But while military emancipation might be short and direct, it might also be short-lived once challenges arose in the courts. And if the federal courts were ever allowed to decide on those challenges and decided as they had in *Dred Scott*, the cause of emancipation might be set back to the dimmest future any of them could see. However, if the slave state legislatures themselves could be bribed into passing emancipation statutes of their own, then all the legal questions would be moot, and emancipation could become permanent. If this required the sugarcoating of compensation and gradualism, Lincoln had no objection. *Gradualism* always accelerated beyond the original timetables set for it; *compensation* would turn the South's lost capital investments in slaves into cash which could then be used to convert slave laborers into free wage laborers, and, if nothing else, it would be cheaper than a war costing $50 million a month. "Why don't you turn in and take pay for your slaves from the Government?" Lincoln implored Missouri senator John Henderson. "Then . . . we can go ahead with emancipation of slaves in the other States by proclamation and end the trouble."[38]

Lincoln liked to think of himself, on the strength of his Kentucky birth and Virginia parentage, as a Northerner who nevertheless possessed a unique empathy and understanding of the Southern mind. "If I could only get [compensated emancipation] before the southern people, I believe they would accept it," he told Pennsylvania Republican Alexander McClure, "and I have faith that the northern people, however startled at first, would soon appreciate the wisdom of such a settlement of the war." In this, he could not have been more wrong, but it allowed him to believe that Kentuckians—and by extension, all Union-loving Southerners—would be willing to slough off the burdens of slavery if someone could make it in their interest to do so. Lincoln was convinced, in classic Benthamite fashion, that people were motivated by "interest" rather than altruism, and it was to that "interest" he believed a gradual, compensated emancipation scheme would appeal. It was only after the blank failure of his appeal to the border states in July 1862, and after it became apparent that the army under McClellan was becoming increasingly unreliable, that he moved to take up the martial-law weapon, not because it was the best weapon, but because urgency had now become his agenda, too. Even then, he was not convinced that an emancipation proclamation based on the "war powers" would survive postwar court appeals. "Nobody was more quick to perceive or more frank to admit the legal weakness and insufficiency of the Emancipation Proclamation than Mr. Lincoln," recalled James Welling. "Determined though he was never to retract the paper, or by his own act to return to slavery any person who was free by its terms, he saw that, in itself considered, it was a frail muniment of title to any slave who should claim to be free by virtue of its vigor alone." So, he continued to propose compensated emancipation schemes, not only during the hundred days between the "Preliminary" and final proclamations, but for the rest of the war. In the largest sense, the Thirteenth Amendment was his ultimate resort to a legislative solution to slavery. That, as he said, would provide the "King's cure for all the evils."[39]

And yet, what is remarkable is that Lincoln was only dubious about the various legal mechanisms of emancipation, not emancipation itself. The trope required to fully understand emancipation is neither *progress* nor *waiting*, but *prudence*. Lincoln was just as conscious as the Radicals of the window of opportunity his presidency provided, and even if his plan took a different path from that of the Radicals, it should not be missed that he was already moving on that road by November 1861. True though it is that the proclamation is couched in a legalese strangely different from the eloquence of his other famous papers, it cannot be said often enough that this was intended to be a legal document, so that it could have real legal consequences. The Gettysburg Address might have been a tremendous exercise in elegiac rhetoric, but it also accomplished absolutely nothing—literally, it changed the status of no one—apart from dedicating a cemetery. The Emancipation Proclamation, which was fully as prosaic as the Gettysburg Address was memorable, changed the legal state of four million slaves who *are, and thenceforward shall be free*. It did not, of course, liberate any Southern slaves until the Union armies marched far enough across the South to make it effectual, nor did it liberate slaves in places where the federal government was sovereign, as in the border states and the occupied

Confederacy. But no one believes, in the first case, that law (even martial law) lacks meaning only because enforcement has yet to catch up with it; and no one allowed at that time that federal power had the constitutional right to impose emancipation where the federal courts were open and functioning. It has to be said, also, that the proclamations of Frémont and Hunter were equally technical and prosaic, yet no one among the legions of Lincoln's critics seems inclined to fault them on this score.[40]

Lincoln's proclamation has no meaning apart from his singular determination to place his nation on a one-way road to emancipation and the death of slavery. It was a determination with the flexibility to consider more than one path, but it was also a determination that did not propose ever to negotiate the fact of emancipation. "While I remain in my present position," he told Congress eleven months later, "I shall not attempt to retract or modify the emancipation proclamation; nor shall I return to slavery any person who is free by the terms of that proclamation." He repeated that declaration a year later, adding that "if the people should by whatever mode or means, make it an Executive duty to re-enslave such persons, another, and not I, must be their instrument to perform it." Of the three terms he laid down for negotiations with Confederate emissaries in February 1865, the second was "No receding, by the executive of the United States on the Slavery question."[41] If that promise, as embodied in the Emancipation Proclamation, appears to later generations to have lacked style, intention, commitment, or scope, the fault may lie, not in a political failure on the part of Abraham Lincoln, but in a failure of civic understanding on our own.

Notes

This essay first appeared in the *Journal of Illinois History* 6.4 (Winter 2003): 242–70.

1. Horace Greeley, "Abraham Lincoln," in *Recollections of a Busy Life: Including Reminiscences of American Politics and Politicians* (New York, 1868), 409, and "Greeley's Estimate of Lincoln: An Unpublished Address by Horace Greeley," *Century Magazine,* July 1891, 381. On Lincoln's "journey," see Stephen B. Oates, "Lincoln's Journey to Emancipation," in *Our Fiery Trial: Abraham Lincoln, John Brown, and the Civil War Era* (Amherst, MA, 1979), 73; David Herbert Donald, *Lincoln* (New York, 1995), 362–65; and Arthur Zilversmit, "Lincoln and the Problem of Race: A Decade of Interpretations," *Papers of the Abraham Lincoln Association* 2 (1980): 22–45; LaWanda Cox, *Lincoln and Black Freedom,* 6–7.

2. Richard Hofstadter, "Abraham Lincoln and the Self-Made Myth," in *The American Political Tradition and the Men Who Made It* (1948; repr., New York, 1973), 117, 129, 131. Hofstadter coined what is easily the most memorable comment ever made on the Proclamation when he complained that it had "all the moral grandeur of a bill of lading." Hofstadter meant to imply triviality, but a "bill of lad-

ing" was actually a significant commercial document in the antebellum economy. "There is no one instrument or contract used in commercial transactions made to subserve so many various, useful, and important purposes, as the Bill of Lading," wrote P. C. Wright in *DeBow's Review* in July 1846. "Yet it appears . . . that there is no one so little understood, as to its legal effect, when applied to some of the purposes to which it is peculiarly adapted. . . . A Bill of Lading is defined to be an instrument signed by the master of a ship, or by someone authorized to act in his behalf, whereby he acknowledges the receipt of merchandise on board his vessel, and Engages . . . to deliver the same at the port of destination in safety." If this was what the Emancipation Proclamation was supposed to do, then Hofstadter was offering Lincoln more of a compliment that he intended.

3. Lerone Bennett, "Was Abe Lincoln a White Supremacist?" *Ebony* 23 (February 1968), 35–38, 40–42; James Baldwin, *The Fire Next Time* (New York, 1964), 22, 115; "An Open Letter Sent to Howard President James M. Nabrit," February 1968, in *The Eyes on the Prize Civil Rights Reader: Documents, Speeches and Firsthand Accounts from the Black Freedom Struggle, 1954–1990*, ed. Clayborne Carson et al. (New York, 1991), 462–63.

4. William Henry Herndon to Jesse Weik, February 25, 1887, in Herndon-Weik Papers, Group 4, reel 9, #1893–96, Library of Congress; Charles Maltby, *The Life and Public Services of Abraham Lincoln* (Los Angeles, 1884), 174; J. G. Holland, *The Life of Abraham Lincoln* (Springfield, MA, 1866), 348, 355; George Boutwell, in *Reminiscences of Abraham Lincoln by Distinguished Men of His Time*, ed. Allen Thorndike Rice (New York, 1886), 125; LaWanda Cox, "Lincoln and Black Freedom," in *The Historian's Lincoln: Pseudohistory, Psychohistory, and History*, ed. Gabor S. Boritt (Urbana, IL, 1988), 177; Ida M. Tarbell, *The Life of Abraham Lincoln* (New York, 1904), 2:96; Julius Lester, *Look Out, Whitey! Black Power's Gon' Get Your Mama!* (New York, 1968), 58, 63.

5. Isaac Arnold, *The History of Abraham Lincoln and the Overthrow of Slavery* (Chicago, 1866), 300, 685–86; Joshua Speed to Herndon, February 7, 1866, and Joseph Gillespie to Herndon, December 8, 1866, in *Herndon's Informants: Letters, Interviews, and Statements about Abraham Lincoln*, ed. Douglas L. Wilson and Rodney O. Davis (Urbana, IL, 1998), 197, 507; Lincoln, "Speech to One Hundred Fortieth Indiana Regiment," March 17, 1865, and "To Albert G. Hodges," April 4, 1864, in *The Collected Works of Abraham Lincoln*, ed. Roy P. Basler (New Brunswick, NJ, 1953–55), 7:281–82, 8:360–61.

6. Lincoln, "Second Debate with Stephen A. Douglas at Freeport, Illinois," August 27, 1858, in *Collected Works*, 3:40.

7. Lincoln, "Sixth Debate with Stephen A. Douglas," October 13, 1858, in *Collected Works*, 3:255; Ward Hill Lamon and Dorothy Lamon Teillard, *Recollections of Abraham Lincoln, 1847–1865*, ed. James Rawley (1911; repr., Lincoln, NE, 1994), 67–68.

8. Gillespie to Herndon, January 31, 1866, in Wilson and Davis, *Herndon's Informants*, 183; Don E. Fehrenbacher, *The Slaveholding Republic: An Account of the United States Government's Relations to Slavery* (New York, 2001), 66; "An

Act concerning the District of Columbia," February 27, 1801, in *The Debates and Proceedings of the Congress of the United States* (Washington, DC, 1851), 1552–55; Lincoln, "To Horace Greeley," March 24, 1862, and "To Nathaniel P. Banks," August 5, 1863, in *Collected Works*, 5:169, 6:365; Lincoln quoted by Gilbert Greene, in *Recollected Words of Abraham Lincoln*, ed. Don Fehrenbacher and Virginia Fehrenbacher (Stanford, CA, 1996), 183.

9. Lincoln, "First Inaugural Address—Final Text," March 4, 1861, in *Collected Works*, 4:270; David M. Potter, *Lincoln and His Party in the Secession Crisis* (1942; repr., Baton Rouge, 1995), 104–5; Swett, in Wilson and Davis, *Herndon's Informants*, 636.

10. Augustin Cochin, *The Results of Emancipation*, trans. Mary L. Booth (Boston, 1863), 324–25; William A. Green, *British Slave Emancipation, 1830–1865* (Oxford, Eng., 1976), 100–101, 118–19, 131, 218; Thomas Holt, *The Problem of Freedom: Race, Labor, and Politics in Jamaica and Britain, 1832–1938* (Baltimore, 1992), 55–57, 65–66, 67, 69–70, 77, 95–102; Douglas Hall, *Free Jamaica, 1838–1865* (New Haven, 1959), 83–84, 87–88, 91; Rebecca Scott, "Comparing Emancipation: A Review Essay," *Journal of Social History* 20 (Spring 1987): 576; Peter Kolchin, "Thoughts on Emancipation in Comparative Perspective: Russia and the United States South," *Slavery and Abolition* 11 (December 1990): 359–60.

11. Lincoln, "To John C. Fremont," September 2, 1861, "To Orville H. Browning," September 22, 1861, and "Proclamation Revoking Gen. Hunter's Order," May 19, 1862, in *Collected Works* 4:506, 531, 5:222.

12. Horace White, *The Life of Lyman Trumbull* (New York, 1913), 173–74; Charles Sumner to Wendell Phillips, August 3, 1861, in *The Selected Letters of Charles Sumner*, ed. Beverly Wilson Palmer (Boston, 1990), 2:74; Salmon Chase, "Report of the Secretary of the Treasury," July 14, 1861, *Congressional Globe*, 37th Cong., 1st sess., appendix, 5; "An Act to Confiscate Property used for Insurrectionary Purposes," August 6, 1861, and "An Act to suppress Insurrection, to punish Treason and Rebellion, to seize and confiscate the Property of rebels, and for other Purposes," July 17, 1862, in *The Statutes at Large, Treaties, and Proclamations of the United States of America, from December 5, 1859, to March 3, 1863*, ed. George P. Sanger (Boston, 1863), 319, 589–92.

13. Arthur Nussbaum, *A Concise History of the Law of Nations* (New York, 1954), 113, 124, 147, 151, 156, 162, 186–87, 192, 198; Knud Haakonssen, *Natural Law and Moral Philosophy: From Grotius to the Scottish Enlightenment* (New York, 1996), 310–41; David Armitage, "The Declaration of Independence and International Law," *William and Mary Quarterly* 59 (January 2002): 15; James G. Randall, *Constitutional Problems under Lincoln* (1926; rev. ed., Urbana, IL, 1951), 297–300.

14. Henry Wheaton, *Elements of International Law*, ed. W. B. Lawrence (Boston, 1863), 321; Lyman Trumbull, *Congressional Globe*, July 15, 1861, 37th Cong., 1st sess., 120; John Syrett, "The Confiscation Acts: Efforts at Reconstruction during the Civil War" (Ph.D. diss., University of Wisconsin, 1971), 6–7; Henry W. Halleck, *International Law; or, Rules Regulating the Intercourse of States in Peace and War* (San Francisco, 1861), 577; Madeline Russell Robinson, "An Introduction

to the Papers of the New York Prize Court, 1861–1865" (Ph.D. diss., Columbia University, 1945), 28–29.

15. Wheaton, *Elements of International Law*, 362, 379; Ludwell H. Johnson, "The Confederacy: What Was It? The View from the Federal Courts," *Civil War History* 32 (March 1987): 5–22. For this reason, Trumbull simultaneously began pressing for revision of the prize laws; see Trumbull, "Prize Law," in *Congressional Globe*, March 17 and 18, 1862, 37th Cong., 2nd sess., 1260.

16. Chase to Green Adams, September 5, 1861, in J. W. Schuckers, *The Life and Public Services of Salmon Portland Chase* (New York, 1874), 428; "The Last of Congress," *New York Times*, August 7, 1861; Moncure Conway, *Autobiography, Memories and Experiences* (Boston, 1904), 1:386; *The Political History of the United States of America during the Great Rebellion*, ed. Edward McPherson (Washington, 1864), 197–98; John Hay, "Washington Correspondence," *Missouri Republican*, November 29, 1861, in *Lincoln's Journalist: John Hay's Anonymous Writings for the Press, 1860–1864*, ed. Michael Burlingame (Carbondale, IL, 1998), 151; Syrett, "Confiscation Acts," 93–98; James G. Blaine, *Twenty Years of Congress: From Lincoln to Garfield* (Norwich, CT, 1884), 1:377.

17. "Emancipation Proclamation of Gen. Fremont," and Maj. Gen. David Hunter, "General Orders No. 11," in McPherson, *Political History*, 245–46, 250; Caleb Cushing, "Martial Law," February 3, 1857, in *Official Opinions of the Attorneys General of the United States Advising the President and Heads of Departments in relation to their official duties* (Washington, 1858), 371; Levi Woodbury, "Martial Law in Rhode Island," in *Writings of Levi Woodbury, LL.D., Political, Judicial and Literary* (Boston, 1852), 2:70–105; Lincoln, "Speech to the Springfield Scott Club," August 14, 1852, and "To Orville H. Browning," September 22, 1861, in *Collected Works* 2:149–50, 4:531–32; Charles Halpine, *Baked Meats of the Funeral: A Collection of Essays, Poems, Speeches, Histories, and Banquets by Private Miles O'Reilly* (New York, 1866), 104–5; Lincoln quoted by John Seymour in a letter to his brother, Gov. Thomas Seymour, January 19, 1863, in Fehrenbacher and Fehrenbacher, *Recollected Words*, 400.

18. John C. Frémont, "Proclamation," in *The War of the Rebellion: A Compilation of the Official Records of the Union and Confederate Armies* (Washington, DC, 1881), ser. 1, 3:467, hereafter cited as *O.R.*; McPherson, *Political History*, 245–46; Vernon L. Volpe, "The Fremonts and Emancipation in Missouri," *Historian* 56 (Winter 1994): 346–47; Blaine, *Twenty Years of Congress*, 1:377.

19. H. Clay Reed, "Lincoln's Compensated Emancipation Plan and Its Relation to Delaware," *Delaware Notes* 7 (1931): 36–39; Lincoln, "Drafts of a Bill for Compensated Emancipation in Delaware," in *Collected Works*, 5:29–30. Fisher later adjusted the total federal offer upwards to $900,000, since federal bonds were trading well below par that winter.

20. Edward Everett Hale, memorandum of a conversation with Charles Sumner, April 26, 1862, in *Memories of a Hundred Years* (New York, 1902), 2:189–91; Orville H. Browning, diary entry for December 1, 1861, in *Diary of Orville Hickman Browning*, ed. Theodore Calvin Pease and James G. Randall (Springfield,

IL, 1925–33), 1:512; Lincoln, "Message to Congress," April 16, 1862, in *Collected Works*, 5:192; Lincoln to David Davis and to Gilbert Greene, in Fehrenbacher and Fehrenbacher, *Recollected Words*, 132, 182.

21. Reed, "Lincoln's Compensated Emancipation Plan," 39–45.

22. Lincoln, "Message to Congress," March 6, 1862, in *Collected Works*, 5:144–46. See also McPherson, *Political History*, 209; and *Congressional Globe*, 37th Cong., 2nd sess. (March 6, 1862), 1102–3; "Aid to the States in Emancipation," *Congressional Globe*, 37th Cong., 2nd sess. (April 2, 1862), 1496; Henry Wilson, *History of the Anti-Slavery Measures of the Thirty-Seventh and Thirty-Eighth United States Congresses, 1861–1864* (Boston, 1864), 91; Sumner to Francis W. Bird, March 12, 1862, in Palmer, *Selected Letters of Charles Sumner*, 2:104; "Some Sense about the Nigger, at Last," *Vanity Fair*, March 15, 1862, 130; Lincoln, "To Horace Greeley," March 24, 1862, in *Collected Works*, 5:169; Carl Schurz, *The Reminiscences of Carl Schurz*, ed. Frederick Bancroft and William A. Dunning (New York, 1907–8), 2:328–29.

23. Lincoln, "To George B. McClellan," July 2, 1862, in *Collected Works*, 5:301–2; Browning, diary entry for July 7, 1862, in Pease and Randall, *Diary of Orville Hickman Browning*, 1:552; *Washington Sunday Morning Chronicle*, July 13, 1862; William C. Davis, *Lincoln's Men: How President Lincoln Became Father to an Army and a Nation* (New York, 1999), 66–70; *A Yankee at Arms: The Diary of Augustus D. Ayling, 29th Massachusetts Volunteers*, ed. Charles F. Herberger (Knoxville, TN, 1999), 54. See also John Hay's account of the Harrison's Landing visit, in "Washington Correspondence," mid-July 1862, in Burlingame, *Lincoln's Journalist*, 281–85; and *With Lincoln in the White House: Letters, Memoranda, and Other Writings of John G. Nicolay, 1860–1865*, ed. Michael Burlingame (Carbondale, IL, 2000), 85.

24. McClellan to Lincoln, July 7, 1862, in *The Civil War Papers of George B. McClellan, 1860–1865*, ed. Stephen W. Sears (New York, 1989), 344, and in *O.R.*, ser. 1, 11 (pt. 1):73. The editor of McClellan's memoirs asserted that the Harrison's Landing Letter was not made public until the end of 1862, after McClellan had been removed from command, but he believed Lincoln had discussed the letter with members of the cabinet, and they in turn leaked descriptions of it more broadly. McClellan did not release his own version of the letter until he published his official report on the Peninsula Campaign in August 1863. See George McClellan, *Report on the Organization and Campaigns of the Army of the Potomac: To which is added an account of the Campaign in Western Virginia* (New York, 1864), 279–82, and *McClellan's Own Story: The War for the Union, the Soldiers Who Fought It, the Civilians Who Directed It, and His Relations to It and to Them* (New York, 1887), 487–89. The letter was also printed in several campaign biographies for McClellan's unsuccessful bid for the presidency in 1864. See *The Life, Campaigns, and Public Services of General McClellan* (Philadelphia, 1864), 105–7; G. S. Hilliard, *Life and Campaigns of George B. McClellan, Major-General, U.S. Army* (Philadelphia, 1864), 262–65; and William Henry Hulbert, *General McClellan and the Conduct of the War* (New York, 1864), 262–64.

25. Jaso Dolson Cox, *Military Reminiscences of the Civil War* (New York, 1900), 1:357; Welles, diary entry for September 3, 1862, in *Diary of Gideon Welles*, ed. John T. Morse (Boston, 1911), 1:107. T. Harry Williams commented acidly in 1962, "McClellan never grasped the political character of the war, he never accepted the civilian as a factor in the war. He did not even seem to comprehend that the political-civilian branch of the government was supposed to have a significant part in determining how the war should be conducted." See T. H. Williams, *McClellan, Sherman and Grant* (New Brunswick, NJ, 1962), 29. Contrast this reading of the Harrison's Landing Letter with the pro-McClellan versions in Porter S. Michie, *General McClellan* (New York, 1901), 370–71.

26. John C. Bigelow, *Retrospections of an Active Life, 1817–1863* (New York, 1909), 508; "General M. C. Meigs on the Conduct of the Civil War," *American Historical Review* 26 (1920–21): 294; George McClellan, "To Mary Ellen McClellan," in *The Civil War Papers of George B. McClellan: Selected Correspondence, 1861–1865*, ed. Stephen Sears (New York, 1989), 351, 362, 375, 390; John Hay, diary entry for September 25, 1864, in *Inside Lincoln's White House: The Complete Civil War Diary of John Hay*, ed. Michael Burlingame and J. R. T. Ettlinger (Carbondale, IL, 1997), 230.

27. Gideon Welles, "History of Emancipation," in *Civil War and Reconstruction: Selected Essays by Gideon Welles*, ed. Albert Mordell (New York, 1959), 237; Noah Brooks, *Washington in Lincoln's Time* (Washington, DC, 1895), 16; Browning, diary entry for July 25, 1862, in Pease and Randall, *Diary of Orville Hickman Browning*, 1:553; Stephen W. Sears, *To the Gates of Richmond: The Peninsula Campaign* (New York, 1992), 351; Lincoln, "To Cuthbert Bullitt," July 28, 1862, in *Collected Works*, 5:345; Arnold, *History of Abraham Lincoln*, 287–88.

28. "Senator Hamlin of Maine," *New York Times*, September 8, 1879; Hamlin, in Henry Clay Whitney, *Life on the Circuit with Lincoln* (Boston, 1892), 442, 468; H. Draper Hunt, *Hannibal Hamlin: Lincoln's First Vice-President* (Syracuse, NY, 1969), 159–65; Francis Carpenter, *Six Months at the White House with Abraham Lincoln* (New York, 1867), 20, 86; Joseph Barrett, *Life, Speeches, and Public Services of Abraham Lincoln* (Cincinnati, 1865), 414; Welles, "History of Emancipation," 254.

29. John Quincy Adams, "Indian Hostilities," in *Congressional Globe*, 24th Cong., 1st sess. (May 25, 1836), appendix, 448, 450; *The Abolition of Slavery the Right of the Government from the War Power* (Boston, 1861), 4; Charles Francis Adams, "John Quincy Adams and Martial Law," *Proceedings of the Massachusetts Historical Society* 15 (1901–2): 436–78; Sumner, in Charles Francis Adams, *Richard Henry Dana: A Biography* (Boston, 1891), 2:260; David Donald, *Charles Sumner and the Coming of the Civil War* (New York, 1960), 388; Sumner, "The Hon. C. Sumner on a War for Emancipation," October 1, 1861, *Anti-Slavery Reporter*, November 1, 1861, 246–47; Sumner to Lieber, September 17, 1861, in Palmer, *Selected Letters of Charles Sumner*, 2:79; "Senator Henderson's Reply to the President," July 21, 1862,, in McPherson, *Political History*, 218–20. For modern commentary on the "war powers," see Phillip J. Cooper, *By Order of the President: The Use and Abuse of Executive Direct Action* (Lawrence, KS, 2002), 16–17, 20–21, 117–19, 120–22,

124, 127, 130, 133; W. E. Binkley, *The Powers of the President: Problems of American Democracy* (New York, 1937), 122–23; and Louis Fisher, *Constitutional Conflicts between Congress and the President* (Princeton, NJ, 1985), 284–325.

30. Lincoln, "Emancipation Proclamation—First Draft," in *Collected Works*, 5:336.

31. Chase, diary entry for July 22, 1862, in *Inside Lincoln's Cabinet: The Civil War Diaries of Salmon P. Chase*, ed. David Donald (New York, 1954), 99; Carpenter, *Six Months at the White House*, 21–23, 77; Welles, "History of Emancipation," 242; Edwin Stanton, "The Cabinet on Emancipation, July 22, 1862," Edwin M. Stanton Papers, container 8, reel 3, Library of Congress. Lincoln did, however, issue the enabling proclamation for the Second Confiscation Act ("Proclamation of the Act to Suppress Insurrection," July 25, 1862, in *Collected Works*, 5:341); a directive concerning the employment of "persons of African descent" was issued on August 16, 1862. See *O.R.*, ser. 3, 2:397.

32. Hamilton to E. D. Morgan, August 4, 1862, in *Reminiscences of James A. Hamilton; or, Men and Events at Home and Abroad during Three Quarters of a Century* (New York, 1869), 526; James Speed to Lincoln, July 28, 1862, Abraham Lincoln Papers, Library of Congress; Welles, "Administration of Abraham Lincoln, I," in *Lincoln's Administration: Selected Essays by Gideon Welles*, ed. Albert Mordell (New York, 1960), 119; Robert L. Kincaid, *Joshua Fry Speed: Lincoln's Most Intimate Friend* (Chicago, 1943), 27; James R. Gilmore, *Personal Recollections of Abraham Lincoln and the Civil War* (Boston, 1898), 75, 82–83. Gilmore, under his pen name "Edmund Kirke," had just published an antislavery novel, *Among the Pines: or, South in Secession-Time*, in June which promised, "Free their Negroes by an act of emancipation, or confiscation, and the rebellion will crumble to pieces in a day" (172). "Conversation with Hon. Leonard Swett," March 14, 1878, in *An Oral History of Abraham Lincoln: John G. Nicolay's Interviews and Essays*, ed. Michael Burlingame (Carbondale, IL, 1996), 58–59; Hiram Barney to Gideon Welles, September 27, 1877, in Gideon Welles Papers, New York Public Library, New York City.

33. Horace Greeley, "The Prayer of Twenty Millions," August 19, 1862, in *Dear Mr. President: Letters to the President*, ed. Harold Holzer (Reading, MA, 1993), 156–61; "Mrs. L. Maria Childs to the President of the United States," and "Compensated Emancipation," in *Washington National Republican*, August 22 and September 8, 1862; Robert Dale Owen to Lincoln, September 17, 1862, in Abraham Lincoln Papers, Library of Congress; George Boutwell to Josiah G. Holland, June 10, 1865, in J. G. Holland Papers, New York Public Library.

34. Chase, in Donald, *Inside Lincoln's Cabinet*, 149; Welles, *Diary of Gideon Welles*, 1:142–43.

35. T. J. Barnett, in Fahrenbacher and Fahrenbacher, *Recollected Words*, 23; Dana to Seward, September 23, 1862, Abraham Lincoln Papers, Library of Congress. James R. Gilmore, whom Lincoln utilized as a back door to Horace Greeley and the editorial page of the *New York Tribune*, forwarded to Lincoln in May 1863 the proposal of a Tennessee Unionist, Augustus Montgomery, to "induce the

blacks to make a concerted and simultaneous rising . . . to arm themselves with any and every kind of weapon that may come to hand." Lincoln was initially inclined to regard the plan as "a hoax," but he also signaled to Gilmore that he "had no objection whatever to your publishing what you propose concerning the negro insurrection," so long as Gilmore did not cite Lincoln as personally authorizing the insurrection. In the end, nothing came of it but some sporadic "outbreaks among the blacks in Georgia and Alabama" in August of 1863. The plan for the rising was drafted by Montgomery on May 17, 1863, and forwarded to Maj. Gen. William S. Rosecrans, then in command of the Federal Army of the Cumberland; Gilmore then sent the letter to Lincoln. See Augustus Montgomery to William S. Rosecrans, May 17, 1863, in Abraham Lincoln Papers, Library of Congress. See also, Gilmore, *Personal Recollections*, 150–53; and John G. Nicolay to Gilmore, June 14, 1863, in Burlingame, *With Lincoln in the White House*, 115. In the summer of 1864, with George McClellan the Democratic candidate for the presidency, Lincoln made a similar proposition to Frederick Douglass, not so much in the form of an insurrection, as in a movement "outside the army to induce the slaves in the rebel states to come within the federal lines." As it had been after the Harrison's Landing Letter, Lincoln's motive was anxiety over McClellan. "He thought now was their time," because if McClellan won the election, *"only such of them as succeeded in getting within our line would be free after the war was over."* Douglass agreed to "undertake the organization of a band of scouts, composed of colored men, whose business should be somewhat after the original plan of John Brown." But the sudden upswing in Lincoln's military and political fortunes, and his reelection that fall, rendered the plan moot. On the 1864 "John Brown plan," see Douglass, *Life and Times of Frederick Douglass, Written by Himself* (1892), ed. R. W. Logan (New York, 1962), 357–59; and Douglass to Theodore Tilton, October 15, 1864, in *Frederick Douglass: Selected Speeches and Writings*, ed. Philip S. Foner (Chicago, 1999), 572.

36. John Hay, diary entry for September 24, 1862, in Burlingame and Ettlinger, *Inside Lincoln's White House*, 41; "Washington Correspondence, 25 September 1862," in Burlingame, *Lincoln's Journalist*, 312; Albert G. Riddle, *Recollections of War Times: Reminiscences of Men and Events in Washington, 1860–1865* (New York, 1895), 204.

37. Welles, diary entries for December 29 and 31, 1862, in *Diary of Gideon Welles*, 1:209, 210; Chase to Lincoln, December 31, 1862, in Schuckers, *Life and Public Services of Chase*, 462; Lincoln, "By the President of the United States of America: A Proclamation," *Statutes at Large* (1863), 1268–69, and "Emancipation Proclamation," in *Collected Works*, 6:28.

38. John B. Henderson, quoted in Walter B. Stevens, *A Reporter's Lincoln*, ed. Michael Burlingame (Lincoln, NE, 1998), 171–72; Henderson, "Emancipation and Impeachment," *Century Magazine* 85 (1912), 196–98; Hay, diary entry for October 28, 1863, in Burlingame and Ettlinger, *Inside Lincoln's White House*, 101.

39. Alexander McClure, in Fehrenbacher and Fehrenbacher, *Recollected Words*, 318; Lincoln, "Response to a Serenade," February 1, 1865, in *Collected Works*, 8:254;

James Welling, in *Reminiscences of Abraham Lincoln by Distinguished Men of His Time*, ed. A. T. Rice (New York, 1886), 551.

40. Salmon P. Chase to Lincoln, February-March 1862, in Abraham Lincoln Papers, Library of Congress.

41. John T. Morse, *Abraham Lincoln* (Boston, 1899), 2:121–25; Lincoln, "Annual Message to Congress," December 6, 1863, and "Annual Message to Congress," December 6, 1864, in *Collected Works*, 7:51, 8:152.

8

Defending Emancipation: Abraham Lincoln and the Conkling Letter, August 1863

braham Lincoln might well have believed that "I never in my life was more certain that I was doing right than I do in signing" the Emancipation Proclamation into military law on January 1, 1863. But doing what was right and what was politically viable were two different things. "At no time during the war was the depression among the people of the North so great as in the spring of 1863," remembered James Blaine, and largely because "the anti-slavery policy of the President was . . . tending to a fatal division among the people." The simple fact of announcing his intention to proclaim emancipation back in September had created more public anger than Lincoln had anticipated. William O. Stoddard, one of Lincoln's White House staffers, gloomily recalled "how many editors and how many other penmen within these past few days" rose in anger to remind Lincoln

> that this is a war for the Union only, and they never gave him any authority to run it as an Abolition war. They never, never told him that he might set the negroes free, and, now that he has done so, or futilely pretended to do so, he is a more unconstitutional tyrant and a more odious dictator than ever he was before. They tell him, however, that his edict, his ukase, his decree, his firman, his venomous blow at the sacred liberty of white men to own black men is mere *brutem fulmen,* and a dead letter and a poison which will not work. They tell him many other things, and, among them, they tell him that the army will fight no more, and that the hosts of the Union will indignantly disband rather than be sacrificed upon the bloody altar of fanatical Abolitionism.[1]

It was not that Lincoln or the proclamation lacked defenders. A long queue of prominent Republicans—George Boker, Francis Lieber, Grosvenor Lowrey, and Robert Dale Owen—promptly entered the lists with pamphlets and articles. But an equally formidable roster of Northern Democratic critics and jurists—including Benjamin Curtis, Montgomery Throop, and Joel Parker—were there waiting for them. But the agitation mounted beyond what Lincoln's friends could hold off, with cries in many places for a negotiated settlement to the war or a national peace convention that would avoid emancipation. "The Darkest hour of our Country's trial is yet to come," warned Benjamin F. Butler. "Nothing is surer than an assembly to settle this struggle on the basis of the *Union as it was!*" Even worse, it was rumored "that the President will recoil from his Emancipation Proclamation" because of the heavy political costs it imposed.[2] In the end, if Lincoln had any hope of turning public opinion in favor of emancipation by argument, the arguments would have to be his, and he would have to be his own best apologist for the Proclamation. The surest mark of how Lincoln rose to that challenge is the public letter he wrote on August 26, 1863, for James Cook Conkling and a "mass meeting of unconditional Union men" in Lincoln's own home town of Springfield, Illinois. The Conkling letter signaled, after months of political uncertainty, that Lincoln's commitment to emancipation was absolute and would not be bargained away in return for concessions or submissions by the Confederates. Thus, a straight line runs from the Proclamation through the Conkling letter to the Thirteenth Amendment and the final abolition of slavery.

The tradition of the public letter—a personal commentary on policy or events, cast in the ostensibly private form of a letter but intended for official or newspaper publication—had a long history in antebellum politics, both for presidents and presidential candidates, and it stood more or less in the place of what might today be described journalistically as a "press briefing." Lincoln's skill with the public letter was second only to the rhetorical skills he manifested in his formal and informal speeches. One of his most famous documents, his reply to Horace Greeley's own impatient pre-emancipation public letter, "The Prayer of Twenty Millions," was cast in the form of a public letter and never sent to Greeley at all as a personal communication. Chauncey M. Depew thought that Lincoln's "series of letters were remarkable documents. He had the ear of the public; he commanded the front page of the press, and he defended his administration and its acts and replied to his enemies with skill, tact, and extreme moderation." As James Rawley observes, the public letter became Lincoln's most perfect vehicle "to explain his views, counter criticism, and manifest his humanity."[3]

Lincoln actually wrote four important public letters in the eight months following the formal issue of the Emancipation Proclamation: a brief reply to a series of resolutions passed by a workingmen's convention in Manchester, England, on January 19, 1863; the letter written on June 12, 1863, in response to Erastus Corning and a convention of New York Democrats; a letter two weeks later in response to the resolutions of the Ohio Democratic State Convention; and the letter of August 26, 1863, to James C. Conkling and the Springfield Union meeting. (Like the Greeley letter, these four letters also achieved independent lives of their own: the Corning letter was republished as a Union League pamphlet under the title *Truth from an Honest Man: The Letter of the President*, provoking a pamphlet reply by the New York Democrats it had been addressed to, while the others were published under the title *The Letters of President Lincoln on Questions of National Policy*, by Benjamin B. Russell.) But the Corning and Ohio letters were mainly preoccupied with justifying the Union Army's use of martial law and the arrest of Clement Vallandigham in May 1863, rather than with emancipation. It was the Conkling letter which addressed the public opposition to emancipation in the most direct manner.

Lincoln's first concern about that opposition was aimed at the border states. "When I issued that proclamation, I was in great doubt about it myself," Lincoln later told John McClintock. "I did not think that the people had been quite educated up to it, and I feared its effects upon the border states." He had more than good reason. In Missouri, one of Lincoln's listening-post correspondents irritably warned him that "your [most] substantial friends about here feel almost disposed to give up the contest, or trying to sustain you." Little more than a week after Lincoln signed the proclamation, William G. "Parson" Brownlow warned Montgomery Blair that "things are not working . . . in Kentucky. I fear the Legislature will take strong action against the proclamation, and even against the Administration." James Garfield thought that, in Washington, "All the men who are worth talking to are in favor of it, now that it has been promulgated," but as an Ohioan, he was sure that "it can only have an adverse effect in Ky. and Tenn." And that was only from Lincoln's friends; the Democratic opposition in the border states was far less self-contained. "The President's proclamation has come to hand at last," complained the *Louisville Daily Democrat*. "We scarcely know how to express our indignation at this flagrant outrage of all constitutional law, all human justice, all Christian feeling." Kentucky Democrats, sniffing the opportunity to overturn the Unionist majorities in the Kentucky legislature, called a state convention in February, for the purpose of "preparing the Kentucky Mind for revolt against the Union," and had to be forcibly dispersed by federal troops.[4]

But the "border" embraced a larger space than merely the four loyal slave states. The attitudes which characterized the border—a general but not absolute Unionism, a marked hostility to free blacks, a refusal to surrender slavery as a legal institution, and a hesitation to commit the lives of its people or its material to either side in the war—belonged to a far wider band of territory than what was contained within the border *states*. The border, in conceptual terms, ran through the Union in a fat seam which stretched on the north to a line running from northern New Jersey through Harrisburg and Pittsburgh, and from there to Columbus, Indianapolis, and Lincoln's own Springfield, while on the south it bulged downward to include northern and western Virginia and eastern and central Tennessee. Within that larger border, the nearest the proclamation came to touching off a legislative rebellion occurred, not in Kentucky or Missouri, but in Lincoln's own home state of Illinois.

Illinois went Republican in the 1860 election, with Lincoln's party capturing the legislature. One of Lincoln's old political associates, Richard Yates, won the governor's mansion by over 12,000 votes; and when the senior Democratic senator, Stephen A. Douglas, died in June 1861, Yates appointed a Republican (and longtime personal friend of Lincoln's), Orville Hickman Browning, to give the state two Republican senators (the other was Lyman Trumbull). But Illinois's political history was Democratic, especially in the southernmost districts of the state, where a large portion of the population was Southern-born immigrants and much of the native-born population was considerably less than enthusiastic about opposition to slavery. Illinois might be technically a free state, but its commitment to free soil was more a matter of small-farmer hostility to the economic scale of the plantation economy rather than to slavery itself; if anything, Illinois was notoriously hostile to free blacks and made generous allowances to slave owners to use slave labor on Illinois farms under the state's slave transit laws.[5]

By mid-1861, signs of resistance to Republican war policies were already appearing. The battered Illinois Democrats cleared their heads and resolved ominously at the party's state convention "that the perilous condition of the country had been produced by the agitation of the slavery question, creating discord and enmity between the different sections, which had been aggravated by the election of a sectional president." In 1862, the decision of Secretary of War Stanton to establish a "contraband" camp at Cairo, Illinois, and begin hiring out blacks as agricultural workers caused an uproar in southern Illinois. "The Germans & Irish are told that they are to interfere with their employment by taking their places," wrote one anxious Republican congressional candidate, and Democratic congressman William Allen complained on the floor of the House of Representatives that "Thousands of negroes have been taken, decoyed or stolen" and transported to Illinois to compete with white workingmen. "Southern Illinois must either be the home of white men or black men—They cannot dwell together!"[6]

The 1862 legislative elections, following hard on the heels of Lincoln's preliminary announcement of the Emancipation Proclamation on September 22, were an unnerving disappointment for the Republicans across the North and especially in Illinois. The Democrats captured the Illinois Senate by a margin of one (13 seats to 12), and the House of Representatives by 54 to 32. Lincoln's own home congressional district defeated a Lincoln friend, Leonard Swett, and sent to Washington instead John Todd Stuart, Lincoln's onetime law partner and mentor but now a Democrat. The U.S. Senate seat that Orville Hickman Browning had inherited by appointment was up for reelection in the Illinois legislature and would now obviously be pulled out from under Browning as quickly as it had been put beneath him. "It is very mortifying to the true American," mourned the *Alton Telegraph* on December 19, 1862,

> to be forced to acknowledge that there is a large and influential party, which in this trying hour, is either so unwise or so lost to all patriotic feeling, as to play into the hands of both our foreign and domestic enemies. The Democratic party may claim to be loyal, and denounce all who question its sincerity as much as it pleases, but it has pursued such a course in the last political campaign, as to cause the common sense of mankind . . . to pronounce it unfaithful to the Government.[7]

The Emancipation Proclamation gave both an edge and a target to the newly renascent Illinois Democrats. There was already substantial disaffection among soldiers in Illinois regiments about the proclamation, and the Democratic victory at the polls back home fanned it higher. "I have been engaged to day in reading letters written by Citizens of Illinois to different members of my Regiment," reported one officer in the 54th Illinois, near Jackson, Tennessee, "advising them to desert & offering protection to them if they will. . . . I am really afraid that if something is not done at once to put a stop to this thing that the fire in the rear . . . will yet form a serious affair." A lieutenant in the 86th Illinois surveyed his company and found to his shock that "only 8 men in Co. K. approve the policy and proclamation of Mr. Lincoln." One relative of an Illinois cavalryman confidently promised that "Every man that has got the sand will throw off on the Lincoln Government now after the proclamation setting the nigger free. Ill's is bound to go with the Southland." Of the more than 13,000 desertions Illinois regiments suffered during the war, the single largest number occurred immediately after the proclamation was issued; one regiment, the 109th Illinois, had to be disbanded for disloyalty.[8]

Even among the Republican faithful, there was enough disharmony and discouragement to make key supporters think of leaving the party. Paul Selby recalled that "it has been charged that there was a conspiracy among leading Republican politicians of Illinois, including those intimately connected with the State administration at that time, to remove Mr. Lincoln by fair means or foul from his exalted position as leader of the political and military forces of the country and replace him with one of its own creatures." Orville Hickman

Browning, facing the inevitable recall to Illinois, was convinced that the Proclamation was an ill-timed political gesture and concluded he should withdraw
from Republican politics: "The counsels of myself and those who sympathize
with me are no longer heeded. I am despondent, and have but little hope left
for the Republic." One of Browning's neighbors, Jackson Grimshaw, warned
that Browning was planning "to build up a great 'third' party" in Illinois as an
alternative, and Joseph Medill accused Browning of defecting to "the secesh
of Illinois." But this was only what Grimshaw himself was coming to expect
as the result of the way Republicans were managing their own cause:

> Our movement is . . . kind to all but its *friends*. It *has* dug up *snakes* and
> it *cant* kill them, it has fostered d——d rascals & crushed honest men. If
> [it] were not that our country, our homes, our all is at stake, that you and I
> have all, all our blood in this fight—Lincoln, [Edward L.] Baker, [William
> H.] Bailhache[,] [Ninian] Edwards & all might go to ——. . . . God help
> us all but it looks blue. . . . Cotton & family speculations, concessions to
> army rascals—arrests one day & releases the next—Kentucky policy and
> all that have shit us to hell. . . . There are some loyal men amongst our
> democrats, but the Government must *use force* and crush out treason at
> home or we are used up.[9]

But when the new Illinois legislature convened in Springfield on January 3,
1863, the initiative was captured at once by the revived Democrats, and their
principal target was Lincoln's proclamation. The leading Democratic newspaper, the *Illinois State Register*, rejoiced that the proclamation would be the
first item to come under legislative scrutiny. "There can be no question of the
popular condemnation of this measure. . . . If Mr. Lincoln will trample on the
Constitution the people will not stand by him. They will become disheartened
in fighting the battles of the country, and they will utterly withdraw from
him the affection and respect which every ruler should, by upright conduct,
command." Governor Yates stubbornly sent in a strongly proadministration
message to open the session on January 6, but the Democratic majority refused to receive it and limited the customary publication of the message to
two thousand copies so that they could "send it forth into the world, entering
their solemn protest against its revolutionary and unconstitutional doctrines."
Two days later, Elias Wenger from the 37th District offered a hostile resolution,
condemning the proclamation in almost frantic terms:

> WHEREAS the Government of the United States has been engaged for
> nearly two years in an unsuccessful attempt to suppress the Southern rebel-
> lion . . . and whereas our country is becoming almost a nation of widows
> and orphans, who, if the President's emancipation proclamation be carried
> into effect, will become prey to the lusts of freed negroes who will overrun

our country . . . we are in favor of an immediate suspension of hostilities, and recommend the holding of a national convention, for an amicable settlement of our difficulties.

This was no mere statehouse squabble. The Illinois legislature was clearly trying to mobilize national discontent and in such a way that Lincoln could not easily ignore, especially coming from his home state. "All the democratic members of the legislature are open secessionists," wrote one anxious observer. "They talked about going to Washington, hurling Mr Lincoln from the presidential chair, and inaugurating civil war north."[10]

And on it went, throughout the legislative session, with emancipation invariably the primary target. The proclamation was declared "unconstitutional, contrary to the rules and usages of civilized warfare, calculated to bring shame, disgrace and eternal infamy upon the hitherto unsullied flag of the Republic, and Illinois . . . will protest against any war which has for its object the execution or enforcement of said proclamations." On February 4, shortly before the session ended, one last resolution announced "that we believe the further prosecution of the present war cannot result in the restoration of the Union and the preservation of the Constitution as our fathers made it, unless the President's emancipation proclamation be withdrawn," and asked for the naming of five commissioners to go to Washington and urge Congress to issue an armistice and arrange for a peace convention.[11]

The mischief the legislature could cause was not limited to provocative resolutions. Three of Lincoln's old Illinois political allies wrote that spring, "The Legislature . . . will, we think pass an act taking the military power out of the hands of the Governor[,] abolish the adjutant generals office and . . . resist a draft or any attempt to apprehend & return deserters to their Regiments in the field." Just as bad, "We cannot sell any Bonds, as the Legislature has not authorized any more to be sold," reported Springfield lawyer James C. Conkling to Lincoln on April 10, 1863, "and have not made even the ordinary appropriations for supporting the State Government so as to be available." As the legislature's second session neared in June, Conkling's wife, Mercy Levering Conkling, looked on disapprovingly as the "the democrats" arrived, "copperheads largely in the majority, boldly expressing their disloyalty, and plotting treason."[12]

This time, however, Governor Yates found a weapon with which to strike back. The legislative session reopened on June 3, only two days after the anti-administration *Chicago Times* was temporarily shut down by General Ambrose Burnside for its "repeated expression of disloyal and incendiary sentiments," and a week after Clement Vallandigham was expelled to the Confederacy on Lincoln's order. Both incidents provided fresh tinder to incendiary antiadministration speech-making in the Illinois House. But on June 10, citing an obscure provision in the Illinois Constitution, Yates prorogued the legislature (and in fact would govern without the legislature's help until the very end of the legislature's term in 1864). The astounded representatives fumed against this "monstrous and revolutionary usurpation of power," but after two weeks of helpless protest, they conceded. "Well knowing that their peace resolutions were pending, and lots more were being 'hatched up,'" Yates chortled, "I sent my polite note to them, telling them in the language of the soldiers to the rebels, to 'skeedaddle.' They had been in session for nine days, and it was a sight good for sore eyes to see them leaving with their nine dollars and postage stamps."[13]

This did not prevent the enraged Illinois Democrats from finding another stage with which to capture national attention, the mass political meeting. Like the public letter, the mass meeting was a staple of antebellum politics, and though the definition of *mass* could be stretched to include everything from a few hundred flag-wavers at a county seat to a major metropolitan quasi-convention, they were organized and staged with extraordinary frequency and partisan absolutism by Republicans and Democrats alike during the war years as a way of connecting local political interests with national issues and national political figures.[14] The centerpiece of mass meetings was usually a roster of nationally known speakers, who were set up at separate stands or platforms at the meeting grounds, while the people were free to move from one to the other, sampling the oratory. The conclusion of the meetings usually involved a series of resolutions; and their general purpose was to offer public encouragement to the leaders of the cause, or, alternately, by a show of numbers, to offer as much political intimidation to the opposition as possible. Both the Republicans and Democrats had staged "mass meetings" in Springfield at the opening of the legislature in January 1863, and the proroguing of the legislature became the occasion for the calling of a Democratic mass meeting by the party's state committee at the Springfield fairgrounds on June 17, 1863.

True to form, the Democratic meeting would be a local event, but with a national audience and national participants. The organizers, chaired by one of Stephen A. Douglas's old loyalists, William A. Richardson, invited two of Lincoln's most prominent congressional critics, Samuel S. Cox of Ohio and Daniel Voorhees of Indiana, as the marquee speakers, and when it was over, the *Illinois State Register* proudly announced that "The meeting yesterday was the most tremendous gathering of the people ever witnessed in Illinois," with attendance estimates varying from 75,000 (the Democratic estimate) to 15,000 (the Republicans'). The resolutions denounced Governor Yates, the arrest and banishment of Clement Vallandigham, and "the further offensive prosecution of this war." And almost as though the legislature were still in session, the meeting proposed "a national convention, to settle the terms of peace, which shall have in view the restoration of the Union as it was, and the securing by constitutional amendments such rights"—and here, the *rights* jeopardized by the Emancipation Proclamation were clearly in view—"to the several states and the people thereof, as honor and justice demand."[15]

Illinois Republicans staged mass meetings of their own in Du Quoin on July 17; in South Macon on July 23; in Havana on July 28; a "Grand Union Meeting" at Pleasant Plains, north of Springfield, on August 10; and a tremendous "Grand Union Demonstration" at the state capitol on July 8 that celebrated the fall of Vicksburg with a thirty-five-gun salute. But just as Yates's daring proroguing of the legislature could never quite wipe out the humiliation Illinois Republicans felt over the legislature's demand for a peace convention, none of these subsequent meetings were quite able to wipe away the humiliation they felt at the size and celebrity of the June 17 Democratic meeting. By the beginning of August, Republicans had prepared a gigantic riposte, a mass meeting for September 3 at the Springfield fairgrounds designed to overshadow even the great June 17 meeting. It would distinguish itself from the Democratic meeting by being a "Union" meeting, inviting both Republicans and War Democrats, thus impugning the June 17 meeting as a purely selfish, partisan affair. True, the bulk of the meeting's leadership would be Republican, but it would feature (or so the organizers hoped) a wish-list of national Republican and War Democrat heroes: Generals Benjamin Butler, John A. Logan, John A. McClernand; Governors David Tod of Ohio, Oliver P. Morton of Indiana, Andrew Johnson of Tennessee, and Andrew Curtin of Pennsylvania; plus U.S. House Speaker Schuyler Colfax. "The meeting will be the largest ever held in the State," the *Journal* promised, "and will be a most impressive demonstration of the sentiment of loyal Illinois," Republican and Democrat alike.[16] Indeed, it would be that, and more, if the organizing committee's chairman, James Conkling, could get his way. He wanted as the principal speaker none other than Abraham Lincoln.

James Cook Conkling was, like Lincoln, a Springfield lawyer, and his wife, Mercy Levering Conkling, had been a close friend of Mary Todd Lincoln's. Born in New York in 1816 and a graduate of Princeton, Conkling had clerked briefly in New Jersey, then moved to Illinois in 1838, and was admitted to the bar that October. Like Lincoln, he had been an ardent Whig, and he successfully ran for both mayor of Springfield in 1845 and then the state legislature in 1851, where "he was identified with a small group of able men who were prominent in anti-slavery legislation." He joined the Republicans, became a member of the state Republican committee in 1856, but lost a race for the U.S. House. In 1860, Conkling was one of fifteen Sangamon County delegates to the state nominating convention in Decatur that pledged itself to Lincoln's nomination for the presidency, and he prided himself on having "voted regularly for Mr. Lincoln for more than a quarter century whenever he aspired to any office." He strongly defended Lincoln's policies, including military arrests. "While the Government is contending against armed traitors it must also crush incipient treason," he icily wrote to one former Democratic acquaintance who had been imprisoned in Ft. Warren as a Confederate sympathizer. "It is therefore . . . justified in arresting those who refuse to take the oath of allegiance." And Lincoln, for his part, spoke highly of Conkling. When Conkling was appointed by Governor Yates as Illinois's state agent to oversee the state's accounts with the federal government, Lincoln endorsed Conkling to Secretary of War Stanton as "a good man" and described Conkling to Quartermaster General Meigs as having "ample business qualification, is entirely trustworthy; and with all is my personal friend of long standing." Yet none of this made Conkling much more than an important Illinois political operative. It was revealing of the disarray and anxiety of Illinois Republicans that the most crucial invitation to the Springfield meeting would come, not from key Illinois party figures and Lincoln allies like Joseph Medill, Leonard Swett, Orville Hickman Browning, Isaac Arnold, or "Long John" Wentworth, but from a comparatively minor political player from Springfield like Conkling.[17]

Given the lack of sponsorship from the great names of Illinois Republicanism, neither Conkling nor his Springfield associates were taking any chances that the "Great Union Mass Meeting" would fall short of the mark set by the June 17 Democratic meeting. The *Illinois State Journal* began running notices for the meeting under its own editorial banner on August 13, announcing that "The Invitations for the great Union Mass Meeting are nearly all issued and the call with a large number of names appended, will appear in a few days." The next day, the *Journal* ran a still larger notice, followed by a list of endorsements from local Republicans and War Democrats, including Governor Yates, Jesse Dubois, Newton Bateman, Isaac Keyes, Paul Selby, and Conkling himself. By August 16, the number of endorsements had grown by three hundred, and the call for the meeting was moved to the *Journal's* front page, where it ran until August 31 (by which time, the list of endorsements consumed a column and a quarter of names in agate type).[18]

By August 21, the plan was beginning to catch national fire. The organizing committee happily announced that Radical Republican senator Zachariah Chandler had agreed to be a speaker, and on successive days, the *Journal* added that Wisconsin senator James R. Doolittle, General Richard J. Oglesby, General McClernand, and Governor Yates would join him. The *Journal* further expected public letters from Edward Everett and others. "Every county will be represented by its hundreds of delegates, and some by thousands," so much so that fears of overcrowding in Springfield were causing the organizers to ask loyal Springfielders to open private homes. But the attraction James Conkling hoped would secure the kind of crowd that would erase all memory of the embarrassments of the preceding eight months was Lincoln himself, and on August 14, Conkling wrote to Lincoln, extending the invitation and a quick list of reasons why Lincoln should accept:

> The unconditional union men in our State are to hold a Grand Mass Meeting at Springfield on the 3rd Day of September next. It would be gratifying to the many thousands who will be present on that occasion if you would also meet with them. . . . A visit to your old home would not be inappropriate if you can break away from the pressure of public duties. We intend to make the most imposing demonstration that has ever been held in the Northwest. Many of the most distinguished men in the country have been, and will be invited to attend and I know that nothing could add more to the interest of the occasion than your presence.

Conkling later explained that "we hardly expected he would be present, but we hoped to receive some communication which would indicate his future policy and give encouragement to his friends."[19]

At that moment, however, Conkling was evidently very much in earnest about the possibility of Lincoln's presence in Springfield. And so, for that moment, was the president. Lincoln had traveled comparatively little outside Washington during the war, but the crisis in Illinois was nearly impossible for him to ignore. On August 20, Lincoln telegraphed Conkling, "Your letter of the 14th is received. I think I will go, or send a letter—probably the latter." Even the barest suggestion of Lincoln's attendance was enough to delight Conkling, and the next day, the *Illinois State Journal* confidently proclaimed, "President Lincoln Will Probably Be Here. . . . President Lincoln has given assurances justifying a strong hope that he will be here. . . . Nothing could be more fitting . . . in this hour of national triumph and hope, than that he should visit his old home and receive the greetings of his friends of the Prairie State." Privately, however, Conkling realized that this was a conditioned promise, and on August 21, he sent Lincoln a second letter, plying him with additional arguments for coming personally to Springfield. Lincoln toyed just seriously enough with the idea to write his old Springfield law partner, William Herndon, about the advisability of committing himself to Conkling's meeting. Herndon, replying to Lincoln on August 26, saw no reason for Lincoln to hold back. "[We] will have a great time here on the 3rd September and it is thought it will be the largest Convt. ever convened here. There is no doubt but it will be a large meeting. I hope it will—hope it will give us confidence, back-bone vigor & energy. The Union men are busy at work all over the State to meet any Emergency. They are determined—cool—not hasty—not rash."[20]

However, by the 23rd, Lincoln had already decided not to make the journey. Part of this was due to his anxiety over the uncertain military situation in Virginia and Tennessee, where Lincoln hoped that both George Meade and William Rosecrans would lurch into pursuit of the Confederate armies; part of it may also have been due to a reluctance to feed the accusations of critics like Vallandigham by looking as though, by personal appearance in Springfield, he was endorsing Yates's unilateral dismissal of the legislature as a good way of dealing with opposition. On the other hand, Lincoln could not disengage himself entirely from the Illinois situation, and so he chose instead to write a public letter for Conkling to read to the meeting on his behalf. (Curiously, it would make no allusion at all to Yates's proroguing of the legislature.) John Hay noted that afternoon that Lincoln "went to the library to write a letter to Conkling & I went to pack my trunk for the North." He worked on it intermittently over three days (William Stoddard noted that Lincoln "composed somewhat slowly and with care, making few erasures or corrections" and usually worked "alone by himself in his room"), completing a rough draft on August 26, followed by a finished draft the same day, and a final version, in a copyist's hand on the 27th. The copyist's version contained some last-minute corrections in Lincoln's hand and a cover note to Conkling by Lincoln himself: "I can not leave here now. Herewith is a letter instead. You are one of the best public readers. I have but one suggestion. Read it very slowly. And now God bless you, and all good Union-men." Lincoln himself leaked the news to the press that he would not be going west, after all, but would instead "address to his fellow-citizens another of those homely but powerful appeals which may have more than once been almost equal to battles won."[21]

The letter arrived in Springfield on August 31, and while it deflated Conkling's hopes for a personal presidential appearance, it set off new speculation as to what the letter would say. "President Lincoln has written a letter to the Mass Convention to meet in this city," wrote the proadministration *Chicago Tribune*'s Springfield correspondent. "Its perusal will gladden the heart of every true Union man in the country, vindicate the President's fame and character, and be the keynote of the next Presidential campaign." Or it might, observed the now restored *Chicago Times*, include a repudiation of the Emancipation Proclamation and "a statement" of "an amnesty to the great mass of the Southern people."[22]

Whatever mystery the letter promised, the meeting itself was everything that the organizers had hoped for. "Never, perhaps, in the history of Illinois, has such a gathering of men been seen," rejoiced the *Illinois State Journal*. "The State of Illinois has redeemed herself. The glory of the 3rd of September has effaced the stain of the 17th of June." The *Journal* estimated the crowds as large as two hundred thousand, although Conkling himself thought it was more reasonable to estimate "50000 to 75000 present." The Democratic press was more dismissive of the estimates: the *Illinois State Register* estimated 12,096, and the *Chicago Times* correspondent "puts it at not exceeding 10,000, the greater portion of whom were women and children." But there was no doubt that Springfield was thronged with people. "The hotels are full," gushed the *Journal.* "Every house in the city, in which a Union family resides, is full to overflowing. Some of our leading citizens are boarding and sleeping more than fifty to one hundred people." At nine o'clock that morning, a great procession formed up at the state capitol and, led by "a magnificent flag and a band of music" and "a blue banner, with a portrait of President Lincoln in the center," it wound its way up and down Springfield's numbered streets and finally west on Washington Street to the fairgrounds. "So vast was the crowd that speaking was had at five different stands at the same time," with a regular schedule of invited speakers at four of them and a fifth reserved for "volunteer speakers." Zachariah Chandler held forth at the first stand, followed by General Isham Haynie, Governor Yates, and Senator Doolittle, plus the reading of letters from Edward Everett, Daniel Dickenson, and Schuyler Colfax; the second stand featured General McClernand and Chicago congressman Isaac Arnold; Richard Ogelsby spoke at the third stand; while the fourth stand was "set apart exclusively for German speakers."

The set piece of the meeting, however, was the reading of Lincoln's letter. And since the letter was addressed to Conkling personally, Conkling arranged that this was exactly how it should be delivered. Instead of following Lincoln's direction to do the reading himself, Conkling assigned the task to Jacksonville lawyer I. J. Ketcham. "Mr Ketcham then read the President's letter to Mr. Conkling," in a sort of epistolary tableau, "which was received with great enthusiasm, particularly the portion of it announcing that a retraction of the proclamation of emancipation was as impossible as the raising of the dead." It was Conkling's moment to bask in the glory of being the mediator between Springfield and the nation, and he was not about to have his role in it missed.[23]

Despite the *Chicago Times's* prediction, the letter was Lincoln's most extensive and forthright defense of emancipation since the issuance of the proclamation itself. The letter, all of 1,662 words long, falls logically into six sections. The first was a simple salutation to Conkling and to the organizers of the meeting, "my old political friends"; but it also made an opening political gesture of recognition to War Democrats, "those other noble men, whom no partizan malice, or partizan hope, can make false to the nation's life."[24]

That much said, Lincoln plunged bluntly into the second section, where it was clear at once that he intended to speak over the heads of the loyalists at the mass meeting, to the very antiemancipation Democrats who had triggered the legislative rumpus of the past spring, in the evident hope that they might be willing to keep fighting if they could have their anger at emancipation reasoned away. "There are those who are dissatisfied with me," he said simply, and their dissatisfaction came down to one thing: "You desire peace; and you blame me that we do not have it." What he asked the dissatisfied to do at that point was to reflect on how peace could actually be obtained. "There are but three conceivable ways." First was to keep on with the war and "suppress the rebellion by force of arms. This I am trying to do." Could there be any disagreement with that? "Are you for it?" he asked rhetorically. Lincoln presumed so, but he accepted for the moment that they didn't and moved on to suggest a second way to bring peace: "give up the Union." Were there any takers for that? "Are you for it?" This time, he presumed not. In that case, "If you are not for *force*, nor yet for *dissolution*, there only remains some imaginable compromise." But could anyone really imagine from where such a Union-saving compromise would come? Not from anyone in the South. "The strength of the rebellion, is its military—its army," Lincoln explained, and the rebel military showed no inclination at all to compromise. Even if the Confederate politicians in Richmond would announce their interest in compromise, "no paper compromise, to which the controllers of Lee's army are not agreed, can, at all, affect that army," and "no word or intimation, from that rebel army, or from any of the men controlling it, in relation to any peace compromise, has ever come to my knowledge or belief." Moreover, any efforts by well-intentioned Northerners to propose compromises and armistices would only "waste time, which the enemy would improve to our disadvantage; and that would be all." There was, in other words, no way forward for saving the Union except to fight determinedly and unitedly to victory over the Confederacy, and all the wild talk of national peace conventions was weakening that resolve.[25]

But Lincoln was quite aware that this was not the real grounds for the "dissatisfaction," or even the calls for national compromise. He began the third section of the letter with an accusation: "But, to be plain, you are dissatisfied with me about the negro." Indeed they were, and he knew that this "difference of opinion between you and myself upon that subject" was the issue before which all the other dissatisfactions were little more than smoke screens. Lincoln's gambit at that moment was to seize the moral high ground and turn the debate from a vicious argument about race to a more imposing argument about the Union. "I certainly wish that all men could be free," Lincoln wrote, which was an assertion so disarming that no one could easily object—and knowing that, Lincoln turned the knife deftly on his critics by adding, "while I suppose you do not." Having cast them neatly to the disadvantage, Lincoln still protested that he did not propose to make even that an issue: "Yet I have neither adopted, nor proposed any measure, which is not consistent with even your view"—and he then added the proviso which would be crucial to the entire development of his argument—"provided you are for the Union."

The strategy of the letter was now becoming apparent. By establishing a common commitment to saving the Union as a paramount virtue, Lincoln was now ready (after the irresistible suggestion that the antiemancipation Democrats had put their party over the last six months in the place of denouncing both Union *and* freedom) to ask whether any of his emancipation policies had been anything else except services to the cause of the Union. He had not, he reminded them, acted wildly or irresponsibly on the subject of emancipation. "I suggested compensated emancipation; to which you replied you wished not to be taxed to buy negroes." Lincoln here referred to the compensated emancipation plans he had designed in the spring of 1862, offering federally financed buyouts of slavery to the border states. This would have meant taxing Northerners to subsidize the purchase of enslaved blacks, but this was only "to save you from greater taxation to save the Union" by means of war. (Corollary: if really *you are for the Union*, there is no reason to oppose compensated emancipation, especially when taxation to pay for compensation promises to be far less expensive than taxation for war.)[26]

But there was a counterargument lurking here: that the proclamation was so radical a gesture that it was the principal reason why the Union was becoming impossible to restore. "Some of you profess to think its retraction would operate favorably for the Union." But practically speaking, the truth was that "the war has certainly progressed as favorably for us, since the issue of the proclamation as before." (Corollary: if really *you are for the Union*, there is no reason to retract the Emancipation Proclamation.) The irony of these protests, Lincoln pointed out, is that all the while "you say you will not fight to free negroes," there were large numbers of emancipated blacks who "seem willing to fight for you." Everyone of them who was willing to subtract himself or herself from the Confederate war-making effort by running away to the Union lines, or who was willing to don a Union uniform and carry a rifle against the rebels, was just so much more aid in saving the Union. "I thought that in your struggle for the Union, to whatever extent the negroes should cease helping the enemy, to that extent it weakened the enemy in his resistance to you. Do you think differently?" Lincoln again jabbed rhetorically.[27]

But for those who swept aside the practical benefits of emancipation on the grounds that, practical or not, it was unconstitutional, Lincoln was ready with a related response. "You dislike the emancipation proclamation; and, perhaps, would have it retracted. You say it is unconstitutional." But this was a matter of interpretation, not constitutional fact. The Constitution, after all, designates the president as commander in chief in time of war, and under international law, emancipation of an opponent's slaves was perfectly within the legal category of military actions which could be taken to weaken the enemy. "The most that can be said, is, that slaves are property. Is there—has there ever been—any question that by the law of war, property, both of enemies and friends, may be taken when needed? And is it not needed whenever taking it, helps us, or hurts the enemy?" Of course, it was possible to quibble whether such a confiscation proclamation in time of war should be considered "valid . . . as law"—in other words, as a measure which would hold up under examination in a court. If it wasn't, there was no use calling for the proclamation's retraction now, because litigation would find out whatever defects it had in the law's own good time; if, on the other hand, the proclamation was valid, then what point would be served by retracting it? "If it is valid, it needs no retraction. If it is valid, it can not be retracted, any more than the dead can be brought back to life."[28]

Significantly, these two points—the proclamation's constitutionality as a wartime measure and its technical legal standing before the federal courts thereafter—were more bothersome to Lincoln than this simple either/or treatment suggested. He had told General Stephen A. Hurlbut in July that "I think [the Proclamation] is valid in law, and will be so held by the courts," but even if not, "I think I shall not retract or repudiate it. Those who shall have tasted actual freedom I believe can never be slaves, or quasi slaves again." And yet, though he was determined that "while I remain in my present position I shall not attempt to retract or modify the emancipation proclamation, nor shall I return to slavery any person who is free by the terms of that proclamation, or by any of the Acts of Congress," nevertheless, he acknowledged that "the Executive power itself would be greatly diminished by the cessation of actual war." He admitted to Confederate vice president Alexander Stephens as late as the Hampton Roads Conference in February 1865 that "his own opinion was that as the proclamation was a war measure and would have effect only from its being an exercise of the war power, as soon as the war ceased, it would be inoperative." He insisted that he would make it apply "to such slaves as had come under its operation while it was in active exercise," including slaves *de facto* liberated by the Union armies. But he was aware that "the courts might decide the other way." Hence, Lincoln's eagerness as early as 1864 for a constitutional amendment which would put emancipation beyond the reach even of the federal courts.[29]

But Lincoln would grant this much to his political critics. If they wished "exclusively to save the Union" and not to emancipate slaves, their love for the Union (if really *you are for the Union*) was quite acceptable to Lincoln and should carry them forward with him to the goal of saving it. "Fight you, then, exclusively to save the Union." And whenever they had succeeded in conquering "all resistance to the Union," if Lincoln should ask them to fight any longer after that, then "it will be an apt time, then, for you to declare you will not fight to free negroes." All this, of course, was a highly subtle joke. By the time such critics had fought and saved the Union, the war for black freedom would also be over. But while the war was still on, there was no other way to get black help to save the Union than through offering blacks freedom. "Negroes, like other people, act upon motives." (Negroes, Lincoln had originally written in his rough draft, are "creatures of motives.") If, for the sake of saving the Union, "they stake their lives for us, they must be prompted by the strongest motive—even the promise of freedom." And here, Lincoln added ominously, "the promise being made, must be kept."[30] There would, in other words, be no taking back of the Emancipation Proclamation. A pledge of life had to be balanced with a pledge of freedom, a pledge so solemn that it would balance forever the risk of life.

And then, abruptly, the argument for emancipation seemed spent. Lincoln turned quickly and briefly in the fourth section of the letter to what many at the fairgrounds might have imagined would have been the longer subject of his letter, a review of the progress of the war. "The signs look better." The Mississippi was now open with the fall of Vicksburg, and "the Father of Waters again goes unvexed to the sea." The Northwest and the Northeast had all contributed their strength, and so even had the Unionist South, "in black and white." Victories at "Antietam, Murfreesboro, Gettysburg, and on many fields of lesser note" had been won, while the navy—"Uncle Sam's Web-feet"—had successfully imposed a blockade that covered the deep sea as well as "wherever the ground was a little damp." Thanks went to all, "For the great republic—for the principle it lives by, and keeps alive—for man's great future,—thanks to all."[31]

But Lincoln had one more round to fire on behalf of emancipation, and this became the fifth and most acerbic section. "Peace does not appear so distant as it did," he concluded, and when it did, the peace would prove the basic point he had been struggling to make since his July 4, 1861, special message to Congress, "that, among free men, there can be no successful appeal from the ballot to the bullet," that in democracies, minorities cannot willfully destroy a polity because they have not triumphed and still pretend that they are functioning democratically. And when that case is proved—and if really *you are for the Union*, that must be one's case—then it will be discovered that "there will be some black men who can remember that, with silent tongue, and clenched teeth, and steady eye, and well-poised bayonet, they have helped mankind on to this great consummation." What, then, would the critics have to say to such men, who had helped them make their own case for the Union and democracy? "While, I fear," Lincoln continued, "there will be some white ones, unable to forget that, with malignant heart, and deceitful speech, they have strove to hinder it."[32] If any of them happened to have been sitting in the Illinois legislature that spring, they knew now what conclusions Lincoln expected them to draw about their own role in history.[33]

The meeting went on until the evening, concluding with resolutions, fireworks, and a final torchlight procession. The next morning, even the hostile *Illinois State Register* had to concede that, "crowded into the narrow amphitheatre of the fair ground, the crowd made a respectable enough appearance," and Conkling jubilantly informed Lincoln by letter that "Our mass meeting was a magnificent success . . . and the largest meeting by far that ever assembled together in the State." But the focus of national attention, from the following morning onwards, was less on the meeting itself and more on Lincoln's letter. Corrected copies were picked up and reprinted across the North—Simon Hanscom's *Washington National Republican* was given the "only correct and authorized copy" to print—and it was even read aloud again at another mass Union meeting in Syracuse, New York, the same day. Congratulations poured in on Lincoln from John Goodrich, Henry Wilson, John Murray Forbes, and Charles Sumner. (Goodrich, the Collector of the Port of Boston, at least had gotten Lincoln's joke: "What a contrast—the black man trying to save, & the white man trying to destroy his country. I think Copperheads must feel that they are compared to the Negro quite to their disadvantage.") And before the end of the year, the Conkling letter was reprinted as a pamphlet at least twice. Lincoln was particularly anxious that his declarations about the permanence of emancipation had been clearly heard, and he quizzed Illinoisan Anson Miller about it when Miller reported to the White House later that month.

> He wanted to know all about [the] great political meeting that had then just been held in Springfield. . . . I told him that the passage in the letter which was most vehemently cheered was the one about the colored men; and I quoted it to him: "We have promised the colored men their rights; and, by the help of God, that promise shall be kept." When I told him this, he replied, very earnestly, "Well God helping me, that promise shall be fulfilled."[34]

The newspapers, like the crowd, also saw how firmly Lincoln had pegged himself to emancipation. The *Chicago Tribune*, especially, saw in the letter Lincoln's reaffirmation of the permanence of emancipation, no matter what. "It has been feared that even he looked upon his Proclamation as a temporary expedient, born of the necessities of the situation, to be adhered to or retracted as a short-sighted or time-serving policy dictated; and that when the moment for attempting compromise might come, he would put it aside," the *Tribune* editorialized.

Somehow this conviction has hold of the popular mind. . . . [But] the Springfield letter dispels all doubts and silences all croakers. In a few plain sentences, than which none more important were ever uttered in this country, Mr. Lincoln exonerates himself from the crimes urged against him, shows the untenableness of the position that his enemies occupy, and gives the world assurance that that great measure of policy and justice, which . . . guarantees freedom to three millions of slaves, is to remain the law of the republic. . . . The battle is to be fought out. No miserable compromise . . . is to stop the progress of our arms. . . . God bless Old Abe!

Even the *Chicago Times* conceded that Lincoln had now made emancipation irrevocable. "The President does not believe that any compromise embracing the maintenance of the Union is now possible. . . . The arming of negroes is defended . . . and a puff is given to the sable warriors, the promise of freedom to whom 'being made, must be kept.'"[35]

The *Times* might have drawn some consolation from what the Conkling letter does *not* say, because there were some significant omissions: Lincoln would defend emancipation, but he made no mention of what the ultimate fate of slavery would be in the places where it remained legal, or even whether renunciation of slavery would be the price of reunion; and while Lincoln vigorously defended the enlistment of black soldiers, he avoided any announcement of what direction he thought the issue of black civil rights ought to take. Nevertheless, the *Times* returned angrily to the same theme two days later, still unwilling to face the fact that Lincoln had drawn his line at the proclamation.

We have here an assumption that the President, who is a creature of the constitution, may, by proclamation, fasten upon the people an irrevocable law which subverts the constitution. If the proclamation cannot be retracted, then every provision in the constitution pertaining to slavery is abrogated. . . . If it cannot be retracted any more than the dead can be brought back to life (by human agency), then the soul of the Constitution has been murdered—assassinated—by him who solemnly swore to "preserve, protect and defend it."

The *Louisville Daily Democrat*, the mouthpiece of antiadministration sentiment in Kentucky, saw Lincoln's adamant defense of emancipation as the promise that "we must go on until there is no power to resist left in the South—not a remnant," and "at the end, if there ever be an end, we shall have, not a restoration of the Union, but something else, which may be desirable or not, no one can foresee." In New York, an antiadministration journal, the *Old Guard,* bitterly remarked that "If it has any meaning at all it means that the object of this struggle is to free negroes. And to do this he is willing to shed the blood of a quarter of a million of white men, and to tax all the white men who survive to a degree that will be the torture of their existence." But the *New York Times* rejoiced: "It is plain that the President has no power to make a man once legally free again legally a slave. The President's argument for the employment of colored troops is unanswerable."[36]

What struck even a few of Lincoln's admirers as odd, however, was the style of the letter. For one thing, there were some unusual grammatical lapses and some overstrained metaphors: "Uncle Sam's Web-feet," the "Father of Waters," "the Sunny South," "apply the means" (an old theological phrase about the constant use of preaching and other "means" to religious conversion), and a particularly *outré* misconstruction at the close of *they have striven* as "they have strove." The *New York Times* only half-praised the letter for its "downright directness of sentiment and style" which appealed to "the real people." The *North American Review* thought that "Mr. Lincoln has . . . been reproached with Americanisms by some not unfriendly British critics," but the *Review* decided that "we cannot say that we like him any the worse for it." George Templeton Strong thought that "there are sentences that a critic would like to eliminate, but they are delightfully characteristic of the man," while the letter itself was "likely to be a conspicuous document in the history of our times." The *Illinois State Register* was more brutal: "Mr. Lincoln speaks of 'Uncle Sam's webbed feet' as if the government were a goose," and "in the radical view of who constitutes 'the government,' perhaps he is right." But even John Hay wondered if Lincoln's stylistic gifts had momentarily deserted him. "His last letter is a great thing," Hay wrote to John Nicolay, but it was marred by "some hideously bad rhetoric—some indecorums that are infamous—yet the whole letter takes its solid place in history, as a great utterance of a great man."[37]

The Conkling letter was also noticeable for the prominence of one particular rhetorical device, the repeated, jabbing interrogatory—*Are you for it? Does it appear otherwise to you?*—and the semi-interrogatory that jumps ahead to put a response to a question into the hearers' mouths—*You desire peace, you are dissatisfied with me about the negro, I suppose you do not, You say you will not fight to free negroes.* This use of *prolepsis* (the anticipation of a question or objection) was a favorite of Lincoln's as early as his Lyceum Speech of 1838 and figures prominently in many of the speeches he gave in 1859, when he was stumping for Ohio gubernatorial candidate Salmon Chase, and in the 1860 Cooper Union address. Obviously, it was a technique which would come easily to a lawyer like Lincoln, for whom interrogation and cross-examination were necessary tools of the trade (and Lincoln, as Isaac Arnold remembered, "had no equal . . . in the examination and cross-examination of a witness").[38] But it played only an infrequent role in his presidential state papers. Where it showed much more frequently were in the public letters of 1863, especially in the reply to the Ohio Democrats, and it was at its peak in the Conkling letter.

One reason, beyond Lincoln's habitual fondness for *prolepsis*, why it should play so large a role in the Conkling letter may be connected to another rhetorical influence on Lincoln in the summer of 1863. In addition to the situation in Illinois, Lincoln had to keep a continuously anxious eye on emancipation's impact on Kentucky and especially the Kentucky gubernatorial election in August. The resistance to emancipation that "Parson" Brownlow had detected in January had little abated by the summer, and antiemancipationists had succeeded in persuading former governor Charles A. Wickliffe to run against the Unionist candidate, Thomas Bramlette. (Another reason why Lincoln was reluctant to leave Washington in August 1863 was his concern to monitor the Kentucky election which, as he put it, "got ugly.") Bramlette had no flaming reputation for being proemancipation, but he staged a surprisingly strong campaign, and on June 25, at Carlisle, Kentucky, Bramlette delivered an aggressive speech which was republished as a pamphlet and became the centerpiece of his campaign. It has some unusual resonances with the Conkling letter, especially in its repeated use of *prolepsis*. "You sympathize with the cotton gentlemen, do you?" asked Bramlette. "This was their plan, and it still is their malignant plan."[39]

> You say the Emancipation Proclamation is all wrong, and Kentucky should not sanction it. You are a Kentuckian, and let us see where you stand. The president carefully excluded from his Emancipation proclamation all the border States. . . .

> You object to negro soldiers. Who began this business? Who raised the first negro regiment? Did Lincoln? Don't you know that in the beginning of this strife, in New Orleans, they heralded it abroad that they had already organized two negro regiments to fight the Yankees with?

> Why is it you have grown so terribly repugnant to negro aid? You are willing it should be employed against us, but now that it is being employed to help us, you are terribly disturbed.

> At this point I am met by a certain class of men who call themselves constitutional Union men. . . . You say you don't approve of the measures or policy of the Administration in the prosecution of the war. . . . Suppose one of you were assaulted by robbers, who threatened to burn your house and murder your family . . . [and] that while you are engaged in a close hand to hand conflict with one of them you should see that brawny negro having one of them down, would you say, "Hold on! I don't want any negro to help me. . . ." Is this what any sane man would do?

The Carlisle speech is far more personal and denunciatory in tone than Lincoln's Conkling letter, but the rhetorical similarities are remarkable, especially given their overlap in the summer of 1863 and Lincoln's concern for the responses to emancipation in both Kentucky and Illinois. And, further underscoring Lincoln's interest in the Carlisle speech, one of John Hay's anonymous editorials on August 7, 1863, for John Forney's *Washington Daily Chronicle* on the Kentucky election, featured long extracts from the Bramlette speech. The awareness in the Lincoln White House of the importance of the Carlisle speech suggests that Lincoln may have had more than just examples of cross-examination in the back of his mind as he composed the Conkling letter.

For all of its complicated and colorful context, the Conkling letter has not received nearly so much attention as the other public letters of 1863, just as Lincoln's use of the genre of the public letter is usually overshadowed by the greatness of his public speeches. Few Lincoln biographers have paid it serious attention, and while some early biographers like J. G. Holland, F. F. Browne, and Isaac Arnold reprinted large extracts of the Conkling letter in their works, the volume of modern notice has dwindled to a few citations, at best.[40] This, in itself, tracks the extent to which Lincoln biography gradually shifted its attention away from Lincoln's role as racial emancipator to the great reunifier or wartime chieftain. But this neglect misses the significance of a document which, as James Conkling himself noted, signaled that "the Presidential Campaign for your successor (*if any*) has already commenced in Illinois." More than that, the Conkling letter signaled the central place Lincoln insisted emancipation would have in that campaign, especially as he pressed forward in 1864 to secure the legal permanence of emancipation through the Thirteenth Amendment. It also offered the most extended and eloquent defense of emancipation as both policy and principle that Lincoln would compose. (In fact, it would be one of the few documents of his own composing which he would afterward quote to illustrate his position.) "The letter to Conkling is one of Lincoln's most intense exertions of political mind," writes literary critic David Bromwich, "and in it we see not only a skilled but a great lawyer arguing."[41] Above all, it was the Conkling letter which had the most long-lasting political impact, since it made clear, finally and beyond any question, that Lincoln had no intention whatsoever of backing away from, or negotiating around, emancipation. This makes the Conkling letter a reminder, even as Lincoln's reputation as an emancipator has become clouded over time, that the Emancipation Proclamation had made slaves, not merely pawns in a political game, but "thenceforth and forever free."

Notes

This essay first appeared in *Civil War History* 48.4 (December 2002): 313–37, where it won that year's John T. Hubbell Prize for the best essay to appear in that volume of *Civil War History*. Reprinted with permission of Kent State University Press.

1. Frederick Seward, in *Recollected Words of Abraham Lincoln*, ed. Don Fehrenbacher and Virginia Fehrenbacher (Stanford, CA, 1996), 397; James Blaine, *Twenty Years of Congress: From Lincoln to Garfield* (Norwich, CT, 1884), 1:488; Lincoln, "To Hannibal Hamlin," September 28, 1862, in *Collected Works of Abraham Lincoln*, ed. Roy P. Basler (New Brunswick, NJ, 1953–55), 5:444; William O. Stoddard, *Inside the White House in War Times: Memoirs and Reports of Lincoln's Secretary* (1890), ed. Michael Burlingame (Lincoln, NE, 2000), 97.

2. Butler to Edward L. Pierce, July 20, 1863, Edward L. Pierce Papers, Houghton Library, Harvard University; Benjamin Flanders to Salmon P. Chase, November 29, 1862, Abraham Lincoln Papers, Library of Congress.

3. "To the Workingmen of Manchester, England," "To Erastus Corning and Others," "To Matthew Birchard and Others," and "To James C. Conkling," in *Collected Works*, 6:63–64, 260–69, 300–306, 406–11; Chauncey M. Depew, *My Memories of Eighty Years* (New York, 1922), 30; James A. Rawley, *Abraham Lincoln and a Nation Worth Fighting for* (Wheeling, IL, 1996), 53.

4. John McClintock, in Fehrenbacher and Fehrenbacher, *Recollected Words*, 314; Truman Woodruff to Lincoln, April 12, 1863, Abraham Lincoln Papers, Library of Congress; William G. Brownlow to Montgomery Blair, January 9, 1863, Blair Family Papers, Library of Congress; Theodore Clarke Smith, *The Life and Letters of James Abram Garfield* (New Haven, CT, 1925), 1:244–45; "The President's Proclamation," *Louisville Daily Democrat*, January 3, 1863; E. Merton Coulter, *The Civil War and Readjustment in Kentucky* (Chapel Hill, NC, 1926), 173–79; Lowell H. Harrison, *Lincoln of Kentucky* (Lexington, KY, 2000), 176–77.

5. Paul Finkelman, "Slavery, the 'More Perfect Union,' and the Prairie State," *Illinois Historical Journal* 80 (Winter 1987): 248–69. On the dearth of antislavery feeling, especially in southern Illinois, see Edgar F. Raines, "The American Missionary Association in Southern Illinois, 1856–1862," *Journal of the Illinois State Historical Society* 65 (1972): 250–51; and Suzanne Cooper Guasco, "'The Deadly Influence of Negro Capitalists': Southern Yeomen and Resistance to the Expansion of Slavery in Illinois," *Civil War History* 47 (March 2001): 7–29; George W. Smith, *A History of Southern Illinois: A Narrative Account of its Historical Progress* (Chicago, 1912), 1:317.

6. Robert Smith to Richard Yates, October 13, 1862, Abraham Lincoln Papers, Library of Congress; *Congressional Globe*, December 23, 1862, 37th Cong., 3rd sess., 182.

7. George W. Smith, *History of Illinois and Her People* (Chicago, 1927), 3:28; J. G. Randall, *Lincoln the President: Springfield to Gettysburg* (New York, 1945), 2:234–35; Paul Angle, *"Here I Have Lived": A History of Lincoln's Springfield, 1821–1865* (Chicago, 1971), 274; "Influence of the Democratic Victory," *Alton Telegraph*, December 19, 1862.

8. G. M. Mitchell to Ozias Mather Hatch, April 14, 1863, in O. M. Hatch Papers, Illinois State Historical Library, Springfield; Charles W. Wills, *Army Life*

of an Illinois Soldier, Including a Day by Day Record of Sherman's March to the Sea (Washington, DC, 1906), 125–26; Joseph Miller to Pvt. William Wilmoth, January 25, 1863, in Lincoln Research Files ("Emancipation Proclamation"), Abraham Lincoln Presidential Library and Museum, Springfield, IL (hereafter cited as ALPLM); Victor Hicken, *Illinois in the Civil War* (Urbana, IL, 1966), 128–29, 139.

9. George Julian, *Political Recollections, 1840–1872* (1884; repr., Westport, CT, 1970), 223; Paul Selby, "Light on a Famous Lincoln Letter," *Transactions of the Illinois State Historical Society for the Year 1908* (Springfield, IL, 1909), 243; O. H. Browning, diary entry for January 30, 1863, in *Diary of Orville Hickman Browning*, ed. T. C. Pease and J. G. Randall (Springfield, IL, 1925), 1:621; Jackson Grimshaw to Ozias M. Hatch, September 8, 1862, and February 12, 1863, O. M. Hatch Papers, ALPLM; David M. Silver, *Lincoln's Supreme Court* (Urbana, IL, 1957), 72. Baker and Bailhache ran the *Illinois State Journal*, the principal downstate Republican newspaper, headquartered in Springfield; Ninian Edwards was Lincoln's brother-in-law and secured the post of commissary commissioner in Springfield.

10. *Illinois State Register*, January 3, 1863; Mercy Levering Conkling to Clinton Conkling, January 11, 1863, in James C. and Clinton L. Conkling Papers, ALPLM.

11. *Journal of the House of Representatives of the Twenty-Third General Assembly of the State of Illinois* (Springfield, IL, 1865), 66, 78, 83, 373.

12. Jesse K. Dubois, Ozias M. Hatch, and William Butler to Lincoln, March 1, 1863, and James C. Conkling to Lincoln, April 10, 1863, Abraham Lincoln Papers, Library of Congress; Mercy Levering Conkling to Clinton Conkling, June 7, 1863, in Conkling Papers, ALPLM.

13. Camilla A. Quinn, *Lincoln's Springfield in the Civil War* (Macomb, IL, 1991), 47; Melvin W. Fuller, in *Journal of the House of Representatives of the Twenty-Third General Assembly of the State of Illinois* (Springfield, IL, 1865), 728; William B. Hesseltine, *Lincoln and the War Governors* (New York, 1948), 318; "Speech of Richard Yates," *Illinois State Journal*, July 13, 1863.

14. Politician-general John A. McClernand reported to Lincoln on a Democratic meeting in Chatham, Illinois, where "a number hurrahed for John Morgan—the same Morgan who is now burning the houses and wasting the fields of peaceful citizens in the loyal state of Ohio." Judging by that meeting, McClernand was alarmed that "a bold demagogue, or a reckless inebriate, in my opinion, has it in his power to precipitate fearful strife and great bloodshed" in Illinois. McClernand to Lincoln, July 23, 1863, Abraham Lincoln Papers, Library of Congress.

15. "The Meeting Yesterday," *Illinois State Register*, June 18, 1863; *History of Sangamon County, Illinois* (Chicago, 1881), 315.

16. "Enthusiastic Union Meeting in Macon County," *Illinois State Journal*, July 25, 1863; "Grand Union Meeting," *Illinois State Journal*, August 10, 1863; "Grand Union Demonstration," *Illinois State Journal*, July 9, 1863; "State Union Mass Convention," *Illinois State Journal*, August 8, 1863.

17. Frederick B. Crossley, *Courts and Lawyers of Illinois* (Chicago, 1916), 191–92; *The United States Biographical Dictionary and Portrait Gallery of Eminent and Self-*

Made Men: Illinois Volume (Chicago, 1876), 159–60; Joseph Wallace, *Past and Present of the City of Springfield and Sangamon County* (Chicago, 1904), 54–55; Victor B. Howard, "The Illinois Republican Party," *Journal of the Illinois State Historical Society* 64 (Autumn 1971): 303; Wayne C. Temple, "Delegates to the Illinois State Republican Nominating Convention in 1860," *Journal of the Illinois State Historical Society* 92 (Autumn 1999): 296; James C. Conkling to George Bancroft, February 19, 1866, and to Robert Hall, July 31, 1862, Conkling Papers, ALPLM; Lincoln, "To Edwin M. Stanton," February 3, 1863, and "To Montgomery C. Meigs," January 31, 1863, in *Collected Works*, 6:85, 90.

18. "The Great Union Mass Meeting," *Illinois State Journal*, August 13, 1863; "Preparing for the Great Mass Meeting," *Illinois State Journal*, August 25, 1863.

19. James C. Conkling to Lincoln, August 14, 1863, Abraham Lincoln Papers, Library of Congress. See also *Dear Mr. Lincoln: Letters to the President*, ed. Harold Holzer (Reading, MA, 1993), 281; Conkling to George Bancroft, February 19, 1866, Conkling Papers, ALPLM.

20. Lincoln, "To James C. Conkling," August 20, 1863, in *Collected Works*, 6:399; "President Lincoln Will Probably Be Here," *Illinois State Journal*, August 21, 1863; "The Great Meeting in Illinois: The President Expected," *Washington National Republican*, August 22, 1863. The possibility of Lincoln absenting himself from Washington in the late summer of 1863 seems to have had general currency, since New Hampshire governor Joseph Gilmore had written him on August 4, "I see from the public prints that you are intending to spend a few weeks among the Mountains of New Hampshire. May we not have the privilege of welcoming you to our state capital?" But it was actually Mary Lincoln, not her husband, who was planning a New Hampshire summer vacation. Gilmore to Lincoln, August 4, 1863, James C. Conkling to Lincoln, August 21, 1863, and Herndon to Lincoln, August 26, 1863, Abraham Lincoln Papers, Library of Congress.

21. John Hay, diary entry for August 23, 1863, in *Inside Lincoln's White House: The Complete Civil War Diary of John Hay*, ed. Michael Burlingame and J. R. T. Ettlinger (Carbondale, IL, 1997), 76; Lincoln, "To James C. Conkling," August 27, 1863, in *Collected Works*, 6:414. Lincoln's rough draft of August 26, 1863, survives in the Abraham Lincoln Papers at the Library of Congress as seven sheets, five of them in pencil, the final two in ink, with a few words crossed out; the formal draft, also of August 26 and also extant in the Abraham Lincoln Papers, is written in ink on eight sheets of Executive Mansion stationery, with one of them, the fifth, pasted together where Lincoln probably removed a section he had originally planned to include on the futility of an armistice or peace convention, and a quick conclusion promising that "the government will return no person to slavery who is free according to the proclamation." Lincoln, "Fragment," August 26, 1863, in *Collected Works*, 6:410–11. The actual letter sent to Conkling was recopied in another hand on four double sheets of Executive Mansion stationery, on which Lincoln made one notable alteration in his own hand, changing a phrase near the conclusion from "well-born bayonet" to "well-poised bayonet." Lincoln's cover note to Conkling, marked "Private," was written on War Department stationery.

Both the copyist's draft and Lincoln's cover note are in the ALPLM. On Lincoln's composing habits, see Stoddard, *Inside the White House in War Times*, 171–72. Stoddard included this news as part of his Washington dispatch for the September 3, 1863, edition of the *New York Examiner*. Lincoln regularly used his staffers to leak significant news to the press through columns and letters they themselves contributed anonymously to a variety of Northern newspapers.

22. "From Springfield," *Chicago Tribune*, September 1, 1863; "The News," *Chicago Times*, September 2, 1863.

23. James C. Conkling to Lincoln, September 4, 1863, Abraham Lincoln Papers, Library of Congress; "The Great Meeting," *Illinois State Register*, September 9, 1863; "The News," *Chicago Times*, September 4, 1863; "From Springfield," *Chicago Tribune*, September 3, 1863; "The Great Union Mass Meeting," *Illinois State Journal*, September 4, 1863. Lincoln's letter was printed in full as the first document in the *Journal*'s article, followed by the texts of the letters from Everett, Colfax, and Dickenson and the speeches of Chandler and Oglesby. The speeches of McClernand and Doolittle were published in the *Journal* on September 7 and 9.

24. Lincoln, "To James C. Conkling," August 26, 1863, in *Collected Works*, 6:406–7. For his own final draft, Lincoln wrote out the salutation on the top half of a sheet of Executive Mansion stationery.

25. Ibid., 6:407.

26. Lincoln was sufficiently anxious to prove the favorable impact of the proclamation on the course of military events that on August 31 he telegraphed Conkling with a paragraph he wanted Conkling to insert in the reading of the letter, attesting "that some of the commanders of our armies in the field who have given us our most important successes, believe the emancipation policy, and the use of colored troops, constitute the heaviest blow yet dealt to the rebellion; and that at least one of those important successes, could not have been achieved when it was, but for the aid of black soldiers." Lincoln, "To James C. Conkling," August 31, 1863, in *Collected Works*, 6:423. Lincoln was quoting a letter he had received from Ulysses S. Grant shortly after sending his own letter to Conkling, in which Grant described emancipation and "arming the negro" as "the heavyest blow yet given the Confederacy." Grant, "To Abraham Lincoln," August 23, 1863, in *The Papers of Ulysses S. Grant*, ed. John Y. Simon (Carbondale, IL, 1982), 9:195–97. This and a similar letter from Nathaniel Banks "gave much satisfaction to the President," according to Salmon Chase, to whom Lincoln showed the letters on August 30. *Inside Lincoln's Cabinet: The Civil War Diaries of Salmon P. Chase*, ed. David Donald (New York, 1954), 178. Conkling marked his copyist's version of Lincoln's letter with a caret, "Here insert Telegram," to note the place where the telegraphed paragraph was to be read.

27. Lincoln, "To James C. Conkling," August 26, 1863, in *Collected Works*, 6:408.

28. Ibid., 6:409.

29. Lincoln, "To Stephen A. Hurlbut," July 31, 1863, and "Annual Message to Congress," December 8, 1864, in *Collected Works*, 6:358, 8:151–52; Alexander Stephens, *A Constitutional View of the Late War between the States* (Philadelphia,

1870), 2:610–11; William C. Harris, "The Hampton Roads Peace Conference: A Final Test of Lincoln's Presidential Leadership," *Journal of the Abraham Lincoln Association* 21 (Winter 2000): 50.

30. Lincoln, "To James C. Conkling," August 26, 1863, in *Collected Works*, 6:409; Douglas L. Wilson, *Lincoln's Sword: The Presidency and the Power of Words* (New York, 2006), 187.

31. Lincoln, "To James C. Conkling," August 26, 1863, in *Collected Works*, 6:409–10.

32. Ibid., 6:410.

33. Ibid. Lincoln actually had one more telegram to send to Conkling about the letter, but it was not for public reading. Lincoln had guarded the text of the letter jealously, choosing not this time to leak it to the press. "He had refused a copy of his letter to the Washington agent of the Associated Press," and both "the President and his secretaries were deaf" to all requests for advance notices; "the paper . . . was sent out of the White House, it was said, by a private messenger," according to Noah Brooks, in *Washington in Lincoln's Time* (New York, 1895), 62–63. However, a "Botched up" version of the letter appeared on the morning of September 3 in the *Washington Daily Chronicle* and then in the *Chicago Tribune* and the *New York Evening Post*. Lincoln was "mad enough to cry," and John W. Forney, the editor of the *Chronicle*, in a note to Lincoln that morning promptly fobbed responsibility onto Laurence A. Gobright of the Associated Press. Forney to Lincoln, September 3, 1863, Abraham Lincoln Papers, Library of Congress. That morning, Lincoln telegraphed Conkling with a demand for an explanation. Lincoln, "To James C. Conkling," September 3, 1863, in *Collected Works*, 6:430. The telegram caught up with Conkling as the meeting was in progress, and Conkling admitted rather lamely in his letter of the next day to Lincoln that "in order that the St. Louis Chicago and Springfield papers might publish your Letter simultaneously and at the earliest period after the meeting, so as to gratify the intense anxiety which existed with regard to your views, copies were sent to the two former places with strict instructions not to permit it to be published before the meeting or make any improper use of it. But it appears that a part of it was telegraphed from Chicago to New York contrary to my express directions. I do not know what particular individual is chargeable with this breach of faith, but I presume it was some one connected with the Chicago Tribune." Conkling to Lincoln, September 4, 1863, Abraham Lincoln Papers, Library of Congress).

34. "Extra. Highly Important. Declaration of Principles by the President," *Washington National Republican*, September 3, 1863. On the Syracuse meeting, see *New York Times*, September 4, 1863. The planner of the Syracuse meeting, Benjamin Field, had written to Lincoln on August 26, asking for a copy of the letter which he had heard Lincoln was preparing for the Springfield meeting; Lincoln sent a copy of the letter, with the same injunction to "not let it become public until your meeting shall have come off." Field to Lincoln, Abraham Lincoln Papers, Library of Congress; Lincoln, "To Ben Field," August 29, 1863, in *Collected Works*, 6:420. "The 'Union' Mass Meeting," *Illinois State Register*, September 4,

1863; Conkling to Lincoln, September 4, 1863, Abraham Lincoln Papers, Library of Congress; Quinn, *Lincoln's Springfield in the Civil War*, 53; "The Springfield Mass Meeting," *Chicago Tribune*, September 4, 1863; John Z. Goodrich to Lincoln, September 3, 1863, Abraham Lincoln Papers, Library of Congress; Moses Coit Tyler, "One of Mr. Lincoln's Old Friends," *Journal of the Illinois State Historical Society* 29 (January 1936): 256–57. The Conkling letter was reprinted as *The War Policy of the Administration: Letter of the President to Union Mass Convention at Springfield, Illinois* (Albany, 1863) and *The Letters of President Lincoln on Questions of National Policy* (New York, 1863), 19–22.

35. "Mr. Lincoln's Letter," *Chicago Tribune*, September 3, 1863; "The News," *Chicago Times*, September 3, 1863.

36. "Subversion of the Constitution by Proclamation," *Chicago Times*, September 5, 1863; "The Letter," *Louisville Daily Democrat*, September 8, 1863; "Does Mr. Lincoln Wish to Save the Union?," *Old Guard* 1 (October/December 1863): 278; "The Springfield Convention," *New York Times,* September 3, 1863.

37. "The Springfield Convention," *New York Times*, September 3, 1863; "The President's Policy," *North American Review* 98 (January 1864): 244; George Templeton Strong, *Diary of the Civil War, 1860–1865*, ed. Allan Nevins (New York, 1962), 355; "What Does It Mean?," *Illinois State Register*, September 8, 1863; Hay to John G. Nicolay, September 11, 1863, in *At Lincoln's Side: John Hay's Civil War Correspondence and Selected Writings*, ed. Michael Burlingame (Carbondale, IL, 2000), 54.

38. Michael Leff and Jean Goodwin, "Dialogic Figures and Dialectical Argument in Lincoln's Rhetoric," in *Rhetoric and Public Affairs* 3 (Spring 2000): 59–69; Isaac N. Arnold, *The Life of Abraham Lincoln* (1884), ed. James A. Rawley (Lincoln, NE, 1994), 84.

39. Lincoln, "To Mary Todd Lincoln," August 8, 1863, in *Collected Works*, 6:372. The full text of the Carlisle speech was printed as "Speech of Judge Bramlette on the Conduct of the War and the Duty of Kentuckians, Delivered at Carlisle," *Louisville Daily Democrat*, July 1, 1863; John Hay, "Editorial," August 7, 1863, in *Lincoln's Journalist: John Hay's Anonymous Writings for the Press, 1860–1864*, ed. Michael Burlingame (Carbondale, IL, 1998), 334–37. The Conkling letter, in turn, may have set a rhetorical pattern for other writers on emancipation, such as Francis Wayland's "Letter to a Peace Democrat," *Atlantic Monthly*, December 1863, where Wayland employs the same devices: "You disapprove of the Emancipation proclamation, you denounce the employment of armed negroes and therefore you have no stomach for the fight. But has not the President published to the world that the Proclamation was a measure of military necessity? . . . If as you are accustomed to assert, the Proclamation is a dead letter, it certainly need not give you very serious discomfort. If it exercises a powerful influence in crippling the energies of the South, it surely is not among Northern men that we should look for its opponents" (778).

40. Substantial citations of the Conkling letter appear in Francis Fisher Browne, *The Every-Day Life of Abraham Lincoln* (1887), ed. John Y. Simon (Lincoln, NE,

1995), 600–602; Josiah Gilbert Holland, *Life of Abraham Lincoln* (Springfield, MA, 1866), 420–21; and Arnold, *Life of Abraham Lincoln*, 336–40. Modern writers' treatment of it is scantier, as in Stephen B. Oates, *With Malice toward None: The Life of Abraham Lincoln* (New York, 1977), 358–60; Phillip Shaw Paludan, *The Presidency of Abraham Lincoln* (Lawrence, KS, 1994), 222–23; and David Donald, *Lincoln* (New York, 1995), 456–57.

41. James C. Conkling to Lincoln, August 21, 1863, Abraham Lincoln Papers, Library of Congress. Conkling went on in the years after Lincoln's death to become one of the fourteen original members of the Lincoln Monument Association, the founders and guardians of the Lincoln tomb in Springfield, and served as postmaster for Springfield in the administration of President Benjamin Harrison. *Portrait and Biographical Album of Sangamon County, Illinois* (Chicago, 1891), 708–9; Lincoln, "To Charles D. Robinson," August 17, 1864, in *Collected Works*, 7:499; David Bromwich, "Lincoln's Constitutional Necessity," *Raritan* 20 (Winter 2001): 23.

9

PRUDENCE AND THE PROCLAMATION

Say the word *prudence* to the ancients, and it would be a virtue; say the word *prudence* to the faculties of the American colleges of the nineteenth century, and it would be a part of the curriculum in moral philosophy; say the word *prudence* today, and it would be part of a joke. This says something for how ideas change over time; but it also serves as a warning for the difficulty we may have in understanding nineteenth-century American thought, where virtue was discussed seriously and where prudence was considered a desirable trait in public leaders. It also explains a major difficulty we have in understanding the prime American example of prudence in political life, and that is Abraham Lincoln. Much as Lincoln was a grass-roots, up-from-the-ranks politician, he was perfectly at ease in speaking of the role of virtue (in general) and prudence (in particular) in political life. Lincoln "regarded prudence in all respects as one of the cardinal virtues," and he hoped, as president, that "it will appear that we have practiced prudence" in the management of public affairs. Even in the midst of the Civil War, he promised that the war would be carried forward "consistently with the prudence . . . which ought always to regulate the public service" and without allowing it to degenerate "into a violent and remorseless revolutionary struggle." Lincoln had little notion that, over the course of a hundred and fifty years, this commitment to prudence would become a source of condemnation rather than approval.[1]

Prudence carries with it today the connotation of "prude"—a person of overexaggerated caution, bland temperance, hesitation, a lack of imagination and will, fearfulness, and a bad case of mincing steps. This would have surprised the classical philosophers, who thought of prudence as one of the four cardinal virtues, and who linked it to shrewdness, exceptionally good judgment, and the gift of *coup d'oeil*—the "coup of the eye"—which could take in the whole of a situation at once and know almost automatically how to proceed. Aristotle called it "practical wisdom" in the *Nicomachean Ethics* and contrasted it with "intuitive reason," the natural endowment Aristotle thought some people had for understanding what was ultimately right and what was ultimately wrong. Intuitive reason marked out "the ultimates in both directions," while prudence "makes us take the right means."[2]

Thomas Aquinas chalked out an even more critical role for prudence, since he regarded prudence as "an intellectual virtue" which performs two vital tasks. First, it was the nail head which fastened the intellectual and moral virtues together. Second, because it was housed in the reason, prudence acted as a restraint on "impulse or passion." It was "right reason about things to be done." Prudence, moreover, was characterized by the possession of a good *memory* (so that someone always had on call a mental encyclopedia of material with which to compare current situations), an *understanding* of the present (being able to discern what a given situation really meant), and *foresight* of the future, so that a prudent person always could see several jumps ahead to where any actions were likely to lead. Aquinas was not trying to say what moderns usually say about prudence, that it is an expression of *moderation*, or the attitude of moderates in action, or an instinct for the middle of the road. It was actually the other way round: prudence *might* resort to moderation for a solution, but not always.[3]

What separates prudence from moderation is that moderation is an attitude preoccupied with the integrity of means, but not ends, in political action. It is a tragic attitude, because it understands only too well the constraints posed by limited human resources and by human nature. This is why moderation so often becomes paralyzed and snarled in an effort to placate competing moral demands or to insist on process without regard to what the process is producing. Being wise "does not mean that prudence itself should be moderate, but that moderation must be imposed on other things according to prudence." Daring, which "leads one to act quickly," might also be the work of prudence, provided that "it is directed by reason." Prudence, then, does not avoid action; if anything, it demands action of a particular kind.

Aquinas also found another difference between prudence and moderation in *foresight*. Moderation is blind, which is why it necessarily leads people to grope forward slowly. Prudence, however, is based on foresight, which yields a discerning and dependable estimate of the way things are going. "Foresight is the principal of all the parts of prudence, since whatever else is required for prudence, is necessary precisely that some particular thing may be rightly directed to its end." And this only made sense, since the term *prudence* (*prudentia*) was itself derived from *providence* (*providentia*), the providing-ahead for things. Aquinas, in fact, introduces a discussion of prudence for the first time in the *Summa Theologica* at the point where he begins his *quaestio* on the providence of God, "for in the science of morals, after the moral virtues themselves, comes the consideration of prudence, to which providence would seem to belong" because both providence and prudence are concerned with "directing the ordering of some things towards an end." Prudence occupied so large a place in providence that one might as well concede that "the perfection of divine providence demands that there be intermediary causes as executors of it."[4]

At the other remove from prudence stands absolutism, which is about the integrity of ends, without sufficient attention to the integrity of means, so that it invests its servants with the attitude of disdain and certainty. This is the universe where it is supposed that wills are free from ultimate constraints, and that only willingness and power are lacking to attain a good end. Prudence, however, pays equal attention to the integrity of ends and of means. It is an ironic, rather than a tragic, attitude, where the calculus of costs is *critical*, but at the same time neither *crucial* nor *incidental*. It prefers incremental progress to categorical solutions and fosters that progress through the offering of motives rather than expecting to change dispositions. Yet, unlike moderation, it has a sense of purposeful motion and declines to be paralyzed by a preoccupation with process, even while it remains aware that there is no goal which is so easily or so fully attained that it rationalizes dispensing with process altogether.[5]

So, if we were to create a palm-card for prudence, it would contain the following elements:
- balancing the integrity of means and ends
- accepting reciprocity, imperfection, and concession rather than demanding resolutions
- favoring reason as predominant among the faculties
- waiting on providence rather than affirming free will
- holding the ironic viewpoint rather than one that is comic, tragic, or didactic

What broke over the boundary between classical prudence and the shrinking-violet image that prudence became saddled with was Romanticism. In their rage against the restraints of Enlightenment reason, the Romantics of the late eighteenth century and the nineteenth century—Herder, Hamann, Fichte, Schiller, Goethe—glorified the passionate, the willful, the sublime, and all the fearful and monstrous qualities which the Enlightenment had tried to banish from the human imagination. And at no point was a greater opening offered for the exercise of the Romantic virtues than in the ethics of Immanuel Kant.

Kant is a hinge figure in European intellectual history, with one face pointing backwards to the rationalism of the Enlightenment, and one facing forward toward the Romantics. Kant's fundamental problem was the one Locke had left unaddressed in the *Essay concerning Human Understanding*, and which Hume exploited with such genteel ruthlessness; and that is, how (given Locke's premises about the source of all knowledge being in sensation) the mind can be aware of relations and connections (like causality) which have no phenomenal or sensation-triggering reality. Kant's reply to Hume was an acknowledgment that Hume had gotten things partly right—that minds have no way of directly apprehending nonempirical relationships (like causality) between phenomena—and partly wrong, in that Hume had missed the active role played by the mind itself in knowledge. Minds come equipped with their own hard-wired categories, which govern the knowledge of phenomena and their relations, and causality is one of the mind's necessary categories, even if there is no direct apprehension of the essence (*noumena*) of the objects themselves.[6]

What this did for the creation of a Kantian ethic was to establish the dominance of a "categorical imperative," which is not known by the senses but which, when applied to ethical dilemmas, yields an absolute and universal answer. "We do not need science and philosophy to know what we should do to be honest and good, yea, even wise and virtuous," argued Kant in his *Fundamental Principles of the Metaphysics of Morals*. What we need to do is obey the imperative: "There is an imperative which commands a certain conduct immediately, without having as its condition any other purpose to be attained by it. . . . It concerns not the matter of the action or its intended result, but its form and the principle of which it is itself a result; and what is essentially good in it consists in the mental disposition, let the consequence be what it may."[7]

This sort of immediate absolutism in ethics sat at a very great distance from the rational metaphysics of Aquinas, and it started prudence on its long roll downwards from its ancient status as virtue toward its modern status nearer to vice. In America it played directly to Romantics like Emerson, whose essay "Prudence," from 1841, describes it unflatteringly as "the virtue of the senses; it is the science of appearances," other than which nothing could be of less consequence for Kantian ethics. "The world is filled with the proverbs and acts of winkings of a base prudence," Emerson complained, "a prudence which adores the Rule of Three, which never subscribes, which never gives, which seldom lends, and asks but one question of any project,—Will it bake bread?" But what gave the assault on prudence its moving power was the intersection of the Romantic ethics with America's own homegrown version of ethical absolutism, in the religion of the Evangelical Awakeners. "There can be nothing to render it, in any measure, a *hard* and *difficult* thing, to love God with all our hearts," wrote Joseph Bellamy, the pupil of Jonathan Edwards, in 1750, "but our being destitute of a *right* temper of mind. . . . Therefore, we are *perfectly inexcusable*, and altogether and *wholly* to *blame*, that we do not."[8]

These two streams of absolutism met in the abolitionists, who combined Romantic ethics with evangelicalism in a fiery blend of German idealism and John the Baptist. But it was exactly this blending which alienated Abraham Lincoln from their ranks. Born at the very end of the so-called long Enlightenment, Lincoln had no reservations about being guided by "Reason," or making reason the preferred instrument to passion. In one of his earliest speeches, from 1838, Lincoln warned that the pillars of the Republic must fall "unless we, their descendants, supply their places with other pillars, hewn from the solid quarry of sober reason. Passion has helped us; but can do so no more. It will in future be our enemy. Reason, cold, calculating, unimpassioned reason, must furnish all the materials for our future support and defence." Twenty-three years later, as he stood on the east portico of the Capitol to take the presidential oath, Lincoln was still warning that "though passion may have strained, it must not break our bonds of affection."[9] On those terms, Lincoln had no shame in being known as prudent.

The most obvious example of Lincoln's prudence at work can be seen through his handling of slavery and emancipation. It has become common—and was common in Lincoln's own day among the abolitionists—to denounce Lincoln as "an equivocating, vacillating leader" whose chief aim was "the integrity of the Union and not the emancipation of the slaves; that if he could keep the Union from being disrupted, he would not only allow slavery to exist but would loyally protect it."[10] The standard of judgment being applied (in this case, by W. E. B. Du Bois) is a standard based upon immediatism. But consider what Lincoln's options for emancipation really were: in an era before the Fourteenth Amendment's incorporation of civil rights into the federal Constitution, civil rights (and that included even the definition of *citizenship*) were state prerogatives and were protected by a jurisprudential firewall from federal review. Much as he "was himself opposed to slavery," Lincoln could not "see how the abolitionists could reach it in the slave states." Demands for immediate abolition might satisfy some Romantic yearning for justice over law, but Lincoln was resistant to appeals which forced a conflict between the spirit and the letter. "In declaring that they would 'do their duty and leave the consequences to God,'" the abolitionists

> merely gave an excuse for taking a course that they were not able to maintain by a fair and full argument. To make this declaration did not show what their duty was. If it did we should have no use for judgment, we might as well be made without intellect, and when divine or human law does not

clearly point out what is our duty, we have no means of finding out what it is by using our most intelligent judgment of the consequences.

And those "consequences" were liable to be fatal to the very cause the aboli-tionists espoused. As long as slavery was a state, not a federal, institution, any attempt on Lincoln's part to emancipate slaves by executive order would be at once challenged by the states in the federal courts—and the federal judiciary, all the way up to the Supreme Court, had shown itself repeatedly and pro-foundly hostile to emancipation. Abolitionists, Lincoln complained, "seemed to think that the moment I was president, I had the power to abolish slavery, forgetting that before I could have any power whatsoever I had to take the oath to support the Constitution of the United States as I found them."[11]

On the other hand, immediate abolition was not the only avenue to emanci-pation. The federal government might have no *direct* power to interfere in state matters, but it did have considerable fiscal powers with which it could tempt slave states to abandon slavery by legislative action and to embrace a federally funded buyout. And within six months of his inauguration, Lincoln had initi-ated a campaign for legislative emancipation, beginning with Delaware, the weakest of the four slave states that remained loyal to the Union. This legisla-tive option was based "upon these conditions: First, that the abolition should be gradual. Second, that it should be on a vote of the majority of the qualified voters . . . ; and third that compensation should be made to unwilling own-ers." Handled this way, emancipation would set up what he expected would have a domino effect among the slave states for emancipation and would cost infinitely less than the blood and treasure to be expended on civil war.[12]

Unhappily for Lincoln, the loyal slave states wanted no part in such a scheme. So, in the summer of 1862, he turned instead to a military order that freed the Confederacy's slaves—what we now know as the Emancipa-tion Proclamation. But because the proclamation was only a military order, prudence dictated that he limit its application to those slave states in actual rebellion against the Union. And since little (if any) legal precedent existed for the use of presidential "war powers" in this way, he continued to back a legislative strategy parallel to his war powers proclamation, and in the end, it was that legislative strategy which bore the ultimate fruit of black freedom in the Thirteenth Amendment. Between these two strategies, legislative and military, Lincoln saw no conflict. He told federal judge Thomas Duval that "he saw nothing inconsistent with the gradual emancipation of slavery and his proclamation." Lincoln's procedure was at every step a model of prudence: it made use of *memory* (a knowledge of constitutional process), an *understanding* of the present (the limitations his position placed upon his ability to move in certain directions), and *foresight* (his confidence that he knew what the results of his actions, military and legislative, were likely to be).[13]

No characteristic of Lincoln's prudence on emancipation, however, was more convoluted than his invocation of Providence. "Mr. Lincoln," wrote William Henry Herndon, Lincoln's law partner, in 1866, "had faith . . . that Providence rules the universe of matter and substance, mind and spirit. That a law enwraps the universe, and that all things, beings, minds, were moving to their appointed end."[14]

This may not have been a particularly shocking revelation, since a good deal of the Victorian world was consumed by a passion to believe in an intelligent, direction-giving, and preserving power, whether inherent in physical nature or supernaturally sovereign over human nature, or both. In Lincoln's own time, providence had come to be an expression of the Enlightenment's confidence in the mechanical regularity of physics and its hope that the same pattern of regularity crossed over into human nature. Joseph Fourier published the first statistics on suicide in Paris in the 1820s, accompanying them with the almost-triumphal announcement that "one observes, year after year, within one or two units, the same number of suicides by drowning, by hanging, by firearms, by asphyxiation, by sharp instruments, by falling or poisoning." There was, in other words, a pattern if one but stopped to look, and Fourier's tentative pleasure in observing this required only time and the methods of Andre-Michel Guerry and Adolphe Quételet to yield a new faith in a physics of human action that looks like nothing so much as a naturalized predestination. "We know in advance," wrote Quételet, "how many individuals will dirty their hands with the blood of others, how many will be forgers, how many poisoners, nearly as well as one can enumerate in advance the births and deaths that must take place." Or perhaps the Victorian passion for providence was better captured by the literati, who yielded to the grim inevitability of Quételet's predictions, but resignedly. "If you look closely into the matter, it will be seen that whatever appears most vagrant, and utterly purposeless, turns out, in the end, to have been impelled the most surely on a preordained and unswerving track," concluded the Puritan-haunted Nathaniel Hawthorne. Even as irreligious a humorist as Mark Twain was preoccupied with free will and determinism, on one occasion sitting up half the night arguing with William Dean Howells about whether there was a controlling providence in the universe. In his final years, it was almost the primary obsession of his writing. If we find Lincoln ruminating similarly, there is nothing in that which forces us to see his providentialism as necessarily religious.[15]

Except, of course, for the way that Lincoln felt compelled to use providence as a living political notion, rather than just a metaphysical one. Certainly no one who knew Lincoln could miss the frequency with which he drew providence into both public and private discourse and spoke of it as a power exerted by a divine personality on both individuals and in general. "I know that Mr. Lincoln was a firm believer in a superintending and overruling Providence," wrote Orville Hickman Browning, briefly an Illinois senator and one of Lincoln's oldest personal and political friends. "He believed the destinies of men were, or, at least, that his own destiny was, shaped, and controlled, by an intelligence and power higher and greater than his own, and which he could neither control or thwart." Out of his own mouth, Lincoln placed "my reliance for support" on "that Divine assistance without which I cannot succeed, but with which success is certain," and he told well-wishers in a speech in Newark, on his way to his inauguration in 1861, "I cannot succeed, without the sustenance of Divine Providence." In 1862, a delegation of Pennsylvania Quakers headed by the famous helper of fugitives, Thomas Garrett, waited on Lincoln to urge him to deal with slavery, but Lincoln, speaking off-the-cuff, turned his reply in a curiously providential direction. "The President responded . . . [that] he had sometime thought that perhaps he might be an instrument in God's hands of accomplishing a great work."[16]

The problem is that this is admirable only up to a point. Holding private consultations with the Ancient of Days on matters of policy has never recommended itself to the American people as proof of presidential greatness. And yet, as Lincoln explained to his cabinet on September 22, 1862, his decision to issue an emancipation proclamation was the direct consequence of "a vow, a covenant" he had made, "that if God gave us the victory" in the battle that resulted at Antietam on September 17,

> he would consider it an indication of divine will and that it was his duty to move forward in the cause of emancipation. It might be thought strange that he had in this way submitted the disposal of matters when the way was not clear to his mind what he should do. God had decided this question in favor of the slaves. He was satisfied it was right, was confirmed and strengthened in his action by the vow and the results.

This, coming from a man with as minimal a religious profile as Lincoln's, was so surprising that Treasury Secretary Salmon Chase asked Lincoln to repeat himself, and Lincoln, "in a manner half-apologetic," conceded that "this might seem strange."[17]

But strange or not, it was precisely this confidence in providence which played a major role in the constitution of Lincoln's prudence. He told the journalist Noah Brooks that he thought it "wise to wait for the developments of Providence; and the Scriptural phrase that 'the stars in their courses fought against Sisera' to him had a depth of meaning."[18] John Todd Stuart, who had been Lincoln's mentor in Illinois law and who served in the 38th Congress, pressed Lincoln with the assertion: "*I believe that Providence is carrying on this thing.*" Lincoln replied "with great emphasis": "Stuart, that is just my opinion." And "considering our manner of approaching the subject" and "the emphasis and evident sincerity of his answer," Stuart was "sure he had no possible motive for saying what he did unless it came from a deep and settled conviction."[19]

That conviction, instead of puffing Lincoln up with personal hubris, forced him into an admission that he knew entirely too little about the ways of providence. Clear as his reliance on providence was, what is equally impressive is how Lincoln made no claims to knowing the precise road that providence had ordained for him. "Certainly there is no contending against the Will of God," Lincoln wrote in a set of notes he prepared during the Lincoln-Douglas debates in 1858, "but still there is some difficulty in ascertaining, and applying it, to particular cases." When a delegation of Chicago ministers presented him with a brace of resolutions from a citywide antislavery meeting in September 1862, Lincoln warned them against presuming to know what the direction of providence was. "These are not . . . the days of miracles, and I suppose it will be granted that I am not to expect a divine revelation. I must study the plain physical facts of the case, ascertain what is possible and learn what appears to be wise and right."[20] The result was that Lincoln believed "we are all agents and instruments of Divine providence" (as he told Senate chaplain Byron Sunderland), but not in the egoistic sense, that God had invested a special interest in the Union cause, but in the sense that North and South alike "are working out the will of God." Moreover, the rule of providence was universal, in both time and space. The Civil War was a "struggle . . . for a vast future" that required "a reliance on Providence, all the more firm and earnest" so that Americans may "proceed in the great task which events have devolved upon us."[21]

Providence was, for Lincoln, a means for balancing respect for a divine purpose in human affairs with the candid recognition that it was surpassingly difficult to know what specific purposes God might have. It was also a means he inherited from his long years as a Whig for recognizing the fundamentally secular structure of the American federal government without surrendering entirely to the notion that it was *totally* secular—"that shallow doctrine of the Monticello School," as a Whig journal put it in 1846—or that the power of religious belief in society had to go untapped by civil government in its avoidance of seeming to establish a civic religion. Alexis de Tocqueville worried that the great flaw of democracy was its inability to offer good reasons for its own virtues; it had no transcendent sanction. By attaching the Emancipation Proclamation to his "vow" to God, Lincoln demonstrated what James C. Welling, the editor of Washington's flagship newspaper during the Civil War, called "that prudent and reverent waiting on Providence" which allowed Lincoln to fend off "the danger of identifying the proclamation in the popular mind with a panic cry of despair."[22]

Prudence is not a matter of looking for guidance from voices from the sky; it is also not about ignoring them, either. The Proclamation was "warranted by the Constitution," but in its final form on New Year's Day, 1863, Lincoln yielded to the suggestion of Salmon Chase that it also fly under the flag of "the gracious favor of Almighty God." Lincoln rooted human dignity in God and natural law; Kant, as one modern commentator quips, "makes us out to be gods ourselves."[23]

Part of what makes our understanding of Lincoln and prudence so difficult is the intrusion of the Kantian ethic into American political thought, an intrusion now grown into dominance through the work of John Rawls. The Rawlsian notion of the "original position" is not one which grows from memory or understanding, much less foresight; it is, on the contrary, a purely theoretical construct. "The original position is not," Rawls admitted, "thought of as an actual historical state of affairs"; it is, in fact, a cutting off of the theorist from the "contingent advantages and accidental impulses from the past." Unlike prudence, it is predicated on a "veil of ignorance" which allows the theorist to debate justice without the admixture of concrete realities or concrete probabilities. "Certain principles of justice are justified because they would be agreed to in an initial situation of equality," Rawls argued, in precisely the same spirit that Kant argued for the mandate of the categorical imperative, as a way of nullifying "the effects of specific contingencies."[24]

Lincoln understood emancipation, not as the satisfaction of a "spirit" overriding the law, nor as the moment of fusion between the Constitution and absolute moral theory, but as a goal to be achieved through prudential means, so that worthwhile consequences might result. He could not be persuaded that emancipation required the headlong abandonment of everything save the single absolute of abolition, or that purity of intention was all that mattered, or that the exercise of the will rather than the reason was the best ethical foot forward. "Kant," remarks Robert Kaplan, "symbolizes a morality of intention rather than of consequences, a morality of abstract justice rather than of actual result."[25] For Lincoln, the integrity of *intention* (in the form of the Constitution and the rule of law) and the integrity of *consequences* (the abolition of slavery) were complimentary rather than conflicting actors—the one possessed moral claims fully as much as the other. "To those who claim omnipotence for the Legislature, and who in the plenitude of their assumed powers, are disposed to disregard the Constitution, law, good faith, moral right, and every thing else," Lincoln declared in one of his earliest speeches to the Illinois legislature, "I have nothing to say."

In this, Lincoln struggled to be true to the two souls of American culture. The one soul is the spirit of the Puritans, self-denying, evangelical, radical, and providential to the point of confidently identifying precisely who and what represent the operations of providence; the other is the spirit of the Enlightenment, secular, commercial, self-interested in the enlightened sort of way. These two have often been locked in combat, only to withdraw from the combat after a brief battering reminds them that in America they have no choice but to coexist. Providence and prudence together are thus joined at the head, if not the heart, of American politics. The Kantian imperative, however, is a threat to both, not because it takes the side of one against the other, but because it dispenses with the virtues of both. In Lincoln, we have a glimpse of prudence in a liberal democracy; but it is also our best glimpse of it, and perhaps our best hope for understanding and recovering it.

Notes

1. Lincoln, "Communication to the People of Sangamo County," March 9, 1832, and "Annual Message to Congress," December 3, 1861, in *The Collected Works of Abraham Lincoln*, ed. Roy P. Basler (New Brunswick, NJ, 1953–55), 1:8, 5:24, 36, 49; Charles Zane, "Lincoln as I Knew Him," *Sunset Magazine*, October 1912, 430–38; Ethan Fishman, "Under the Circumstances: Abraham Lincoln and Classical Prudence," in *Abraham Lincoln: Sources and Style of Leadership*, ed. Frank J. Williams et al. (Westport, CT, 1994), 3–15; Ralph Lerner, *Revolutions Revisited: Two Faces of the Politics of Enlightenment* (Chapel Hill, NC, 1994), 107–11.

2. Aristotle, *Nicomachean Ethics* 6.11–12.

3. Thomas Aquinas, *Summa Theologica* 2.1, Q. 57, 65.

4. Ibid., 1, Q. 23, 2.1, Q. 47, 57, 2.2 Q. 49, 127; Aquinas, *Summa Contra Gentiles* 3.1.76.

5. William Lee Miller, *Lincoln's Virtues: An Ethical Biography* (New York, 2002), 222–23; Thomas Sowell, *The Vision of the Anointed: Self-Congratulation as a Basis for Social Policy* (New York, 1995), 105.

6. Isaiah Berlin, "The Restrained Romantics," in *The Roots of Romanticism*, ed. Henry Hardy (Princeton, NJ, 1999), 68; Ralph C. S. Walker, *Kant* (London, 1978), 151–64.

7. Immanuel Kant, *Fundamental Principles of the Metaphysics of Ethics*, ed. T. K. Abbott (London, 1932), 20, 33; John Rawls, *Lectures on the History of Moral Philosophy*, ed. Barbara Herman (Cambridge, MA, 2000), 156.

8. Ralph Waldo Emerson, "Prudence" (Essays: First Series, 1841), in *Selected Writings*, ed. Brooks Atkinson (New York, 1940), 237–48; Joseph Bellamy, *True Religion Delineated; or, Experimental Religion as distinguished from formality and enthusiasm* (1750; repr., Morristown, NJ, 1804), 100; James Hoopes, *Consciousness in New England: From Puritanism and Ideas to Psychoanalysis and Semiotic* (Baltimore, 1989), 121; Lerner, *Revolutions Revisited*, 95–98.

9. Lincoln, "Address before the Young Men's Lyceum of Springfield," January 27, 1838, and "First Inaugural Address," March 4, 1861, in *Collected Works*, 1:115, 4:271; James Jasinski, "Idioms of Prudence in Three Antebellum Controversies:

Revolution, Constitution, and Slavery," in *Prudence: Classical Virtue, Postmodern Practice*, ed. Robert Hariman (University Park, PA, 2003), 168–76.

10. Lerone Bennett, in "Differing Perspectives on Abraham Lincoln," in *Booknotes: Stories from American History*, ed. Brian P. Lamb (New York, 2001), 115–17; W. E. B. Du Bois, "Abraham Lincoln," May 1922, and "Lincoln Again," September 1922, in *W. E. B. Du Bois: Writings*, ed. Nathan Huggins (New York, 1986), 1196, 1197–98.

11. Henry W. Blodgett, in *Recollected Words of Abraham Lincoln*, ed. Don Fehrenbacher and Virginia Fehrenbacher (Stanford, CA, 1996), 34; Lincoln, "Speech at Worcester, Massachusetts," September 12, 1848, in *Collected Works*, 2:3–4; Francis B. Carpenter, *Six Months at the White House with Abraham Lincoln* (New York, 1867), 76.

12. Lincoln, "To John Hill," September 1860, in *Collected Works*, 4:106–7; Joseph R. Fornieri, "Lincoln and the Emancipation Proclamation: A Model of Prudent Leadership," in *Tempered Strength: Studies in the Nature and Scope of Prudential Leadership* (Lanham, MD, 2002), 125–49.

13. Thomas Duval, in Fehrenbacher and Fehrenbacher, *Recollected Words*, 146.

14. Woodrow Wilson, "Abraham Lincoln: A Man of the People," in *Abraham Lincoln: The Tribute of a Century, 1809–1909*, ed., Nathan William MacChesney (Chicago, 1910), 30; David Donald, "Getting Right with Lincoln," in *Lincoln Reconsidered: Essays on the Civil War Era* (New York, 1960), 17; William Herndon, December 3, 1866, in *The Hidden Lincoln: From the Letters and Papers of William H. Herndon*, ed. Emanuel Hertz (New York, 1938), 43.

15. Ian Hacking, *The Taming of Chance* (Cambridge, 1990), 77–78, 105; Nathaniel Hawthorne, *The Marble Faun; or, The Romance of Monte Beni* (1860; repr., Boston, 1901), 333; Paul F. Boller, *Freedom and Fate in American Thought* (Dallas, 1978), 189; Alfred Kazin, *God and the American Writer* (New York, 1997), 188–93.

16. Orville H. Browning to Isaac Arnold, November 25, 1872, in Isaac Arnold Papers, Chicago Historical Society; Lincoln, "Farewell Address," February 11, 1861, "Remarks at Newark, New Jersey," February 21, 1861, and "Remarks to a Delegation of Progressive Friends," June 20, 1862, in *Collected Works*, 4:190, 234, 5:278–79.

17. Salmon P. Chase, diary entry for September 22, 1862, in *Inside Lincoln's Cabinet*, ed. David Donald (New York, 1954), 150. On Chase asking for the repeat of the "vow," see Isaac Arnold, *The History of Abraham Lincoln and the Overthrow of Slavery* (Chicago, 1866), 295–96; Gideon Welles, diary entry for September 22, 1862, in *Diary of Gideon Welles*, ed. John Torrey Morse (Boston, 1911), 1:143; Welles, "History of Emancipation," in *Civil War and Reconstruction: Selected Essays by Gideon Welles*, ed. Albert Mordell (New York, 1959), 248.

18. Noah Brooks, "Personal Recollections of Abraham Lincoln," in *Lincoln Observed: Civil War Dispatches of Noah Brooks*, ed. Michael Burlingame (Baltimore, 1998), 216.

19. John G. Nicolay, "Conversation with Hon. J. T. Stuart," June 24, 1875, in *An Oral History of Abraham Lincoln: John G. Nicolay's Interviews and Essays*, ed. Michael Burlingame (Carbondale, IL, 1996), 14–15.

20. Lincoln, "Fragment on Pro-slavery Theology," October 1, 1858, and "Reply to Emancipation Memorial Presented by Chicago Christians of All Denominations," September 13, 1862, in *Collected Works*, 3:204, 5:420; W. W. Patton, *President Lincoln and the Chicago Memorial on Emancipation* (Baltimore, 1888), 19–20.

21. Lincoln, "Annual Message to Congress," December 3, 1861, in *Collected Works*, 5:53; Lincoln to Byron Sunderland, in Fehrenbacher and Fehrenbacher, *Recollected Words,* 436; William E. Barton, *The Soul of Abraham Lincoln* (New York, 1920), 332.

22. James C. Welling, in *Reminiscences of Abraham Lincoln by Distinguished Men of His Time*, ed. A. T. Rice (New York, 1886), 530; Stewart Winger, *Lincoln, Religion, and Romantic Cultural Politics* (DeKalb, IL, 2003), 111.

23. Janet Chase Hoyt, "Setting Free a Race: How the Emancipation Proclamation Was Made," *New York Tribune*, February 22, 1893; Robert Hariman, "Theory without Modernity," in Hariman, *Prudence*, 31; Herman Belz, "The 'Philosophical Cause' of Free Government: The Problem of Lincoln's Political Thought," in *Abraham Lincoln, Constitutionalism, and Equal Rights in the Civil War Era* (New York, 1998), 56–57; J. Budziszewski, *The Revenge of Conscience: Politics and the Fall of Man* (Dallas, 1999), 53, 93–94.

24. John Rawls, *A Theory of Justice* (New York, 1971), 12, 21, 136, and *Political Liberalism* (New York, 1993), 23.

25. Robert Kaplan, *Warrior Politics: Why Leadership Demands a Pagan Ethos* (New York, 2002), 113; Lincoln, "Speech in the Illinois Legislature concerning the State Bank," January 11, 1837, in *Collected Works*, 1:67.

10

LINCOLN AND THE "WAR POWERS" OF THE PRESIDENCY

O n the day that Charles Sumner heard of the firing on Fort Sumter, he took himself at once to the White House to tell Abraham Lincoln (as he would tell him so many more times during the course of the next two years) that the war had delivered slavery into the president's hands for destruction. Why civil war, and not Congress or the state legislatures, should be the mechanism for emancipation came down to two words: "I . . . told him," Sumner said, "that under the war power the right had come to him to emancipate the slaves." And if Lincoln had pressed Sumner for more details, the president would have learned that Sumner believed the *war power* gave him more than just the room to emancipate slaves. The war power of the president, argued Sumner, "is above the constitution, because, when set in motion, it knows no other law."

> The civil power, in mass and in detail, is superseded, and all rights are held subordinate to this military magistracy. All other agencies, small and great, executive, legislative, and even judicial, are absorbed in this transcendent triune power, which, for the time, declares its absolute will, while it holds alike the scales of justice and the sword of the executioner.

"The existence of this power," Sumner triumphantly concluded, "nobody questions."[1]

Which, people might have said, was typical of Charles Sumner, announcing as an accepted fact something which very few people understood, and which still fewer agreed upon. The lack of agreement began with the very term *war power* which, inconveniently for Sumner's argument, does not even exist in the Constitution that Sumner believed it superseded; and it ran from there through the four most pressing issues of the Civil War (the suspension of habeas corpus, the confiscation of rebel property, the imprisonment and trial of rebel sympathizers and Northern dissidents, and ultimately, emancipation); and it continued—and continues—to run through the seizures of German property in both world wars, detention of the *Nisei* in 1942, Truman's nationalization of the steel industry, the Vietnam War, the failed Iranian hostage rescue, Lebanon, Grenada, and to the gates of Guantanamo Bay. Despite the passing of more than 140 years, Supreme Court opinions, and the War Powers Act of 1973, we are, in fact, no closer to a comprehensive definition of the war powers of the presidency than Charles Sumner was in 1861. And so it might be instructive if we took this opportunity to see in what ways Abraham Lincoln thought it was possible to take Sumner's advice.

The Constitution splits the responsibility for war. Article 1, section 8, gives to Congress the power to announce the legal state of war (in other words, to "declare War"), to authorize the raising of an army and a navy, to supervise the state militias, and to "provide for" calling out those militias "to execute the Laws of the Union, suppress Insurrections and repel Invasions." But Article 2, section 2, lodges the responsibility for putting those forces into play in an entirely different branch of the government, with the president, who shall be "Commander in Chief of the Army and Navy of the United States, and of the militia of the several States, when called into the actual Service of the United States." And once such wars were over, the power to conclude peace was also split, with the president given the power to "make Treaties," but only with the consent of two-thirds of the Senate. Dividing the power to wage war between the legislative and executive branches looked odd against the background of the English past, where the making of both war and peace were prerogatives of the Crown. But it made sense to the architects of the Constitution, who had been bred on John Locke's division of governmental powers into domestic (governed by the legislature) and "federative" (the relations between a society and other nations, which Locke confined to the executive), and who were convinced that "the history of human conduct does not warrant that exalted opinion of human virtue, which would make it wise in a nation to commit interests of so delicate and momentous a kind . . . to the sole disposal of a . . . president of the United States."[2]

But supposing that the power to make war actually could, on this new model, be divided between Congress and the presidency, what then were the powers comprehended under the president's title of "Commander in Chief of the Army and Navy of the United States, and of the militia of the several States, when called into the actual Service of the United States"? To that, no one had any very clear answer. Chancellor James Kent's celebrated *Commentaries*, in discussing the powers of the presidency, never breathed a word about any "war powers"; Kent, in fact, limited the operation of any wartime powers of seizure and confiscation to an act of Congress. Hamilton, in the *Federalist*, no. 69, believed that the office of commander in chief "would amount to nothing more than the supreme command and direction of the military and naval forces, as the first general and admiral of the Confederacy," but he saw this as little more than acting as a sort of general coordinator of military actions, similar to the power which "the governor of New York" exercised over the militia, rather than a military officer in direct command of armies in the field. And Supreme Court Justice Joseph Story actually believed that Congress ought to pass a consent resolution before allowing a president to take up personal military command. But in 1795, George Washington took the commander in chief title literally and rode out at the head of the United States forces (with Hamilton at his side) to suppress the Whiskey Rebellion; and when HMS *Leopard* shot up the U.S. frigate *Chesapeake* in 1807 for refusing an order to heave-to and allow a search of the American crew for British "deserters," Thomas Jefferson immediately took steps to purchase military supplies entirely on his own authority as president.[3]

The nearest legal cognate to the war powers of the president was martial law. But even here, the parallels were almost useless. In fact, there was only one significant example of the American use of martial law, and it did not bode well for any attempt to create a broad-based doctrine of presidential war powers. In December 1814, General Andrew Jackson proclaimed a state of martial law in New Orleans that suspended habeas corpus and imposed a curfew, a civilian draft, and a requirement that any movements in or out of the city be registered with his adjutant general. Federal district judge Dominick Hall defied Jackson, and Jackson expelled Hall from the city. But when news of the Treaty of Ghent arrived in New Orleans on March 13, 1815, Hall promptly cited Jackson for contempt of court and fined him, and Secretary of War Alexander Dallas unsympathetically advised Jackson to pay it. As Jackson learned, the use of martial law—which chiefly involved suspension of the writ of habeas corpus and closure of the civil courts, temporary seizures of property, and rule by the military—stuck grotesquely in American throats as a throwback to British tyranny.[4] Martial law, wrote Supreme Court Justice Levi Woodbury in 1849, could be used by "a commanding officer of troops" only to govern his "camp" and "its environs and the near field of his military operations," but not an inch beyond. "The writ of habeas corpus . . . is as much in force in intestine war as in peace," Woodbury declared, "and the empire of the laws is equally to be upheld."[5]

But not without opinions, though. In 1842, John Quincy Adams warned Southerners that, in the event of a slave insurrection or a war with Britain,

Congress had a "full and plenary power" to emancipate slaves if it thought such an emancipation useful in restoring national order or repelling invasion. "It is a war power" and though that power had never actually been "called into exercise under the present Constitution of the United States," it was "a settled maxim of the law of nations" that in time of war, "the military supersedes the civil power."[6] Adams made no attempt to explain whether he thought this "war power" belonged jointly or separately to Congress or the president; at times, he seemed to be doing no more than justifying the use of martial law as a weapon of emancipation. That was enough for Charles Sumner, though, who liked to think of himself as Adams's Elisha. Nineteen years to the day after Adams's "war powers" speech, Sumner was in Abraham Lincoln's office, beseeching the president to do as Adams had said.

Sumner liked to boast that he was "the first, who in our day, called for this exercise of power." This, strictly speaking, was not true. William Lloyd Garrison issued a pamphlet-sized reprint of John Quincy Adams's speeches on the war powers in order to make the case, and Adams's son, Charles Francis Adams (whom Lincoln would pick to represent the United States as American minister to Great Britain) agreed that "under the war power we can do what is . . . necessary for the purposes of the war, as justified by humanity, good sense, and the consent of Christendom. I know no other limits."[7] Necessity, however, could take a number of astonishing forms: military tribunals acting under different rules of justice than civil courts, arrests without warrants and imprisonment without trials, surveillance, and (even if indirectly) intimidation of the press. Nor was it clear what the appropriate reactions from the courts ought to be: should the courts yield the ground to the executive to act unilaterally on the grounds that the president and the military have to operate by their own rules and expertise in time of war; or is it the task of the courts to exercise a skeptical restraint on executive powers? Judges, after all, are not soldiers and do not have access to the information soldiers possess about enemy intentions, nor are the courts in the position to move as swiftly as the military in responding to enemy threats. On the other hand, the very atmosphere of wartime emergency has a nasty habit of causing public panics and a jittery willingness to acquiesce when the military begins chipping away at civil liberties; and the executive and military may display an equally nasty penchant for ratcheting up their demands for more powers once one level of special powers is conceded. And this spoke only to potential conflicts between the executive and the judiciary; what role, if any, should be played by Congress? All of these questions were presented to Lincoln, Congress, and the courts in 1861 wrapped in a combined atmosphere of novelty and crisis, and it took the first two years of the Civil War—and the increasingly messy and unpopular use by Lincoln of suspensions of the writ of habeas corpus, the creation of federal military districts with authority to detain and try suspected rebels, the enlistment of volunteers and the diversion of funds to equip them without congressional sanction, the blockade, and, most momentous of all, the emancipation of the Confederacy's slaves by presidential proclamation—before a set of specific justifications for the exercise of presidential war powers began to crystallize into a reasonable doctrine.

That doctrine came to rest on three legs: *(a)* the presidential oath, *(b)* the requirement of the Constitution to guarantee the states a republican form of government, and *(c)* the dictates of necessity. The "oath" justification was posed most forcibly by New York lawyer Grosvenor Lowrey (who would become more famous after the war as Thomas Edison's lawyer and fund-raiser) in 1863. "It is the duty"—and Lowrey wanted the weight placed squarely on the word *duty*—"of the Commander-in-chief to subdue a great number of persons actively engaged in supporting the war." His oath to "preserve, protect and defend" obligated Lincoln to use any and all means to subdue the rebellion, and neglecting the use of any means would be grounds for impeachment.[8] Similarly, the Boston jurist Joel Prentiss Bishop argued that Lincoln was obligated to flex the powers of war by the Constitution's "guarantee to every State in this Union" of "a Republican Form of Government" (Article 4, section 4). After all, "A republican form of government implies the voluntary suffrage of the people," Bishop reasoned; such a government did not exist in rebellious South Carolina; therefore, "the Constitution . . . lays its power . . . upon the President" and authorizes any measure which will restore "Republican Government."[9] For the Radical Republicans in Congress, those measures could include the creation of "a military tribunal . . . to follow the army, and as we conquer their territory, sell to the highest bidder the lands of every rebel, to military occupants, who with arms in their hands, shall take resident possession by themselves, or their tenants, and be ready to defend it against all comers." But it was Horace Greeley, through the pages of the *New York Tribune*'s short-lived monthly magazine, the *Continental Monthly*, who shouldered his way past any constitutional niceties and justified the use of war powers by the president purely on the grounds of necessity. "Who but a *fool* would question the right of a man to strike a dagger to the heart of the assassin whose grasp was on his throat, because there is a law against the private use of deadly weapons?" the *Monthly* asked in its October 1862 issue. Just so in war: the right of survival overrides any constitutional restraint ordinarily applied to the president. "In such a time, they must all give way to the supreme necessity of saving the national existence."[10]

But were the people who questioned the war powers doctrine really *fools?*[11] Lincoln's own party in Congress was a good deal less than united over the presidential war powers doctrine, partly because the Radical Republicans wanted the war powers for themselves, and partly because a number of moderate Republicans were convinced that equipping the president with nonconstitutional powers for the purpose of defending the Constitution might create a cure worse than the disease. Orville Hickman Browning balked at "the doctrine . . . in favor of absolute power in the hands of the President, under the name of Commander-in-Chief" as "the most dangerous doctrine ever advocated under a constitutional Government. . . . Unless we can save the Constitution with the Union, we had better let them both go." Benjamin Curtis, who had cowritten the minority dissent in *Dred Scott* in 1857, did not doubt that Lincoln was "honestly desirous to do his duty to the country," but he drew the line at recognizing Lincoln's possession of some "implied powers of the President as commander-in-chief in time of war." The title *commander in chief* only allowed Lincoln to "do what generals in the field are allowed to do within the sphere of their actual operations." That did not, however, include the various powers which Lincoln seemed to be exercising under the rubric of that title. "I do not yet see that it depends upon his executive decree whether . . . my neighbors and myself . . . should be subjected to the possibility of military arrest and imprisonment, and trial before a military commission." Even Grosvenor Lowrey had to admit that though the war powers "are the faithful friends and servants of the Constitution, they are not constitutional powers; and I am compelled to call them extra-constitutional for want of a better name."[12]

And that was only what Lincoln's *friends* were saying. Former Whigs (whose party had come into being in the 1830s on the back of opposition to the armed despotism of Andrew Jackson, the "military chieftain"), outright Southern sympathizers, racist demagogues horrified at the prospect of emancipation, and Northern Democrats struggling to regain their equilibrium after the electoral defeat of 1860 joined in a wail of denunciation, complaining that *(a)* no such presidential war powers existed or had ever existed, *(b)* if they did exist, nothing that Lincoln had done qualified as a war power, and *(c)* if they did exist, they required the cooperation of Congress and the judiciary in their exercise. By ignoring those objections, Lincoln was a far greater threat to the Constitution and liberty than the Confederacy was.[13] The nonagenarian Kentucky jurist Samuel Smith Nicholas was shocked that any president would think of using "that immemorial tyrants' plea, *necessity*," which Nicholas believed the Founders had "intended to extirpate utterly from our system. . . . I have not the language to express the surprise, not to say horror, with which I have witnessed the promulgation of these opinions." Robert Winthrop, the venerable Massachusetts Whig and onetime Speaker of the House, agreed that invoking such a thing as war powers was "abhorrent to every instinct of my soul, to every dictate of my judgment, to every principle which I cherish as a statesman or as a Christian." Joel Parker, the Royall Professor of Law at Harvard Law School, upheld Lincoln's suspension of habeas corpus in 1861. But he stopped at the extension of military powers further than an officer's "camp . . . its environs and the near field of his military operations." And Parker not only attacked the legitimacy of issuing a presidential emancipation proclamation but in 1862 launched a failed bid to dump Charles Sumner from his Senate seat. The idea that a president could emancipate slaves generally across the Confederacy and declare them "forever free" even after the conclusion of hostilities was injecting "the poison of despotic principles . . . into the system of the Constitution."[14] Having in the president's hands any such war power, complained the New York lawyer Montgomery Throop, "in connection with the power of arbitrary arrests, will give the Constitution a speedy and effective coup-de-grace." The Democratic newspaper *Old Guard* simply announced "There is no such thing as a war power known to this country." The war power was, complained Philadelphia Democrat Thomas Jefferson Miles, merely a tool of the "so-called Republican, but really Abolition party," to silence free speech as part of a "premeditated conspiracy to destroy the Constitution," the first step of which had been "the nomination of Abraham Lincoln at Chicago."[15]

No one would have been more surprised at being fingered as the figurehead of a conspiracy to impose a war powers despotism than Abraham Lincoln. He had burned his own fingers as a congressman in 1848 by questioning President Polk's rationale for war with Mexico. "Allow him to make war at pleasure, whenever he shall deem it necessary," Lincoln argued, and you will have a war "whenever he may choose." And, as we've already seen in the third of these essays, Lincoln never shared much of Victorian romanticism's glorification of men-at-arms. He suspected—and not without reason—that most of the professional military men of the Republic were Democrats and unsympathetic to his administration. Jefferson Davis, he complained, "had known all the officers of the regular army. I had never seen but three of them before I came to Washington as President."[16] Nor, for that matter, did Lincoln ever try to construct a comprehensive doctrine of the presidential war powers for use in the ways Thomas Jefferson Miles and Joel Parker feared. If anything, his old Whig political inclinations inclined him to defer to Congress in taking up any national initiatives. "By the constitution, the executive may recommend measures which he may think proper; and he may veto those he thinks Unproper; and it is supposed he may add to these, certain indirect influences to affect the action of congress." But for more than that, Lincoln wanted Congress to "originate, as well as perfect" any "wartime measures."[17]

But this was 1861 was not 1846, and anyway, Lincoln's concern in 1848 had been about Polk's threat to "the war-making power" of Congress—in other words, the constitutional stipulation that Congress must be the agency to declare war—rather than to the president's responsibilities in conducting it. Polk's offense had been to start the Mexican War on his own initiative, while Lincoln had found a war deposited on his doorstep by the Confederacy less than six weeks after his inauguration. And even if he had no ready-made war powers doctrine in mind, he took seriously his oath of office, and from that Lincoln began his development of such a doctrine. "You can have no conflict, without being yourselves the aggressors," he warned the Confederates in his First Inaugural. "You have no oath registered in Heaven to destroy the government, while I shall have the most solemn one to 'preserve, protect and defend' it." He asserted no Polklike power to invent a war, but he also had a duty to respond to one if it erupted. The oath imposed on him a "duty . . . to administer the present government, as it came to his hands, and to transmit it, unimpaired by him, to his successor." Preserving the Union, he repeated, is what "the Constitution itself expressly enjoins upon me," and he wanted to add (but struck out from the final version) the ominous promise that while secessionists "can forbear the assault upon it, I can not shrink from the defense of it."[18] This was not a particularly aggressive way of announcing that disunion would be resisted by whatever means Lincoln decided to use; as in so many of his key writings, the voice is a passive one, as though he were being forced into a task he would normally find unpleasant were it not for the dictates of the situation. But anyone who mistook Lincoln's use of the passive voice as a statement of uncertainty soon learned that it was exactly his conviction that the scope of response is narrowed down by the actions of others which nerved him to the most vigorous forms of action. And anyone who imagined that Lincoln took the oath of office as a mere rhetorical formality would soon discover how painfully dear the idea of honor—of fidelity to promises above all things—was to him.[19]

If anything, Lincoln hoped against hope that the oath would *not* plunge him into civil war. "It shall be my endeavor to preserve the peace of this country so far as it can possibly be done, consistently with the maintenance of the institutions of the country," he promised a preinaugural crowd in Harrisburg. "With my consent, or without my great displeasure, this country shall never witness the shedding of one drop of blood in fraternal strife."[20] He negotiated strenuously to avoid a clash over Fort Sumter, even to the point of promising Alexander Boteler that he would discourage the final session of the 36th Congress from passing a bill authorizing a militia call-up.[21] And unlike Andrew Jackson in 1832, he sent, not an army, but an unarmed transport to relieve the Sumter garrison—only to have the Confederates bombard Sumter into submission before the supplies could reach the fort. He was surprised yet again when, under the terms of the Militia Act of 1795, he called up 75,000 state militia for the statutory three months' service—only to have the governors of Delaware and Maryland reply that their militias would be available only for defending the capital, and the governors of Virginia, Tennessee, Kentucky, and Arkansas state frankly that their militias would "not be furnished to the powers at Washington for any such use or purpose as they have in view."[22] But worst of all, Lincoln had to endure an agonizing four weeks after the firing on Sumter, waiting for the militia of the Northern states to force their way through to the capital, while government employees were mustered to defend the White House, General Winfield Scott sandbagged the Treasury Building as a last-stand bunker, and Lincoln's two small sons anxiously built a pitiful little fort of their own on the White House roof. "All the troubles and anxieties of his life had not equaled those which intervened between this time and the fall of Sumter," he told Orville Hickman Browning on July 3, 1861.[23] And it was out of that dilemma that Lincoln grasped the second leg of the war powers doctrine, *necessity*.

The appeal to necessity was what had aroused his suspicions in 1848. He now learned just how superficial the criticisms of necessity could be in a *real* national emergency. It was necessity which impelled Lincoln to issue, after the fiasco of the militia call-up, a call for state volunteer units and for an expansion of the regular army (and an appropriation of funds for their equipment) and the suspension of the writ of habeas corpus to assist in the detention of rebel saboteurs along the Maryland rail and telegraph lines.[24] Congress had been out of session at the time of the firing on Fort Sumter, and it was impossible to call a special session before the summer because too many congressional districts in the vital border states were still holding congressional elections through the spring. "No choice was left but to call out the war power of the Government." He would not state categorically whether "these measures" were "strictly legal or not," but they did meet "a public necessity." After all, it seemed to Lincoln absurd that "all the laws" were to be overthrown by the rebels and "the government itself" allowed to "go to pieces" while Lincoln observed the constitutional requirement of congressional approval. But *necessity* was not Lincoln's only argument: harking back to the sanctity of his oath, he asked, "In such a case, would not the official oath be broken, if the government should be overthrown" while Lincoln had the power to preserve it by "yielding to partial, and temporary departures, from necessity"? And, he added (reaching for the third leg of the war powers doctrine), was the war power not also mandated by the constitutional guarantee of republican government? "The Constitution provides, and all the States have accepted the provision, that 'The United States shall guarantee to every State in this Union a republican form of government.'" Secession, however, was the very antithesis of republican government, and "to prevent" secession "is an indispensable means, to the end, of maintaining the guaranty mentioned; and when an end is lawful and obligatory, the indispensable means to it, are also lawful, and obligatory." As he confidentially told Lyman Trumbull, "he did not know of any law to authorize some of the things he had done; but he thought there was a necessity for them, & that to save the constitution & the laws generally, it might be better to do some illegal acts, rather than suffer all to be overthrown."[25]

Hovering behind these points, however, was a larger, vaguer notion of constitutional authority in Lincoln's mind which could justify actions that were not just invisible to the Constitution but which actually contradicted its express statements. In the spring of 1861, the westernmost counties of Virginia repudiated the Virginia secession ordinance, organized themselves as the "restored" government of Virginia, and in May of 1862, petitioned Congress for recognition as an entirely new state. The West Virginia statehood bill was bitterly opposed in Congress by antiadministration Democrats for its "utter and flagrant unconstitutionality"—and for once, they could quote an explicit ban in the Constitution, in Article 4, section 3, on the subdivision of existing states "without the consent of the Legislatures of the States concerned." This caught Lincoln in a dilemma of his own manufacturing, since he had all along insisted that secession was a constitutional impossibility, and that therefore Virginia had never legally left the Union—or, presumably, its right to consent to its own division. When the West Virginia statehood bill finally ended up on his desk in December 1862, Lincoln was so troubled about signing it that he convened a special cabinet meeting, with written opinions required of all members, to discuss it. Unhelpfully, they divided three-to-three. In the end, however, Lincoln signed the bill, and his justification was cloaked in a form of near-mysticism. The West Virginia seceders were, strictly speaking, asking for something which the Constitution forbade by its letter. But there was more to the Constitution than its letter. In 1861, Lincoln reflected on the struggles of the Revolutionary War, and it struck him that "there must have been something more than common that those men struggled for . . . something even more than National Independence," and that was the "great promise to all the people of the world to all time to come," the promise of democracy itself, "that in due time the weights should be lifted from the shoulders of all men, and that all should have an equal chance." The Constitution, as he wrote during the secession winter of 1860–61, was a means to preserving that principle, not an end in itself, and certainly not a suicide pact which disunionists could twist to its own destruction:

> The assertion of that principle, at that time, was the word, "fitly spoken" which has proved an "apple of gold" to us. The Union, and the Constitution, are the picture of silver, subsequently framed around it. The picture

was made, not to conceal, or destroy the apple; but to adorn, and preserve it. The picture was made for the apple—not the apple for the picture.

The West Virginians, by seceding from secession, had put themselves on the side of the angels, and Lincoln was not about to punish them for violating the letter of the Constitution while they had risked so much to save its spirit. "It is said, the devil takes care of his own," Lincoln wrote. "Much more should a good spirit—the spirit of the Constitution and the Union—take care of its own. I think it can not do less, and live."[26]

Overriding the letter of the Constitution in favor of its democratic spirit was not an argument Lincoln liked to resort to, and using it on this occasion drove his critics to ask whether this was simply a fancy way of saying that Lincoln "can proceed step by step to grasp the reins of absolute power." Even the argument from necessity was "one of the most startling exercises of the one-man power—which the history of human government, free or despotic, ever witnessed."[27] And so it went through the course of the war, as the Lincoln administration proceeded to expand its suspensions of habeas corpus, arrest truculent members of the Maryland legislature who were agitating for secession, impose an ever-escalating series of conscription measures, levy direct taxes on incomes, and conduct a program of military arrests which were estimated in 1865 to have imprisoned 38,000 people (including a former U.S. congressman, Clement Vallandigham) and shut down two Northern newspapers. "This assumption of power," complained the New York State Democratic Committee in a public letter in May 1863, "not only abrogates the right of the people . . . but it strikes a fatal blow at the supremacy of law and the authority of the State and Federal Constitution."[28]

But did it? Lincoln "was greatly moved—more angry than I ever saw him," according to Attorney General Edward Bates in the fall of 1863, over state judges who freed civilians detained by military tribunals, because he frankly believed that these interpositions had more to do with partisan Democratic resistance to his politics than it did with a concern for the civil-liberties implications of the war powers. He "declared that it was a formed plan of the democratic copperheads, deliberately acted out to defeat the Govt., and aid the enemy." As Mark Neely showed in 1991, the estimates made at that time of military arrests carried out under the Lincoln administration were more than a little exaggerated—in fact, the total arrests probably amounted to no more than 13,535, by Neely's reckoning—and of those, vanishingly few occurred north of the Mason-Dixon line. By far, the bulk of Lincoln's military detentions were of what we today might call "enemy combatants"—British nationals crewing blockade-runners, smugglers, draft rioters, guerillas—as well as corrupt war contractors, deserters, and bounty jumpers. If anything, Lincoln once remarked, people were more likely to look back on the Civil War and wonder why he didn't exercise the war powers with a harder hand: "I think the time not unlikely to come when I shall be blamed for having made too few arrests rather than too many," Lincoln replied to the New York Democrats. In fact, rather than stifling liberty, it was precisely the doctrine of presidential war powers which gave Lincoln the opening he needed to proclaim emancipation, "by virtue of the power in me vested, as Commander-in-Chief, of the Army, and Navy of the United States in time of actual armed rebellion against the authority and government of the United States, and as a proper and necessary war measure," and thus dodge the bullet of a federal court challenge if he had issued the Emancipation Proclamation as a civil decree.[29]

In the end, Lincoln's implementation of presidential war powers acted in precisely the opposite direction from that which his critics feared. More than necessity or the oath or the republican guarantee (which might contain little or nothing in the way of self-limitations), it was the constant reminder in Lincoln's mind that the war powers were a means, not an end, toward the promotion of democracy that kept Lincoln from becoming the outright dictator his enemies, and some of friends, feared. "I do not intend to be a tyrant," Lincoln said in 1863 to a delegation of Radicals who wanted more vigorous prosecution of dissidents. "I must make a dividing-line somewhere between those who are the opponents of the government and those who only oppose peculiar features of my administration while they sustain the government." And when Treasury Secretary Salmon Chase urged him to expand the scope of the Emancipation Proclamation to include the slaves of the border states as well as the Confederacy, Lincoln sharply demurred: "The exemptions were made because the military necessity did not apply to the exempted localities. . . . If I take the step must I not do so, without the argument of military necessity, and so, without any argument, except the one that I think the measure politically expedient, and morally right . . . would I not thus be in the boundless field of absolutism?"[30] He frequently reiterated his belief that, however sweeping his war powers might be, they terminated the moment the war was over, and after that moment, he and his policies would become as subservient to the dictates of Congress and the courts as anyone else, even including emancipation. At the Hampton Roads peace conference in February 1865, he admitted to Alexander H. Stephens that, once the war was over, emancipation would become "a judicial question. How the courts would decide it, he did not know and could give no answer." If they overturned the proclamation, then his choices would be acquiescence or resignation from office, and although he left no doubt what option he would exercise, forcible presidential resistance was not one of them.[31] And the federal judiciary, despite Chief Justice Taney's hunger to rule on a case which would cripple the "war powers," largely stood aside and refused to use the war as an opportunity to hedge the war powers doctrine too tightly by judicial dictum. Consistent with Lincoln's pattern of interposing his war powers only in specific instances, the judiciary likewise set a pattern of avoiding explicit challenge to the war powers. Even today, at moments when the Supreme Court has questioned certain presidential actions, it has done so on grounds other than the president's claim to the war powers of a commander in chief.[32]

Lincoln thus succeeded, without formally articulating a detailed description of the war powers, in demonstrating that such powers could exist outside the normal boundaries of the Constitution without automatically destabilizing it. As Chief Justice Charles Evans Hughes once remarked, "While we are at war, we are not in revolution." Neither the Constitution nor the idea of democracy were so fragile that they could not survive the taking up of arms—and of unusual powers—in their own defense, and especially when those powers were consigned to the hands of one who had such painstaking reverence for constitutional and democratic authority. Thaddeus Stevens, who had weighed Lincoln so often in the balances and found him wanting for *not* exercising his war powers more relentlessly, paid a difficult tribute to Lincoln as "the calm statesman . . . who will lead you to an honorable peace and to permanent liberty. . . . For purity of heart and firmness of character he would compare well with the best of the conscript fathers."[33] Lincoln's construction of the war powers was neither as sweeping nor as dictatorial as the jurists feared or the opposition complained, and in an ironic way, it was precisely his refusal to press the war powers to the extent that they feared which may have cost him his life. He would not surround himself with military escorts, he remarked to Charles Graham Halpine, because it would send too imperial a message about his idea of himself as president. "It would never do for a president to have guards with drawn sabres at his door, as if he fancied he were, or were trying to be, or were assuming to be, an emperor."[34] Perhaps, had Lincoln applied those war powers to his own protection, he might not have come to so tragic, and so untimely, an end.

Notes

This essay first appeared in *Federal Lawyer*, November/December 2007. Reprinted with permission.

1. David Donald, *Charles Sumner and the Coming of the Civil War* (New York, 1960), 388; "The Hon. C. Sumner on a War for Emancipation," *Anti-Slavery Reporter,* November 1, 1861, 246.

2. John Locke, *Two Treatises of Government*, ed. Peter Laslett (New York, 1965), 277, 411–12; Alexander Hamilton, "No. 74," in *The Federalist*, ed. G. W. Carey and James McClellan (Indianapolis, 2001), 389.

3. James Kent, *Commentaries on American Law*, ed. G. F. Comstock (Boston, 1867), 1:67, 295–303; Louis Fisher, *Constitutional Conflicts between Congress and the President* (Princeton, NJ, 1985), 286; Hamilton, "No. 69," *The Federalist*, 357; Joseph Story, *Commentaries on the Constitution of the United States* (Boston, 1833), 1486; Caspar W. Weinberger, "Dangerous Constraints on the President's War Powers," in *The Fettered Presidency: Legal Restraints on the Executive Branch*, ed. G. L. Cravitz and Jeremy A. Rabkin (Washington, DC, 1989), 97–98.

4. Robert V. Remini, *Andrew Jackson and the Course of American Empire, 1767–1821* (New York, 1977), 207, 313–15.

5. Levi Woodbury, "Martial Law in Rhode Island," in *Writings of Levi Woodbury, LL.D., Political, Judicial and Literary* (Boston, 1852), 2:101, 104.

6. "Abolition of Slavery," and "Speech of the Hon. J. Q. Adams," *Congressional Globe*, May 25, 1836, 24th Cong., 1st sess., 498–99, 448 (appendix); John Q. Adams, "Intercourse with Foreign Nations," *Congressional Globe*, April 15, 1842, 27th Cong., 2nd sess., 429; Charles Francis Adams, "John Quincy Adams and Martial Law," *Proceedings of the Massachusetts Historical Society* 15 (January 1902), 439–44.

7. Charles Sumner to John Murray Forbes, December 30, 1862, in *The Selected Letters of Charles Sumner*, ed. Beverly Wilson Palmer (Boston, 1990), 2:136; Charles Francis Adams, *Richard Henry Dana: A Biography* (Boston, 1891), 2:259–60; William Whiting, *War Powers under the Constitution of the United States* (1864; repr., Glorieta, NM, 1971), 11.

8. Grosvenor Porter Lowrey, *The Commander-in-Chief: A Defence upon Legal Grounds of the Proclamation of Emancipation* (New York, 1863), 20; Bacon, "Reply to Professor Parker," *New Englander and Yale Review* 22 (April 1863): 196.

9. Joel Prentiss Bishop, *Thoughts for the Times* (Boston, 1863), 24.

10. Thaddeus Stevens, "Speech on Conquered Provinces, April 4, 1863, to the Union League of Lancaster," in *Selected Papers of Thaddeus Stevens*, ed. Beverly Wilson Palmer (Pittsburgh, 1997), 1:392; "The Constitution as It Is—The Union as It Was," *Continental Monthly*, October 1862, 379.

11. Isaac N. Arnold, *The History of Abraham Lincoln and the Overthrow of Slavery* (Chicago, 1866), 702.

12. Orville Hickman Browning, "Confiscation of Property," March 10, 1862, and "Confiscation of Rebel Property," June 25, 1862, *Congressional Globe*, 37th Cong., 2nd sess., 1136, 2972–73; Benjamin Curtis, "Executive Power," *A Memoir of Benjamin Robbins Curtis, LL.D., with Some of His Professional and Miscellaneous Writings* (Boston, 1879) 2:310, 313, 320–21; Lowrey, *Commander-in-Chief*, 13; W. E. Binkley, *The Powers of the President: Problems of American Democracy* (New York, 1937), 122–23.

13. These objections are similar in substance to the arguments for limiting presidential discretion in treaty making, foreign affairs, and international conflicts made by Louis Henkin, Harold H. Koh, and Michael Glennon; see John Yoo, *The Powers of War and Peace: The Constitution and Foreign Affairs after 9/11* (Chicago, 2005), 5, 144.

14. Samuel Smith Nicholas, "Martial Law," in *Conservative Essays, Legal and Political* (Philadelphia, 1863), 164, 178–79; Robert Winthrop, "The Presidential Election of 1864," in *Addresses and Speeches on Various Occasions, from 1852 to 1867* (Boston, 1867), 621; Joel Parker, "Habeas Corpus and Martial Law," *North American Review* 92 (October 1861): 505–6, and *The War Powers of the Congress and of the President: An Address Delivered before the National Club of Salem, March 13, 1863* (Cambridge, MA, 1863), 9–10, 31–32, 58, and *Constitutional Law and Unconstitutional Divinity: Letters to Rev. Henry M. Dexter and to Rev. Leonard Bacon* (Cambridge, MA, 1863), 33–34; Philip S. Paludan, *A Covenant with Death: The Constitution, Law, and Equality in the Civil War Era* (Urbana, IL, 1975), 130–33, 143–51.

15. Montgomery Throop, *The Future: A Political Essay* (New York, 1864), 265–66; "The War Power," *Old Guard,* July 1863, 164; Thomas Jefferson Miles, *The Conspiracy of Leading Men of the Republican Party to Destroy the American Union* (New York, 1864), 10.

16. Lincoln, "To William H. Herndon," February 15, 1848, in *The Collected Works of Abraham Lincoln, ed.* Roy P. Basler (New Brunswick, NJ, 1953–55), 1:451; John F. Seymour, in *Recollected Words of Abraham Lincoln*, ed. Don Fehrenbacher and Virginia Fehrenbacher (Stanford, CA, 1996), 400; Michael Burlingame, *The Inner World of Abraham Lincoln* (Urbana, IL, 1994), 90.

17. Lincoln, "Manuscript Prepared for the Pittsburgh Speech," February 15, 1861, in *Collected Works*, 4:214.

18. Lincoln, "First Inaugural Address—Final Version," March 4, 1861, and "First Inaugural Address—First Edition and Revisions," in *Collected Works*, 4:261, 265, 270, 271.

19. Lois J. Einhorn, *Abraham Lincoln the Orator: Penetrating the Lincoln Legend* (Westport, CT, 1992), 38, 63–64, 84; Douglas L. Wilson, *Honor's Voice: The Transformation of Abraham Lincoln* (New York, 1998), 289–92.

20. Lincoln, "Reply to Governor Andrew J. Curtin at Harrisburg, Pennsylvania," February 22, 1861, in *Collected Works*, 4:243.

21. A. R. Boteler, "Mr. Lincoln and the Force Bill," *Annals of the War*, ed. Alexander K. McClure (Philadelphia, 1879), 226–27.

22. "The 'War Power' Called Out," in *The Political History of the United States of America during the Great Rebellion*, ed. Edward McPherson (Washington, 1864), 114–15. Lincoln's April 15 proclamation (*Collected Works,* 4:331–32) strictly copied the language of the Militia Act; see "An Act to Provide for the Calling Forth of the Militia," February 28, 1795, *Statutes at Large*, 1:424.

23. Margaret Leech, *Reveille in Washington, 1860–1865* (New York, 1941), 55–65; Julia Taft Bayne, *Tad Lincoln's Father* (Boston, 1931), 69; O. H. Browning, diary entry for July 3, 1861, in *The Diary of Orville Hickman Browning*, ed. T. C. Pease and J. G. Randall (Springfield, IL, 1925), 1:476.

24. Clinton Rossiter, *The Supreme Court and the Commander-in-Chief,* ed. R. P. Longacre (Ithaca, NY, 1976), 20–25.

25. Lincoln, "Message to Congress in Special Session," July 4, 1861, in *Collected Works*, 4:426, 429, 430, 438, 440; Lyman Trumbull to Julia Trumbull, July 2, 1861,

Lyman Trumbull Papers, Abraham Lincoln Presidential Library and Museum, Springfield, IL.

26. Lincoln, "Fragment on the Constitution and the Union," c. January 1861, "Address to the New Jersey Senate at Trenton, New Jersey," February 21, 1861, "Speech in Independence Hall, Philadelphia, Pennsylvania," February 22, 1861, and "Opinion on the Admission of West Virginia into the Union," December 31, 1862, in *Collected Works*, 4:168, 236, 240, 6:27.

27. Throop, *Future*, 268; Winthrop, "Presidential Election of 1864," 620–21.

28. "Correspondence between New York Democrats and President Lincoln," May 19, 1863, in McPherson, *Political History*, 163.

29. Burlingame, *Inner World*, 179; Mark Neely, *The Fate of Liberty: Abraham Lincoln and Civil Liberties* (New York, 1991), 133–37, 167–74; Lincoln, "To Erastus Corning and Others," June 12, 1863, in *Collected Works,* 6:265.

30. John Hay, "Memorandum," September 30, 1863, in *At Lincoln's Side: John Hay's Civil War Correspondence and Selected Writings*, ed. Michael Burlingame (Carbondale, IL, 2000), 63; Lincoln, "To Salmon P. Chase," September 2, 1863, in *Collected Works*, 6:428–29.

31. Alexander Stephens, *A Constitutional View of the Late War between the States* (Philadelphia, 1870), 2:613; Lincoln, "Annual Message to Congress," December 6, 1864, in *Collected Works*, 8:152.

32. Rossiter, *Supreme Court and the Commander-in-Chief,* 2–5.

33. Hughes, in Rossiter, *Supreme Court and the Commander-in-Chief,* 8; Peter Irons, *War Powers: How the Imperial Presidency Hijacked the Constitution* (New York, 2006), 142 ; Thaddeus Stevens, "Speech on the Copperhead Threat at the County Union Convention, September 7, 1864, in Lancaster," and "Remarks on the President's Message and Emancipation, January 5, 1865, in Congress," in Palmer, *Selected Papers*, 1:502, 513. See Jonathan Zimmerman's op-ed, "How Lincoln Finessed Security," *Philadelphia Inquirer* (August 1, 2006): "You might reply that our liberties define our nation; if we abandon them, we give up on America itself. But Lincoln said otherwise—and lucky for us."

34. Charles Graham Halpine (Private Miles O'Reilly, pseud.), *Baked Meats of the Funeral: A Collection of Essays, Poems, Speeches, Histories and Banquets* (New York, 1866), 106–7.

INDEX

ALLEN C. GUELZO is the Henry R. Luce Professor of the Civil War Era and a member of the history department at Gettysburg College, where he also directs the college's Civil War Era Studies program. He is the author of *Abraham Lincoln: Redeemer President* (1999), *Lincoln's Emancipation Proclamation: The End of Slavery in America* (2004), and *Lincoln and Douglas: The Debates That Defined America* (2008) and has contributed to the *Wall Street Journal, Washington Post, Journal of American History, Civil War History,* and *Journal of the Abraham Lincoln Association.* He is a member of the National Council on the Humanities.